CELEBRATING PEACE

BOSTON UNIVERSITY STUDIES IN
PHILOSOPHY AND RELIGION
General Editor: Leroy S. Rouner

Volume Eleven

Celebrating Peace

Edited by
Leroy S. Rouner

UNIVERSITY OF NOTRE DAME PRESS
Notre Dame, Indiana

Library of Congress Cataloging-in-Publication Data

Celebrating peace / edited by Leroy S. Rouner.
      p.   cm. — (Boston University studies in phi-
losophy and religion ; v. 11)
   Includes bibliographical references and index.
   ISBN 0-268-02356-5 (paper : alk. paper)
   1. Peace — Religious aspects — Christianity.
2. Peace — Religious aspects — Hinduism.   3. Peace —
Religious aspects — Buddhism.   I. Rouner, Leroy S.
II. Series.
BT736.4.C42   1990
291.1'7873 — dc20   90-36381
                                         CIP

Manufactured in the United States of America

Contents

PART III: HINDU AND BUDDHIST VIEWS OF PEACE

PART IV: MAKING PEACE: PROPHECY, PROTEST, AND POETRY

Preface

Boston University Studies in Philosophy and Religion is regularly a joint project of the Boston University Institute for Philosophy and Religion and the University of Notre Dame Press. This year that project has been expanded to include the University of Notre Dame's Institute for International Peace Studies. Professor John Gilligan, Director of that Institute, has not only participated in our program as a lecturer and author; he has also helped with program planning and with the program budget. The Boston University Institute and the Notre Dame Press welcome the Notre Dame Institute to this series, and express appreciation for their help in making possible this study of peace.

The essays in each annual volume are edited from the previous year's lecture program of the Boston University Institute. The Director of the Institute, who also serves as editor of these Studies, chooses a theme and invites participants to lecture at Boston University in the course of the academic year. The papers are then revised by their authors, and the editor selects and edits the essays to be included in these Studies. In preparation is Volume 12, *On Community*.

The Boston University Institute for Philosophy and Religion is a Center of the Graduate School, and is sponsored jointly by the Department of Philosophy, the Department of Religion, and the School of Theology. The Institute is an interdisciplinary and ecumenical forum. Within the academic community it is committed to open interchange on fundamental issues in philosophy and religious study which transcend the narrow specializations of academic curricula. Outside the university it seeks to recover the public tradition of philosophical discourse which was a lively part of American intellectual life in the early years of this century before the professionalization of both philosophy and religious reflection. At a time when too much academic writing is incomprehensible, or irrelevant, or both, we try to present readable essays by acknowledged authorities on critical human issues.

Acknowledgments

Our volumes are made possible by our individual authors, who have honored us by their participation and been gracious in response to my editing of their papers. We are also grateful for permission to quote the poems included in Denise Levertov's essay. Those publishers are indicated in her notes.

Barbara Darling-Smith has once again proven her skills as a superb copy editor. This year she has been assisted by Sydney Smith III and Andrew Crouch in manuscript preparation.

Editor Ann Rice at the University of Notre Dame Press has been expert and expeditious in bringing these volumes into print. And our debt to Jim Langford, Director of the University of Notre Dame Press, grows with each new addition to the series. He is a colleague, friend, and occasional author in these volumes, as well as our publisher.

This year's program on Peace has been funded by a generous grant from the John D. and Catherine T. MacArthur Foundation's Program on Peace and International Cooperation. We are grateful to the Foundation's Board for their financial support, and to the Foundation staff for their help in preparing our proposal.

Contributors

DANIEL BERRIGAN, S.J., is a poet, priest, and activist living in New York City, where he works with AIDS patients. Among his recent works are an autobiography, *To Dwell in Peace*, and a journal based on his work with the film *The Mission*. He has won many literary awards, including the Lamont Prize, for thirty-five published books. Among his better-known prose works are *No Bars to Manhood*, *The Geography of Faith* (with Robert Coles), and *Night Flight to Hanoi*. He has published ten volumes of poetry and a play, *The Trial of the Catonsville Nine*.

SISSELA BOK is Associate Professor of Philosophy and the History of Ideas at Brandeis University. She received her Ph.D. in Philosophy from Harvard University and her A.B. and M.A. in Clinical Psychology from George Washington University. She is the author of *Lying: Moral Choice in Public and Private Life* (1978), which received the George Orwell Award and the Melcher Book Award. Her recent publications include a biography of Alva Myrdal and *A Strategy for Peace* (1989). In 1989 she served as a member of the American Philosophical Association and Soviet Academy of Sciences exchange on nuclear policy.

JOHN J. GILLIGAN is Director of the Institute for International Peace Studies at Notre Dame. He served as the sixty-second governor of Ohio from 1971 to 1975 and was appointed by President Jimmy Carter to the post of Administrator of the

Agency for International Development in 1977. Prior to his current position he was Thomas J. White Professor of Law and Government and Chairman of the Institute for Public Policy at Notre Dame. He is a recipient of the Association of Catholic Colleges and Universities' annual award for outstanding Catholic lay leaders.

GERALD JAMES LARSON has taught and written extensively on comparative philosophy and South Asian philosophy. Since 1972 he has been Professor of Religious Studies at the University of California, Santa Barbara. From 1982 to 1985 he was President of the Society for Asian and Comparative Philosophy. Among his recent publications are *Interpreting Across Boundaries: New Essays in Comparative Philosophy* (edited with Eliot Deutsch) and *Sāṃkhya: A Dualist Tradition in Indian Philosophy* (published in both India and the United States). He recently completed a major research project on the future of graduate education in religious studies.

DENISE LEVERTOV is a poet who also teaches creative writing at Stanford University. She publishes new collections of poems nearly every year, including most recently *Breathing the Water* and *Oblique Prayers*. She has also translated poems of Guillevic and Joubert. Among her many honors and awards are a Guggenheim Fellowship, the Longview Award, and the Elmer Holmes Bobst Award. Recordings of her poems have been released on the Folkways and Watershed labels.

PAUL S. MINEAR is Winkley Professor of Biblical Theology *Emeritus* at Yale University. He has served as Program Secretary for the North American Faith and Order Conference, Director of the Faith and Order Department of the World Council of Churches, Vice Rector of the Ecumenical Institute for Advanced Theological Research in Jerusalem, and consultant to the World Council of Churches assemblies in Evanston, New Delhi, and Uppsala. His many books include *Eyes of Faith;*

*The Kingdom and the Power; Images of the Church in the
New Testament; Christian Hope and the Second Coming;
The Gospel of Mark; Matthew, the Teacher's Gospel; John,
the Martyr's Gospel; On Setting Death to Music;* and *The
God of the Gospels.*

JÜRGEN MOLTMANN, Professor of Systematic Theology at the
University of Tübingen, is a member of the Faith and Order
Commission of the World Council of Churches and the Department of Theology of the World Alliance of Reformed
Churches. He edits the journal *Evangelische Theologie* and
has been Woodruff Visiting Professor at Emory University.
Among his many books are *The Theology of Hope, The Crucified God, The Church in the Power of the Spirit, The Future
of Creation, On Human Dignity, The Trinity and the Kingdom, God in Creation,* and *Creating a Just Future.*

BHIKHU PAREKH studied for the B.A. at St. Xavier's College,
Bombay, and took his Ph.D. at the London School of Economics. He has taught political theory at Hull University
since 1964. In 1981 he returned to India and was Vice-
Chancellor (President) of Baroda University until 1984. In
Britain his long service as Deputy Chairman of the Commission for Racial Equality concludes in 1990. His many publications include *Hannah Arendt and the Search for a New
Political Philosophy* (1981), *Marxist Theory of Ideology* (1982),
Contemporary Political Thinkers (1982), and two major studies
of Gandhi: *Gandhi's Political Philosophy* (1989) and *Colo-
nialism, Tradition, and Reform: An Analysis of Gandhi's Political Discourse* (1989).

TRUTZ RENDTORFF is Professor of Theology on the Protestant
faculty of the Institute for Systematic Theology at the University of Munich. He is the author of many books, including *Protestantismus und Revolution; Gott, ein Wort unserer
Sprache? ein theologischer Essay; Politische Ethik und Chris-*

tentum; and *Charisma und Institution. Church and Theology: The Systematic Function of the Church Concept in Modern Theology* and *Ethics* have been translated into English. He is widely known as an ethicist and human rights specialist. His interests include developments in contemporary American theology, and he has traveled and lectured throughout the United States.

LEROY S. ROUNER is Professor of Philosophy, Religion, and Philosophical Theology at Boston University, Director of the Institute for Philosophy and Religion, and General Editor of this Series. He did his Ph.D. with John Hermann Randall, Jr., at Columbia University on the philosophy of William Ernest Hocking, and is the author of *Within Human Experience: The Philosophy of William Ernest Hocking*, editor and coauthor of the Hocking *Festschrift, Philosophy, Religion, and the Coming World Civilization*, and, with John Howie, of *The Wisdom of William Ernest Hocking*. His most recent books include a memoir, *The Long Way Home*, and *To Be at Home: Christianity, Civil Religion, and a World Community.*

NINIAN SMART has written extensively on the history and philosophy of religion, Indian philosophy, and interreligious dialogue. Educated at Oxford, he founded the first major department of religious studies in England, at Lancaster University. He is currently J. F. Rowny Professor of Comparative Religions at the University of California, Santa Barbara, where he chairs the Department of Religious Studies. His books include *The Long Search* (also a BBC television series), *Religion and the Western Mind*, and *Beyond Ideology*. He has held numerous visiting professorships in the United States, New Zealand, Australia, South Africa, and India.

STEPHEN E. TOULMIN was educated at King's College in Cambridge where he received his Ph.D. in Moral Sciences. He is currently Avalon Professor of the Humanities at Northwestern University. From 1973 to 1986 he was a Professor in the Committee on Social Thought at the University of Chicago. Among his many books are *Knowing and Acting* (1976), *The Return to Cosmology* (1982), and *Human Understanding.* Works currently in progress include a collection of essays on mental life and the Freud Lectures, *Reasons of the Heart.* Since 1981 he has been a Senior Visiting Scholar and Fellow of the Hastings Institute for Society, Ethics, and the Life Sciences.

JOHN H. YODER is Professor of Theology at the University of Notre Dame, where he specializes in Reformation history, missiology, and ecumenical theology. His best known books are *The Politics of Jesus* (1972) and *The Priestly Kingdom* (1984). He has served the Mennonite Central Committee in overseas relief and mission administration, in ecumenical representation, and in theological education as Professor of Theology and President of Goshen Biblical Seminary. He has also served the World Council of Churches as advisor, consultant, and observer in numerous assemblies. He previously lectured in the Institute for Philosophy and Religion's 1980–81 series.

Introduction

LEROY S. ROUNER

THE WORLD CHANGED in the autumn of 1989.

Communism collapsed in Eastern Europe. China smashed its prodemocracy movement in June, but the bloody handwriting on the wall around Tiananmen Square told of a new future. The reunification of Germany was suddenly imminent. Russian communism was dissolving, the Soviet Union itself was beginning to fragment, and the Western world found itself in sympathy with the Soviet government for the first time since the heady days of Allied victory in World War II. Less than ten years after President Reagan called Russia "the evil empire," his successor was entertaining the Russian president as a friend in his summer home and publicly claiming him as a colleague in the work of disarmament and the quest for peace. Political pundits are now holding seminars on the end of the Cold War, as both America and Russia cut defense spending and withdraw troops from Europe.

These changes are so radical and recent that it is not yet clear what causes brought them about, how permanent they will prove to be, or what they mean for the future. They are cause for celebration, but they also bring new dangers. Eastern Europe's underground dream of democracy has surfaced into daylight as a real possibility. But a populace made passive by years of authoritarian rule now begins a self-taught crash course in the fragile volatilities of democratic government. These exercises in political flexibility will be strenuous, and their success is uncertain.

More dangerously, the collapse of militarily enforced communist ideology ironically encourages ethnic and regional antagonisms which that rule had kept at bay. In the Soviet Union, the transition to a more democratic government is threatened not only by hard-line political conservatives, intent on maintaining

1

the old authoritarianism, but by ancient and visceral animosities among large populations whose "national" loyalty has always been primarily to their particular regional, linguistic, ethnic, and/or religious community. The Baltic states are already announcing secession, and their transition to independence could be relatively smooth, since their incorporation into the Soviet Union has been relatively recent. There is a worst-case possibility, however, that threatened secessions elsewhere could initiate a full-scale civil war.

These dangers to the contrary notwithstanding, the prospect of world peace has been given new life. The Bulletin of Atomic Scientists has set back the Doomsday Clock. History seems ready to "give peace a chance." And a volume of essays on Peace is at least timely.

Most of our essays were written before the momentous autumn of 1989, and to that extent they are dated. On the other hand, they provide a perspective on the nature of peace which current events cannot yet yield. It will be some time before we can confidently say anything new about peace. In the meantime, while the world sorts out the radical events of recent months, reflection on basic issues concerning peace can help prepare us for a new tomorrow.

Our first section, "Just War, Perpetual Peace, and the Nation-State," begins with John Gilligan's essay on "Teaching Peace in a Christian Context." Gilligan is a Catholic lay thinker, and his point of departure is the now famous pastoral letter of the Catholic bishops, *The Challenge of Peace: God's Promise and Our Response.* That letter defends the classical Christian "just war" theory, the grounds on which it might be morally justifiable to wage war. He notes that the need to reconcile the teachings of the Prince of Peace with the perceived need for the use of armed force goes back as far as Augustine. A former governor of Ohio, Gilligan is mindful of the need to find an alternative to *Realpolitik*, and much of the first part of his essay is a primer in just war theory.

A just war requires a *just cause*, as assessed by a *competent authority*, and the threat to *comparative justice* must be deemed serious enough to justify the taking of human life. Further, *right intention* must be established, it must be undertaken only as a *last resort*, it must have real *probability of success*, and both *pro-*

portionality and *discrimination*, that is, continuous reevaluation of the good to be achieved in relation to the ongoing costs of war.

Gilligan readily admits that just war theory is complex and difficult when applied to actual human affairs and that it has never been, and probably cannot be, a serious element in any nation's policy making. What then is its relevance? Returning to the Catholic bishops' letter, he notes their hope that the question of a just war might now be part of a larger public debate. To teach peace in a Christian context is to educate the public in the virtually insurmountable difficulty of giving any serious moral grounding to modern warfare.

John Yoder, a Mennonite colleague of Gilligan's at the University of Notre Dame's Institute for International Peace Studies, follows with a careful criticism of just war theory, "The Credibility of Ecclesiastical Teaching on the Morality of War." Yoder is a pacifist, but here he states his case negatively by accepting the premises of the classical just war argument, as set forth in both the 1983 Catholic bishops' letter and the 1986 Methodist letter, "In Defense of Creation." He then asks what it would take to make these arguments morally and institutionally credible.

Whereas Gilligan focused on the public educational value of just war debate, Yoder focuses on analyzing, or perhaps better, dismantling, the theory itself. One of his broad arguments is that just war theory presupposes both personal and public education of the sort that Gilligan calls for. Yoder points out that this has never been available. The possibility of either personal or public moral choice against a given war would require "some kind of effective moral education, acquainting the individual with the basic notion of moral accountability, as well as the criteria by which it must be guided. How many high schools do that kind of civics instruction? How many parishes do that kind of catechesis? How many curricula in our war colleges and ROTC units teach the grounds, or the procedures, for disobeying an unjust order?"

Yoder's point — that just war theory is not actually a resource for concrete political decisions — has already been conceded by Gilligan. But Yoder, the pacifist, concludes that "perhaps the just war ethicist is just as utopian as the pacifist, to think that the normative system can be applied with integrity. If that is true, some will argue that an honest 'realism' would be morally preferred to a self-deceiving use of just war rhetoric."

Is there, then, something "realistic" to be said for utopians after all? Sissela Bok thinks so. She shares her predecessors' skepticism about the moral possibility of a just war, and turns instead to utopian advocates of perpetual peace. Her essay deals with "Early Advocates of Lasting World Peace: Utopians or Realists?" She notes that the just war theory assumes that war is an immutable aspect of the human condition. But in the nuclear age nations cannot run the risk of a major war. Gilligan and Yoder had argued that previous assumptions about a just war are untenable. Bok counters that previous assumptions about the impossibility of perpetual peace are now equally untenable.

She turns to Erasmus and Kant for challenges to the common assumption that war will always be with us, and for suggestions about a social climate conducive to the forging of a stable peace. Erasmus, in his *Adages* of 1500, wrote that "War is Sweet to Those Who Have Not Experienced It." He later proposed a "congress of kings" who would sign a peace treaty, and he wrote *The Education of the Christian Prince* to guide the young Prince Charles of Spain, soon to become Charles V. Erasmus was not a pacifist, but argued that war appeals to dreamers, not realists; it promises good, but produces "the shipwreck of all that is good."

Kant's essay on "Perpetual Peace" in 1795 furthered Erasmus's argument. Although Kant held that peace was more difficult to achieve than Erasmus had assumed, he nevertheless held that it was possible. Kant proposes the kind of educational program which both Gilligan and Yoder have found necessary for an ethical evaluation of war; only in this instance, Kant is proposing ethical education for peace.

Bok's essay is a sympathetic historical account of utopian views, in the sense of a society that is possible but at present merely visionary. She does not argue that they are right. She argues only that we have no choice but to take them seriously. "Only time will tell whether a cumulative process and principled efforts at domestic and international change can, in the long run, disprove the age-old assumption that war will always be with us."

Stephen Toulmin's question is structural rather than theoretical. Who makes war? Nations. There, he suggests, is the heart of our problem. "For three hundred years, Europe and the countries that it strongly influenced learned the lessons of 'nationhood' all too well and must now in many respects unlearn them." His essay, "From Leviathan to Lilliput," concludes a major study on *Cosmopolis* dealing with the rise of the nation in the modern West. In order to bring peace, he suggests, we must cultivate a host of "nonnational institutions which will undermine extreme nationhood, hamper claims to absolute sovereignty, and obstruct the tyranny and brutality into which absolute authority has tempted the established rulers of all nation-states."

Toulmin is not a Hannah Arendt or a Gandhi in suggesting that we return to the *polis* or the village as our central political institution. Nor does he advocate doing away with the nation-state, but he does advocate undermining its power. In that sense he sides with Gilligan on the education issue. We must develop vital subnational institutions to counter the authoritarian power of the nation, in the same way that intellectual life must develop "interlocking modes of investigation and explanation [which] will undermine exaggerated claims on behalf of abstract, universal theory, and help reinstate respect for the pragmatic multiplicity of methods that is appropriate when dealing with practical concerns in a rational and reasonable manner."

In contrasting the Lilliputian advocates of diverse subnational communities, who have no troops, with the authoritarian national forces of Leviathan, who have troops to spare, Toulmin notes wryly that power and force eventually run up against their limits. "From now on, the name of the game is not force but influence; and in playing that particular game the Lilliputian institutions hold some of the best cards."

Our second section on "Christian Conceptions of Peace" turns to the question: What are the different ways in which various religious and cultural traditions understand the nature of peace? Trutz Rendtorff recognizes the complexity of Christian conceptions of peace. His essay on "Conceptions of Peace: Political Challenge and Theological Controversy in German Protestantism" reports on the discussion in West Germany between theological ethicists and churches on the one hand, and political strategists on the other. The initial church response involved those who regarded the peace issue as a *status confessionis*, an axiom of Christian thought, rather

than a theory open to change and interpretation. Opposed to them
was a larger group which regarded the peace issue as a worldly
affair to be judged according to the criteria of human reasoning,
which eventually led away from just war arguments to the possibility of a just peace.

Rather than suggest an impossibly idealistic conception of
peace, Rendtorff suggests an analogy to health as the capacity to
cope with life disturbances, and a capacity to live with them. Peace
is "not the complete absence of conflicts, but the sum of the abilities and instruments for dealing with them in something other
than a violent manner."

Rendtorff concludes that there is no final Christian politics
of peace. "We are halfway between a doctrine of just war and a
doctrine of just peace. Only if we have reason to hope that the
world has not been abandoned by God and that God's peace holds
sway over all that we undertake can we be encouraged to think
toward peace."

Jürgen Moltmann's "Political Theology and the Ethics of
Peace" also takes its point of departure from the political situation
in Europe, especially that in West Germany. His particular concern, however, is the development of a new "political theology"
which is turning into a "theology of peace." The nuclear age, he
notes, is the last age of humankind. We will now always have to
live with the deadly threat of nuclear weapons. But it is also the
first common age of all nations and of all people because we are
all possible objects of nuclear extermination.

Political theology arose in Germany after the shock of Auschwitz, which marked a theological crisis for Christians. "For us
Auschwitz did not turn into a question about the meaning of suffering, as it did for the Jews. For us it was a question about guilt
and shame and sorrow." Moltmann notes Adorno's comment that
"after Auschwitz there are no more poems," but he and Johann
Baptist Metz argued that there could be theology after Auschwitz.
Remembering the victims and "recalling the prayers that were
spoken in the gas chambers" we can find "the courage to live and
hope for a different future."

That theology assumes that politics, economics, law and the
sciences are now ethical issues for us all. As a Christian he argues
that "the common formulation of an absolute ethical code for the

community and for the life of humankind on this earth is necessary, so that the great problems of humankind can be solved today in a responsible way."

We conclude this section on "Christian Conceptions of Peace" with Paul Minear's essay on "The Peace of God," examining conceptions of peace in the New Testament. Minear's essay is not concerned with the politics of peace. His focus is on the radical transcendental demands of the peace of God. "It is God who determines and defines the true meaning of peace." Crucial to that peace is the transformation of the inner world of the heart. Quoting Paul's letter to the Romans, Minear notes: "No longer does the memory of sins against God guarantee the wrath of God. Paul had been weak, ungodly, an enemy of God. No longer. Anxiety about the future had spawned despair. No longer. Once suffering had prompted resentment and fear. No longer. Now intensified suffering and danger produced hope. Now the love of God, poured into the heart, gave birth to forgiveness, trust, hope, and even love of persecutors."

In a section on "God's War" Minear considers Jesus' announcement that he came not to bring peace, but a sword (Matt. 10:34). This warfare brought strife within families and within the religious community. Minear sees this strife as a precursor of Jesus' death, which was his final battle with Satan and the dark forces of this world. Christian peace is not bought lightly. It results only from faithful confrontation with those forces in this world which oppose the transcendent peace of God.

Minear readily acknowledges that "this world of thought is alien to most modern people." He suggests, however, that "the ultimate issue is this: does that God exist? Is this the true God? . . . What if the God of peace is the only true God? . . . If he is God, his authority is quite independent of the alternate ways of measuring wisdom, or power or relevance." He concludes: "The ultimate issue is not the idea of peace, but how we are to think about this God of peace, and what is more important, how to enter the realm that is created by his 'grace and peace.'"

Our third section on "Hindu and Buddhist Views of Peace" begins with Gerald Larson's essay on "The Rope of Violence and the Snake of Peace: Conflict and Harmony in Classical India." Larson remembers when he was present at the traditional Repub-

lic Day ceremony in New Delhi called "Beating Retreat." After
much military pageantry in the presence of government officials
and foreign diplomats, the combined military bands conclude the
ceremony at the moment of sunset by playing the old Christian
hymn, "Abide with Me."

Larson is struck with the anachronism of a modern secular
society dominated by Hindus and Muslims celebrating its independence with a traditional Christian hymn; but he also recalls
Whitehead's reference to that particular hymn in *Process and Reality* as the best known rendering of "integral experience." The first
two lines—"Abide with me: / Fast falls the eventide"—combine the
permanence of "abiding" with the flux of time "fast falling." Larson then traces the etymology of the Sanskrit term for peace,
śānti, and concludes that the classical Indian interpretation of
peace has two levels. One is that of ordinary experience, where
things are often not what they seem to be. He illustrates this problem of appearance and reality with the classical image of the rope
which looks like a snake, but isn't. On this level of existence, where
permanence and change exist together, the Hindu notion of peace
is a dialectical balance of forces, not unlike Rendtorff's view.

On another level, however, "Indian thought invites us to take
a journey into silence, beyond permanence and flux, beyond peace
and conflict, beyond the rope and the snake" to the transcendental peace which passes all understanding, the ultimate meaning
of *śānti*.

Ninian Smart, describing himself as a "Buddhified Episcopalian," tries to understand how the peaceful spirit of Buddhism
could become enmeshed in Sri Lanka's violence. His empathetic
essay on "Buddhism, Sri Lanka, and the Prospects for Peace" examines both philosophical ideas and historical conditions in the
genesis of militant Buddhist nationalism. He points first to the
dominance of Theravāda Buddhism in Sri Lanka, and notes that
because it is nontheistic it is doctrinally and mythologically distinct from the monistic systems of Hindu thought celebrated in
the Sri Lankan Tamil community. He also notes that the Buddhist
Sinhalese majority in Sri Lanka feel themselves to be a threatened
minority community because they see Sri Lanka's Hindu Tamils
as an extension of the huge Tamil community in South India.
Sinhala Buddhism is thus a syncretism between Buddhism and a

national feeling which, in modern times, has become political nationalism.

Smart's plea is that Sri Lankan Buddhism extricate itself from Sinhala nationalism, and in so doing develop both an empathy for Hindu ways of life and thought, and a persuasion of the rights of Sri Lankan Tamil Hindus to a measure of autonomy within a new Sri Lankan federation. "Above all, it seems to me, we must experiment in the world with new styles of and arrangements for pluralism. At the same time openness to other traditions and viewpoints is needful. Here religions and ideologies in particular need encouragement toward openness in their teaching. We can have a vision of a world community with great internal variety and many worldviews in harmonious competition. We can look forward to a polydoxic world."

Perhaps no world figure has been more closely identified with the politics of peace than Gandhi, and Bhikhu Parekh's essay on "Gandhi's Quest for a Nonviolent Political Philosophy" advances the thesis of his recent book, *Gandhi's Political Philosophy*. Parekh notes that people in the West tend to regard Gandhi as "a dated figure of local significance." Over against that view Parekh argues that Gandhi was a creative and original thinker who lived a political life of rare intensity and range. His reputation has suffered because he was not a systematic thinker, and many of his most imaginative political acts were inspired by an incommunicable (and therefore unrepeatable) intuitive insight into the appropriate move in a given moment.

Parekh notes Gandhi's deep uneasiness with the modern state, "in his view the most abstract, rigid and dehumanizing form of political organization invented by humankind so far." Here Gandhi and Toulmin make common cause. Because the nation-state speaks only the language of authority and has, as its only means of action, the law, it finds compliance only in compulsion, and is increasingly absorbed in the problem of order. Gandhi, on the other hand, wanted a compassionate freedom in which law allowed for human difference. This could only be possible locally, among friends and neighbors, whose self-governing communities were constituted on territorial, ethnic and functional lines.

"Since a human community was necessarily a fellowship of unique and interdependent beings, the concept of equality had to be defined in noncomparative, noncompetitive and nonatomic terms." Citizenship would be based on cooperation. For him non-violence was a spirit which infected every aspect of a person's life. "As he put it, he was not a preacher, a teacher, a guru or even a guide, but an initiator of a conversation on moral and political matters. . . ."

Our final section is somewhat unusual for us. Our essays are in the philosophy of religion, broadly conceived, and while we encourage occasional lyricism in our writers, we academic philosophers tend to feel awkward about ecstasy. A section on "Making Peace: Prophecy, Protest and Poetry" moves beyond dialectic, however, into transcendent realms of meaning and insight where we are smack up against the ecstatic. Daniel Berrigan and Denise Levertov are poets. They may analyze peace for us, here and there, but that is not why we need them. We need them because they will celebrate it for us, and so remind us why we care.

Readers of Plato's *Republic* will remember Socrates' image of the divided line, in which he distinguished our empirical knowledge of particulars in the world of experience from the transcendental realm of Ideas, where the true nature of the thing was to be known. That knowing was not dialectical; it wasn't something that anyone could calculate or "figure out." It was not the result of technical or instrumental reason. It was a "synoptic intuition" whereby we grasped, and were grasped by, the real truth of the idea. So with these final two visionary friends. Their gift is not their argument but their insight.

Daniel Berrigan's "Christian Peacemakers in the Warmaking State" is his theology of protest at the General Electric weapons factory in King of Prussia, Pennsylvania. His essay explains the rationale behind the action of hammering on nuclear warheads (beating swords into plowshares), the intense Bible study which preceded the action, and the sometimes bizarre aftermath. Berrigan claims Martin Luther King, Jr., Gandhi, and Dorothy Day as spiritual heirs and predecessors in the work of peace, but his early focus in this essay is on Isaiah as the source of inspiration for an action in which swords were beaten into plowshares. "Isaiah is a visionary, and a practical one. He sees what few saw in his lifetime, and only a few since; only a few kings and couriers and academics and students, churchgoers and consumers. He sees a new form of things, the shape of a world that has turned away from killing, turned its face toward the stranger and orphan and widow."

In summing up Berrigan notes that his essay has treated their religious beliefs, and how these might be thought to impinge on public conduct, especially with respect to the law. Berrigan has claimed Gandhi as a predecessor and his experience with the law is perhaps a test case for Gandhi's theory that "justice" is impossible for the modern state because its mechanism is geared only to the maintenance of order. Whatever one's view of the Berrigan action, the fact is that the actors were never persuaded that their judges were evaluating what they had done, as they understood it. Their sentence responded to an alien interpretation of the event. Gandhi's view is that "justice" in the modern nation-state is inevitably alienating in this way, because its only interest is order. Toulmin also suggests empathy with this view. Berrigan sums up:

> We see ourselves as conservatives. We love our country and its people. Root and branch, for good and ill, weal and woe, we belong here. We take to ourselves a history of heroes and martyrs, civil libertarians, cross-grained writers and solitaries and pamphleteers, town criers, tea party tosspots, stamp act resisters, seditious printers of broadsheets, poets, myth makers, chroniclers.
>
> Also, and of course, native Americans, slaves, indentured servants, poor artisans, radical farmers, multitudes of women, labor organizers, students, people of the cloth, political prisoners, philosophers. All those who from the start, saw, dimly or ecstatically, something new.

We conclude with Denise Levertov's question, "Is there a poetry of peace?" which begins her essay on "Poetic Vision and the Hope for Peace." She tells of a panel discussion at Stanford University on "Women, War, and Peace" when someone in the audience said that poets should present images of peace to the world, and that we needed to be able to imagine peace if we were going to be able to achieve it. But Levertov concluded that we cannot imagine peace as a positive condition of society because it is something so unknown that it casts no images on the mind's screen. "Credible, psychologically dynamic poetic images of peace exist only on the most personal level. None of us knows what a truly peaceful society might feel like; and since peace is indivisible, one society, or one culture, or one country alone could not give its members a full experience of it, however much it evolved in its own justice and positive peacemaking: a full experience of peace could only come in a world at peace."

But we do have poems of protest, struggle, denouncement, and even of comradeship in the quest for peace, and Levertov includes several of these. She concludes: "If a poetry of peace is ever to be written, there must first be this stage we are just entering — the poetry of *preparation* for peace, a poetry of protest, of lament, of praise for the living earth; a poetry that demands justice, renounces violence, reverences mystery."

So the world has changed, and peace has a chance. But if Levertov is right, we can't imagine what it would be like. And Larson and Minear, for all their different cultural interests and religious persuasions, agree that the peace which passes all understanding — God's peace — is not a doctrine but a synoptic intuition which we cannot explain, and which implies no particular social program.

Perhaps more modestly we will have to make do with Rendtorff's view that peace will always be only an uneasy harmony; and Bok's persuasion that we must take perpetual peace seriously not because we have good reason to believe it will happen, but because we can no longer afford to believe anything else.

PART I

Just War,
Perpetual Peace,
and the Nation-State

1

Teaching Peace
in a Christian Context

JOHN J. GILLIGAN

THE NOW FAMOUS pastoral letter of the Catholic bishops, first published in 1983 and entitled *The Challenge of Peace: God's Promise and Our Response*,[1] is surely one of the most remarkable documents of our time. First of all, it is difficult to refer to a statement running to 103 printed pages, with 127 extensive footnotes, as a letter, never mind a *pastoral* letter. Secondly, the process by which it was produced involved a drafting committee of five bishops who worked for more than two years and held public hearings all over the country to provide opportunities for experts and others to make their views known. Next, at least two preliminary drafts were circulated to Catholic dioceses of the country, with instructions that they be discussed as widely as possible with the faithful, and that any comments or criticisms be forwarded to the drafting committee.

Finally, at a special meeting of the National Catholic Welfare Conference in Chicago in May 1983, 247 Catholic bishops convened to publicly debate the text, to offer amendments, and to vote on the question of whether or not the perfected text should be promulgated as the official position of the Catholic bishops of the United States on the complex and vexing issues of war and peace in the nuclear age. In the final vote, 238 bishops voiced approval, and 9 demurred. But that vote marked, as the bishops had hoped, not the end but the beginning of the debate, for Catholics and for many of their fellow citizens.

Before the bishops had taken their final vote a counterargument was written by Michael Novak, signed by more than 100 prominent American Catholic laypersons, and widely disseminated under the title, *Moral Clarity in the Nuclear Age.*[2] A highly complimentary foreword to the book was written by Billy Graham, and an entire issue of William Buckley's *National Review*[3] was given over to its publication. Two members of Congress submitted the entire text for publication in the *Congressional Record.* All of this was just the *initial* response to the pastoral. It is not easy to recall an ecclesiastical document which created greater public furor, or which precipitated a greater production of printed commentaries, arguments, statements of praise, and rebuttals. They continue to appear to the present day.

The tumult occasioned by the publication of the bishops' letter served to focus attention on one of the more intriguing aspects of the study of peace and peacemaking among peoples and nations, which is the role that religion has played throughout human history in providing a framework for the peaceful resolution of conflict and, paradoxically, the role it has played in justifying the most barbaric kinds of bloodletting and devastation. That paradox has never been more evident than in the present age with, on the one hand, for instance, the holy war between Iran and Iraq, or the interreligious slaughter between Jews, Moslems, and Christians in Lebanon, or the sectarian savagery between the Christians of Northern Ireland; and on the other hand, the efforts made by religious leaders to counsel peace and reconciliation.

Tracing Christian attitudes toward war that have helped to shape our common history is a fascinating, if disconcerting, exercise. Jesus explicitly rejected violence and urged his disciples to turn the other cheek, to return good for evil, to bless their enemies and persecutors rather than curse them. In the early centuries of the Christian dispensation Christians were regarded as unfit for military duty because of their exotic attitudes toward violence and warfare, and they were judged to be probably disloyal to the emperor because of their insistence upon loyalty to a higher standard than the imperial will.

History has it that all of that was changed by the actions of the Emperor Constantine, who in 313 A.D. proclaimed Christianity to be the official religion of the Empire and raised the cross as the heraldic symbol of the Roman legions. It is said that Constantine did not become a Christian until his deathbed; he had other matters to attend to first. But he did recognize the value of converting mercenaries into true believers. Convinced that they served a higher cause, the same soldiers fought more ferociously and effectively. Idealism, realized Constantine, is an exceedingly important element in military morale.

The Constantinian bargain was simple and straightforward: the church received the protection and patronage of the emperor, and in return his military campaigns and designs were pronounced in advance to be part of the divine plan for the triumph of justice. While sometimes stated somewhat differently, that is essentially the bargain that has remained in effect in many regimes in many lands down through the ages. There have been dissenters, of course, essentially individuals or small sects like the Mennonites and Friends and Amish of the present era, who have insisted upon the original Christian position of nonviolence; but for most some form of the bargain has provided the moral framework within which they lived and fought. It is not to be thought that such an arrangement was regarded simply as a fundamental compromise with the forces of evil, or a sellout. Beginning with Augustine, the problem of reconciling the teachings of the Prince of Peace with the perceived need for the use of armed force has occupied the time and energies of countless philosophers and moral theologians.

What emerged over time, in various modifications, is a set of guiding principles, variously referred to as the *theory*, or the *doctrine*, of just war. The undergirding notion is that while violence against one's fellow human beings is reprehensible, it is essential that justice prevail in human society lest the weak and the innocent suffer hopelessly at the hands of the violent. So there must be — at least theoretically — situations in which violent efforts must be made in defense of the innocent. Within any organized society some sort of order must prevail, and the maintenance of order may involve the use of coercion on the recalcitrant. There may be no courts and cops in heaven, but here on earth they remain a necessity.

However, problems of a different order arise in the arena where different societies or nations make contact and try to protect their own interests. Frequently there is no higher authority or body of law through which the clash of interests can be adjudicated. Clausewitz, among others, declared warfare to be simply the ultimate effort to carry forward national policy. When compromise seems elusive, and the abandonment of one's position is the only alternative in the face of an obdurate foe, draw and fight!

As a realistic Christian alternative to *Realpolitik*, the just war doctrine has two parts: *jus ad bellum*, in which an effort is made to determine under what conditions it could be morally permissible for one society to declare war on another; and *jus in bello*, which outlines the moral limits governing the conduct of combatants once the conflict is underway. It will be seen that the various principles enunciated by the doctrine really raise more questions than they settle. For instance, in *jus ad bellum*, seven standards are generally enumerated:

1. *A just cause.* The motive must be to protect the good against a clear and imminent threat of evil, such as the protection of innocent life, the defense of a civilized and humane society (not necessarily one's own) against the onslaught of barbarism, or the defense of human rights. A problem inherent in the effort to establish the justice of one's own cause is the difficulty, in the absence of a disinterested arbiter, of distinguishing between justice and self-interest.

2. *Competent authority.* War cannot morally be initiated by an individual, or a small band of malcontents; it must result from the considered action of a legitimate government, which is acting within its own constitutional and statutory limitations. What does that proposition do to the right of an oppressed people to resort to violent revolutions against a tyrannical regime?

3. *Comparative justice.* Is the threat to justice serious enough to justify the taking of human life? Clearly not every injustice can justify bloodshed. How can the question be answered rationally and deliberately, given the limitations on human knowledge of the future? For example, would any of those involved in launching World War I have done so if they had known the cost and the outcome?

4. *Right intention.* It is one thing to declare the justice of one's cause when compared to the position of the adversary, but the original reasons justifying bloodshed must be kept constantly in view, and when they are realized, the conflict must be terminated. No revenge, no retribution, is to be tolerated, only the preservation of justice. No demand for unconditional surrender could possibly satisfy this condition.

5. *Last resort.* Before resorting to hostilities all peaceful alternatives must have been exhausted. Clearly, those of a more hawkish attitude will exhaust alternatives more quickly than will their more dovish colleagues. Among other things, this principle requires a great deal of prior consideration of all possible alternative courses, together with a very cautious appraisal of the likely cost/benefit results of military action.

6. *Probability of success.* No mass suicide, or its equivalent, is permitted under this moral code, even in the defense of justice. Further, this principle requires a belligerent government to consider, *before* as well as during the hostilities, the kind of situation which would mandate surrender.

7. *Proportionality.* The good to be achieved by the initiation or prolongation of hostilities, and the good reasonably to be expected as a result, must be constantly reevaluated. Such a continuing concern with costs and benefits would lead constantly back to a reflection upon just cause and the chances of success, however defined.

The just war doctrine would hold that, even if the earlier conditions had been met, and hostilities between nations had commenced, certain additional principles are still to be applied to the conduct of the fighting. These principles, grouped under the title *jus in bello*, are *proportionality* and *discrimination*. When one considers the kinds of weaponry available to combatants today, and the manner in which modern military strategies and tactics contemplate the use of such weapons, we are thrown back to a reconsideration of the whole question of whether or not, or under what sorts of very extreme conditions, it can be said that it is morally justified to begin any war at all.

The principle of *discrimination* holds, for instance, that the taking of innocent human life cannot be justified even in a war waged to defend justice. Of course, even the most bellicose recognize that My Lai and similar outrages are beyond the pale of justifiable military action, but difficulties arise with the consideration of such modern military tactics as the fire-bombing of cities, or the use of chemical and biological weapons, or the declaration of "free fire zones," or indiscriminate submarine warfare. If it is argued that the resort to such activities is a necessary part of modern warfare, the prior question recurs in a new form. If warfare *absolutely requires* such actions, are there any grounds which would make it morally acceptable to declare war on another nation? The alacrity with which that question will be answered in some quarters is a good indication of how seriously the principles of *jus ad bellum* are regarded. More often than not, a much simpler and easier rationale is employed: the evident malignancy of our foes makes anything that we do to them, or plan to do to them, morally justifiable.

The principle of *proportionality* was referred to earlier as a condition to be considered prior to the opening of hostilities, but it also requires that the balance between relative goods, or relative evils, be kept in mind until the war ends and peace is restored. It was this principle which finally moved the Catholic bishops of the United States to call for an end to the American war in Vietnam, on the grounds that whatever the original aims and motivations might have been for our involvement, a point had been reached at which there was nothing to be gained which could conceivably justify the continued destruction of the Vietnamese society and countryside. Others had reached the same conclusion far earlier by the application of one or another of the principles of *jus ad bellum*, or in many cases by the use of a quite different moral calculus.

The just war doctrine has over the centuries been offered as the more realistic alternative to the gospel of peace on the grounds that there must exist some sort of order among, as well as within, nations and, in the absence of a better way of sorting out the moral principles governing the efforts to achieve that order, these principles will serve. At least they represent an effort to achieve justice. The Christian pacifist in the age of Augustine, or on the threshold of the twenty-first century, would be inclined to say that justice is not the question; personal justification is. An individual, or a relatively small group of people, cannot be reasonably expected to establish justice in a dark and sinful world, but one can attempt to be a just and nonviolent person, in imitation of the Lord Jesus. If enough people in a community, or a broader society, come to the observance of those same principles, both peace and justice will prevail. In the meantime, at least the individual pacifist will not perpetrate an injury upon another person, and that in itself is a contribution to the order and justice and peace which we all seek.

Beginning then the study of the moral issues involved in war and peace with a careful review of the traditional Christian formulations of the just war theory reveals two things. First, as John Howard Yoder has so carefully and effectively demonstrated in such works as his brief and cogent *When War Is Unjust*, there is nothing simple or easy about the principles of the just war theory and their application to the affairs of persons and nations:

> This review of ups and downs should have made it clear that the just war tradition is not a simple formula needing only to be applied in some self-evident and univocal way. It is rather a set of very broad assumptions, whose implications demand — if they are to be respected as morally honest — that they be spelled out in some detail and then tested for their ability to throw serious light on real institutions and institutional decisions.[4]

Secondly, while the just war theory has provided endless hours and years of debate in the *academic* arena, it simply is not, has not been, and probably cannot be, a serious element in the policy-making process of our nation, or any other. Currently the tradition is adverted to by those who want to argue that the rejection of violence as a tool of national policy is unrealistic in light of the fact that it amounts to unilateral disarmament and surrender to the forces of evil which would then overrun the world. Secondly, Christian tradition, as expressed in the just war doctrine, *requires*, as a matter of justice, those who are capable of doing so to defend the innocent and the weak against injustice, by resort to appropriate means, even violence, as outlined in the principles of the doctrine.

David Hollenbach, S.J., in his *Nuclear Ethics: A Christian Moral Argument*, summarizes the confrontation:

> It is on the level of practical political wisdom that one of the major points of dispute between the ethics of nonviolence and the just war theory is located. Just war thinking more explicitly employs conclusions of political reasoning in formulating its norms for military policy than does the tradition of nonviolence. Just war thinking sees the values of peace and justice as interrelated in a way that is not symmetrical. The protec-

tion of justice (that is, the securing of freedom and other fundamental human rights in a just social order) is regarded as a *prerequisite* of the establishment of a true and lasting peace. There is a causal linkage between the values which implies that a commitment to peace which does not rest on a prior commitment to justice will produce neither peace nor justice.[5]

Most policy makers would be mystified, and more than a little annoyed, by such a debate. The prevailing standard is not some airy concept of justice but the *national interest*, as defined by those in power. Discussions of justice, not to say brotherly and sisterly love and nonviolence, are the sport of philosophers and fools. That attitude and approach to affairs of policy is Machiavelli writ large, and those in public office may very well be devoted believers in *Realpolitik*, the use of power to impose order in an otherwise turbulent and dangerous world. But it is also evident that people, generally speaking, need to feel good about their nation and themselves. They need to believe that whatever efforts or sacrifices they are called upon to make are for the common good. In any society, but particularly in one under democratic governance, the people *must* believe themselves, and their nation, to be righteous. They must believe in the lyrics of the Battle Hymn of the Republic. Otherwise, no hymn, and no battle. Observe what happened when one generation of Americans lost that sense of the righteousness of their cause in Vietnam. The fighting finally stopped, but the *psychological damage*, caused by a loss of confidence in ourselves and in our values, has exacted an appalling toll on the entire nation, from which we have still not recovered.

Realizing, as they do, the need of people for justification — especially people who subscribe to the Christian belief in good and evil, sin and damnation, judgment and redemption — our political leaders have over the years resorted to a ritualistic reference to the just war doctrine, or something akin to it. Wrapped up in the political rhetoric of the time will be assertions of the need to vindicate justice, of the basic evil of our adversaries' actions and intentions, of failed efforts to find another solution to the problem, of the necessity of choosing the lesser evil of armed conflict to the greater evil, whatever it is, or is alleged to be. Our leaders know, as Constantine did, that raising the cross before the troops as their battle standard is an effective maneuver, so long as the emperor still gives the orders.

The fact is that the just war tradition is simply *not used* in the policy-making process leading to the declaration of war, or to the initiation of military interventions of various sorts. Indeed it could not be used in any meaningful way, as Yoder explains, unless well in advance of any possible confrontation with an enemy a very serious commitment of time and resources was made for the purpose of researching a wide range of alternative decisions and options, so that as the policy-making process got underway it could reasonably be said that the policy makers had available an entire array of reasonable choices. What is unmistakably evident today is that our government and virtually all governments devote thousands of hours and millions of dollars to the study of military tactics and strategy, to the design and procurement of new weapons systems, to training personnel, to field maneuvers and war games, to every conceivable activity which might offer some advantage in the event of an outbreak of hostilities, but virtually nothing to considering the kinds of things that might be done, or planned, to find a peaceful means of resolving tension and conflict.

It is not just the study of the techniques of conflict resolution, valuable as they are, which is at issue, but a far wider area of concerns. To take the just war principles individually for just a few examples, if a *just cause* is the first requirement, and if it is at least conceivable that our nation is capable of taking an unjust position in a given controversy, what procedures have we established, or could we establish, in order to test the justice of our position, before unsheathing the sword? Clearly involving a disinterested third party, or a legal tribunal of some sort, as a means of testing the case would seem a prudent move. And if such tribunals as the World Court are imperfect, or others need to be developed, what efforts are we expending to do so? Failure to pursue such efforts would seem to indicate a greater devotion to self-interest, supported by armed might, than to justice.

If war must be declared by *competent authority* in order to be deemed just, it would appear that the government, to be fully competent, must act within the limitations of its own constitution, which is a contractual grant of authority awarded by the people, under the terms and conditions set forth. Without pausing to discuss in detail the number of "secret" military operations conducted by various presidents in recent American history, or our two most recent large-scale wars, neither of which were declared by Congress as required by the Constitution, how much time or effort has been devoted to exploring alternative methods of handling such problems? It is said, for instance, that when enemy missiles are launched and on their way, we cannot call the committees of the Congress into session to consider our next move. True enough, but what of the period *before* the missiles have been launched, like the present time? If it is argued that modern weaponry seems to render inoperative the constitutional requirement that Congress publicly declare war before we dispatch our armed forces on their missions of destruction, what prevents us from having Congress debate at whatever length it wishes the terms and conditions under which we would declare a *state of peace* to exist between our nation and any other on earth with whom we have disagreements?

If the just war tradition requires that there be some *proportionality* between the evil to be suffered, by ourselves and others, due to the exercise of military might, and the good that can be attained and evil avoided as a result of our actions, how is that determination to be made? By whom? Using what criteria? If such a determination can only be made by those in authority in our government, and it must be made in secret according to the criteria which they deem best, then clearly we have come full circle. Those who will have to fight the war, and pay for it, and suffer the consequences, are of necessity excluded from the decision-making process, and the only *moral* decision to be made by them is whether or not to support the government's position. So much for government of, by, and for the people. Raise the cross, and unsheathe the sword!

How could the decisions about *proportionality*, both *ad bellum* and *in bello*, be made other than in the current fashion? Clearly, no one has an exact answer to that question, but a good beginning would open the discussion to embrace people at all levels of society, and in every age group. What would they do, as individuals, if faced with certain hypothetical situations? As the public dialogue broadened and deepened, people might turn out to be considerably less bellicose and more morally sensitive than we expect, and they might begin to draw some rather clear policy lines for the guidance of their elected representatives in both the executive and legislative branches.

Today we are inclined to regard such proposals as whimsical. If that be the case, then our present procedures are about as much as we can expect. But then, what are we to say about the moral responsibilities of the young Air Force officers who go on control duty in a missile silo containing a weapon which is not only quite capable of obliterating an entire city with all of its inhabitants, but which is actually *aimed* at such a city? What is their moral situation if the order comes to fire that missile? Can they conscientiously report for duty, knowing that such an order may come?

Are they to seek refuge in the thought that they don't really *know* where the missile is aimed, or that they aren't *sure* that it will reach its target and detonate? Or is it a case of, theirs not to reason why; theirs but to shoot and cry?

What of those who actually aimed the missiles, chose the targets, assembled the weapons, paid for them with their taxes, put them in place, gave the order to fire? At what level in this process are the principles of the just war tradition to be considered and discussed? And by whom?

John Howard Yoder summarizes his view of the just war tradition as follows:

> If the tradition which claims that war may be justified does not also admit that it could be unjustified, the affirmation is not morally serious. A Christian who prepares the case for a justified war without being equally prepared for the negative case has not soberly weighed the prima facie presumption that any violence is wrong until the case for an exception has been made.[6]

Interestingly, the Catholic bishops begin where Yoder ends, although perhaps stating the case somewhat less emphatically. They declare at the outset, "This letter is a contribution to a wider common effort, meant to call Catholics and all members of our political community to dialogue and to specific decisions about this awesome question."[7]

They then go on to set the stage for the dialogue by saying, "The Church's teaching on war and peace *establishes a strong pre-*

sumption against war which is binding on all; it then examines
when this presumption may be overridden, precisely in preserving the kind of peace which protects human dignity and human
rights."[8]

Then they take a look at the world "as it is, not simply as we
would want it to be":

> The view is stark: ferocious new means of warfare threaten-
> ing savagery surpassing that of the past, deceit, subversion,
> terrorism, genocide. This last crime, in particular, is vehe-
> mently condemned as horrendous, but all activities which
> deliberately conflict with the all-embracing principles of the
> natural law, which is permanently binding, are criminal, as
> are all orders commanding such action. Supreme commen-
> dation is due the courage of those who openly and fearlessly
> resist those who issue such commands.[9]

So, first the bishops praise those whose individual consciences
require them to resist the commands of their government when
ordered to perform an action which violates moral principle, and
then they turn to those who feel the obligation to protect the society from evil. Individuals have the right to choose the course of
nonviolence, to opt out; but governments, which exist to promote
the common good, have the *obligation* to protect the weak and
the innocent. Thus, when the society is threatened by violence,
internal or external, *justice* may require a violent response, or resistance.

Confronted with the prospect of violence in a violent world,
the bishops, in seeking restraints against wanton slaughter, turn
for guidance to the traditional doctrines of the just war. They realize that this is a new age, and that science has now provided us
with weapons of unimaginable destructive power, but they need
a fulcrum on which to rest their plea for a new way of looking
at war and international relations; and the just war tradition is
familiar to many of the faithful, and to others of good will to
whom their argument is addressed.

So they begin with the just war tradition and acknowledge
that there is a substantial difference between the enunciation of
moral principles and their application in a highly contingent world.
Yet they firmly condemn as immoral the use of nuclear weapons

against population centers, which was standard U.S. nuclear doctrine during the era of "massive retaliation"; the first use of nuclear weapons as a response to conventional attack, which has been the basic NATO strategy for forty years, and the whole notion of "counterforce" warfare, which contemplates some sort of extended but limited nuclear war.

They run up on a shoal, however, on the question of nuclear deterrence. Confronted with the question of whether it is immoral to possess and threaten the use of weapons which it would be immoral *actually* to use, the bishops try uneasily to balance the demands of the East/West superpower confrontation with the moral imperatives of the just war tradition, especially the principles of discrimination and proportionality.

Without backing away from the condemnation of the *use* of nuclear weapons under any circumstances, the bishops acknowledge, at least implicitly, two significant points. First, they admit that to condemn outright and without qualification the possession and deployment of nuclear weapons would be tantamount to a demand for unilateral disarmament, which would strip them of any credibility in the arena of public opinion and effectively exclude them from participation in the continuing debate. Secondly, they are painfully aware that at the present moment there is no alternative in the international arena to the interplay of raw force, and therefore they grant a "highly qualified" approval to the deterrence policy of the U.S. and its Western allies, as a "balance of forces, preventing either side from achieving superiority."[10]

Recently, at an annual meeting at St. John's University in Minnesota, the bishops restated their carefully qualified acceptance of nuclear deterrence as a military strategy. At the same time, they gave a scathingly critical analysis of SDI, as a transparent effort to seek a position of military superiority over the Soviet Union, and therefore as a wholly unacceptable threat to the present balance of power, or balance of terror. Neither the Congress nor the President seemed to be much persuaded by the arguments of the bishops. American military and nuclear policy did not change much during the five years since the issuance of the first pastoral letter, although recent events in eastern Europe and the Soviet Union bring hope for change in the future.

Not many Christian pacifists occupy high political offices in the United States, but what is called the just war tradition continues to have minimal impact upon the deliberations and decisions of the policy makers. Is consideration and discussion of these questions then only an exercise in academic vanity? No, the moral issues have been raised in the arena of public debate; and while they have not proved to be immediately determinative, they have had some influence on the terms of public discourse, and will have more in the future.

The problem is that only a relatively small segment of the electorate is capable of dealing with issues of international and military policy in terms of moral principles. Nothing much in their experience or education has prepared them for such discourse. In fact, all our cultural standards and mores have operated to the contrary. One need only consider the steady erosion of moral scruples among the so-called civilized nations of the world during the twentieth century, as applied to the tactics of war. We were drawn into World War I in part because the Germans practiced "unrestricted" submarine warfare. In World War II, all nations including the United States practiced unrestricted submarine warfare from the very outbreak of hostilities. We recoiled in horror at the Nazi bombing of civilians in London and Coventry, and within a few years we were fire-bombing Dresden and Tokyo and other metropolitan centers. We not only used nuclear weapons against totally defenseless civilian populations at Hiroshima and Nagasaki, but as a matter of policy have reserved the right to use such weapons again at times and places of our own choosing — and *not* just as a deterrent to nuclear attack upon ourselves.

It is a sign of hope, therefore, that the ethical principles of just cause, and discrimination, and proportionality, and the other elements of the just war tradition, are being introduced into the public dialogue. But that is only the tiny first step in the process of moving toward a more thoughtful and morally sensitive consideration of the problems of war and peace. Having only begun, and with meager results to show in the policy field, one cannot and should not underestimate the difficulties that lie ahead.

Curiously, the debate which consumes the time and energy of the academics and the moralists seems to center about the issue of whether one places greater value upon the preservation of justice in human society, which might require a forceful intervention into the affairs of humankind, or whether one holds nonviolence and the acceptance of suffering to be the supreme value. Neither line of argument, as has been noted, seems to carry much weight with the governmental leaders who make the decisions about the use of force as an instrument of foreign or domestic policy, and it would appear that the rejection of these concerns by our political leadership may represent the classic example of the use of the word *academic* as a dismissive epithet. The preachers of the Christian gospel are told to concern themselves with problems of personal salvation and to stay out of politics.

And yet the debate has to begin somewhere, if we are to retain any claim to the status of moral beings. We simply cannot abandon the field to those for whom not only is might right, but who also argue that the utterly ruthless use of might is the only key to success.

It would seem then that if the moralists are to make any effective headway against the reign of the realists, it would first be necessary to avoid wasting precious time and energy on arguing with each other, and to turn their attention to the principal adversary. But where are the just war traditionalists and the Christian pacifists to find common ground for the reconciliation of their own disputes?

The Catholic bishops clearly understood the need for carrying forward the discussion on two interrelated levels:

> Catholic teaching on war and peace has had two purposes: to help Catholics form their consciences and to contribute to the public policy debate about the morality of war. These two purposes have led Catholic teaching to address two distinct but overlapping audiences. The first is the Catholic faithful, formed by the premises of the gospel and the principles of Catholic moral teaching. The second is the wider civil community, a more pluralistic audience, in which our brothers and sisters with whom we share the name Christian, Jews, Moslems, other religious communities, and all people of good will also make up our polity. Since Catholic teaching has traditionally sought to address both audiences, we intend to speak to both.[11]

To the committed Christian the letter speaks of the relationship of God with humankind, through Jesus Christ and through the life of the Christian community. It draws strongly and directly upon scriptural insights concerning that relationship and what it requires of the believer, including "the disarmament of the human heart and the conversion of the human spirit to God who alone can give authentic peace."[12]

For those who, in T. S. Eliot's phrase, stand at the gate but cannot pray, the letter invokes the standards of the just war tradition, which demand that lines be drawn, limits be observed, which will distinguish a fully human society from a totally barbaric one. The letter grants that it is possible for persons of good will to arrive at differing conclusions in attempting to apply moral and ethical principles to highly contingent, specific situations, but what is unacceptable is the failure to acknowledge the existence of moral principles in the field of human action, and the refusal to attempt to deal seriously and thoughtfully with such questions. The bishops did not urge the academics to abandon their theological and philosophical disputes, but said,

> In developing educational programs, we must keep in mind that questions of war and peace have a profoundly moral dimension which responsible Christians cannot ignore. They are questions of life and death. True, they also have a political dimension because they are embedded in public policy. But the fact that they are also political is no excuse for denying the Church's obligation to provide its members with the help they need in forming their consciences. We must learn together how to make correct and responsible moral judgments.[13]

Teaching peace in a Christian context involves, first of all, an examination of why we call ourselves Christians, and the manner in which being Christian shapes our understanding of who we are, as individuals, and how we relate to others, all others. If the answer is, as so often it will be, that we are no different from others, that we share the same values and attitudes as the rest of humankind, the discussion will stop there. If there is something distinctive about the way Christians perceive reality, and are expected to deal with the problems of everyday life and with other people, then we begin with a close and careful exploration of what those distinctive qualities are, and whether or not they are *actually* present in our days and ways. "The Christian community," writes Father Charles Curran, "calls itself and its individual members to an ever more intense life of discipleship." He continues:

> Christians are to be doers of the word, witnesses to Jesus. The bishops eloquently call for the disarmament of the human heart and conversion of the human spirit. Christians working for peace should be people of prayer, penance, and reverence for life. The consciences of all Christians must be educated to carry out their commitment to work for peace in our age.[14]

When Christians in this society, and throughout the world, become capable of making that kind of personal commitment to the values of the gospel, things may change. The bishops, facing that prospect, conclude on a note of hope: "It is our belief in the risen Christ which sustains us in confronting the awful challenge of the nuclear arms race. Present in the beginning as the word of the Father, present in history as the word incarnate, and with us today in his words, sacraments, and spirit, he is the reason of our faith and hope."[15]

It is not necessary that all share that vision and that faith in order to work for peace and the reduction of violence in human society, but Christians, if they understand the significance of their own traditions, have a real contribution to make to that effort.

NOTES

1. *The Challenge of Peace: God's Promise and Our Response* (Washington, D.C.: U.S. Catholic Conference Office of Publishing Services, 1983).

2. Michael Novak, *Moral Clarity in the Nuclear Age* (Nashville: Thomas Nelson, 1983).

3. *National Review* (April 1, 1983).

4. John Howard Yoder, *When War Is Unjust* (Minneapolis: Augsburg Publishing House, 1984).

5. David Hollenbach, S.J., *Nuclear Ethics: A Christian Moral Argument* (New York: Paulist Press, 1983), p. 22.

6. Yoder, *When War Is Unjust*, p. 82.

7. *The Challenge of Peace*, no. 6.

8. Ibid., no. 70 (emphasis added).

9. Ibid., no. 71.

10. Ibid., no. 174.

11. Ibid., no. 16.

12. Ibid., no. 284.

13. Ibid., no. 281.

14. Charles E. Curran, "The Moral Methodology of the Bishops' Pastoral," in *Catholics and Nuclear War*, ed. Philip J. Murnion (New York: Crossroads Publishing Co., 1983), p. 53.

15. *The Challenge of Peace*, no. 339.

2

The Credibility of Ecclesiastical
Teaching on the Morality of War

JOHN H. YODER

THE DOCUMENTARY BACKGROUND of my assignment comes not from the realm of government but from two texts recently circulated by Christian bishops. Both texts were original, both important.

The Challenge of Peace, the 1983 Roman Catholic pastoral letter, introduced more than one important innovation in Catholic public moral thought, including a description of the two perspectives called "just war" and "nonviolence" as complementary and convergent. This was not previously the Catholic tradition.

"In Defense of Creation," the 1986 Methodist letter, improves the accuracy of the historical account by noticing the "crusade" beside the other two types, making three logical options. It is in fact odd that bishops of the church of Urban II, Bernard of Clairvaux, and Innocent III should have leapfrogged over the Middle Ages in such a way as to miss the Crusades. It is also odd that it should be Methodists who remind them of that past.

After having set out those three types, however, the Methodist text goes on to set the threefold typology aside as inadequate. Instead, the bishops respond to the unprecedented issue of deterrence by spreading out a sevenfold spectrum. Six of the seven types on the spectrum are, however, after all variants of the "just war" view, differing only in how they read issues of strategic detail. Then the bishops choose to espouse clearly "none of the above," asking their readers instead to be very concerned and politically active. In response to this fudging, the late Paul Ramsey, Protestantism's premier interpreter of the just war view in his genera-

33

tion, wrote his last book, *Speak Up for Just War or Pacifism.*[1] He accused the bishops (or their writer Alan Geyer) of appealing inconsistently to two contradictory modes of moral choice, being thereby both intellectually and pastorally irresponsible.

To these two texts it may be helpful to add two other documents, the German bishops' "Out of Justice, Peace" (April 18, 1983), and the French bishops' "Winning the Peace" (November 8, 1983).[2] Occasional references to these European letters will measure the extent to which *The Challenge of Peace* is "catholic," in the practical sense of saying what is believed everywhere.

Taken together the two American bishops' letters represent the standard account of the conceptual lay of the land, from which my present analysis seeks to move forward. They both recognize pacifism (or "nonviolence," the term preferred by the Catholic text) as an authentic Christian moral possibility beside the mainstream just war tradition. Both groups of bishops affirm this; for Catholicism the affirmation is new. The European letters do not support it.

Pacifism and the just war tradition begin at the same point logically, we are told, in their presumption against the use of violence. They converge toward the same point practically today, in their common rejection of disproportionate, indiscriminate, or unwinnable war.

My present agenda arises from the divergence which remains between these two admissible Christian views: *pacifism* and the *just war*. The episcopal account of their differences and commonalities raises three questions, only one of which I propose to pursue here. I must however identify the other two. One is more historical, one more abstruse.

The abstruse one concerns the perennial challenge of how to adjudicate clashes between systems of moral discourse which are prima facie incommensurable. Some claim, for example, that the pacifist rejection of killing is a pure case of principled deontology. It holds all killing to be forbidden regardless of circumstance, and therefore is subject to all the strictures addressed in general to moral absolutisms. The just war tradition on the other hand, accepting war under certain circumstances and not under others, depending on what is at stake, is consistently consequentialist. Then the difference about the morality of war reduces to a methodological difference between an ethic of means and one of ends. In every decade some seek to avoid facing the war issue by taking refuge in the method issue.

Is this characterization correct? Is it the case that the difference between the two views on war is not really about war at all, but about conflicting modes of moral discourse in general? If so, could that classical clash be adjudicated or transcended from some other perspective? Is there anything about the common presumptions, or about the present pragmatic convergence between the two stances, to which the bishops point, which could contribute to a restatement of the nature of the debate between consequentialist and principled morality?[3]

The other question, the historical one, is a matter of accuracy. It is factually not true that these two positions, pacifism and just war reasoning, are what Christians since the fourth century have held to. As the Methodists have already noted, *The Challenge of Peace*, in saying that that was the case, ignores the fact that the most prominent church leaders of the Middle Ages preached up crusades. Although rhetorically the two concepts, justifiable war and crusade, overlapped in the Middle Ages, their moral logic does not. They differ significantly, as the Methodists recognize, and as historians have recognized, especially since Roland Bainton,[4] with regard to last resort, probable success, just cause, legitimate authority, legitimate means, and sometimes with regard to noncombatancy. If *The Challenge of Peace* had named this medieval phenomenon and disavowed it, that would have made its contemporary teaching more credible. Simply ignoring such a pivotal historical phenomenon makes us wonder how adequate the rest of the account is.

But there is more than that; there are two other phenomena, impossible for the historian of ethics to miss, which both documents ignore. Unless these realities are named and their power acknowledged, ethicists and pastors are in the clouds.

One of them is what Michael Walzer, author of the best survey in the field,[5] calls "realism." Others use the label *raison d'etat*, or "prudence," or "national interest." From the cynics of antiquity with whom Hugo Grotius argues in his "Prolegomena" to *The Laws of War and Peace*,[6] through Machiavelli, down to this century's Hans Morgenthau, there are those for whom the very notion of a network of binding criteria, able either conceptually or institutionally to impose *any* serious restraint, is simply silly and, because counterfactual, also immoral. Warriors will do what they have to do, and any talk of restraint *on moral grounds* is deception.

The other phenomenon, again logically quite distinct, is named variously by Michael Walzer: he calls it frenzy, hysteria, or excess killing. Our simplest code name for it is perhaps "Rambo." It glorifies brutal virility. It is usually racist and xenophobic. It is mythopoeic in ascribing absolute evil to the adversary and absolute virtue to one's own cause. It is infantile in getting a kick from violence for its own sake. Sylvester Stallone makes his millions by pandering to and reinforcing our culture's adolescent appetite for that kind of drama. We train our Marines that way. George Bush cited Tom Clancy's novels as foreign policy guides during the electoral campaign.

Now certainly neither the Methodist bishops nor their Roman Catholic counterparts make any brief for "realism" in that formally cynical sense, nor (even less) for the macho cult of violence. Yet by ignoring the presence and power in our society of those less moral alternatives, both groups perpetrate and perpetuate a self-deceiving misreading of the pastoral situation. This perhaps partly explains the slimness of their long-range impact. They name the more careful and concerned strands of teaching one can find in intellectual history, yet without taking pastoral responsibility to identify the threatening alternatives.

Confessional statements from Nicaea to Barmen regularly name the false doctrine which has called them forth; so do effective pastoral letters. By laying out the doctrinal situation regarding justifiable war as if things were conceptually under control, while ignoring the powers behind the decisions people really make, these bishops lead their readers to underestimate the crucial need for the teaching they claim has already been in effect. Thereby they dull the intended critical edge of their pastoral comment.

This lack of critical edge enabled the Catholic statement with a good conscience to compare the worst aspects of the Soviet system of 1983 with the best intentions of our own. This sets up the political analysis so that the Soviet threat to democratic values is a part of *just cause* considerations; yet the letter does not avow "Rambo" or "Machiavelli" as internal threats to our own ability to measure responsibly last resort, proportion, or discrimination.

The bishops do nothing pastorally to change the fact that, historically, just war rhetoric has routinely served to cover for wars which were really of the three other kinds, while bishops, pastors, and chaplains did not discernibly use the "just war" tools to denounce that fact.

The Criteria of Credibility

The third question, my primary assignment, is to clarify what it would take to make just war reasoning, the option which the Catholic letter purports to apply, morally and institutionally credible. The just war theory *purports* to be a system of interlocking criteria capable of illuminating concrete moral decisions between and among authentic political/strategic/tactical options, as the other positions cannot do.[7] My assignment is therefore to ask how the just war ethicist or lawyer, politician or general can so articulate that self-interpretation that it might be possible to validate or invalidate it, not by going through past history to look for whether there was ever a just war, but by unfolding from within the system itself the conditions of its inner coherence.

In this exposition I am not advocating backhandedly my own pacifist ideals. To make the case for my own views would call for a biblical and a pastoral argument. What I am doing here is rather seeking ecumenically to give the benefit of the doubt to the mainstream theological tradition. My stake in the consistency of the just war system is triple: (a) pragmatically: if and when its restraints are effective, its application will save lives; (b) ecumenically: any theology ought to be honored by being measured, by others who do not hold it, by the criteria by which it claims to be validated; and (c) prophetically: should it be the case, as some "realists" argue, and a few pacifists, that the just war system is an elaborate self-justifying self-deception, incapable of effective implementation, then the sooner that deception is unveiled, the sooner moral persons will face honestly the other choices. What would it take for the majority just war tradition to be morally credible, intrinsically worthy of respect?[8]

Just war thinkers need, for the sake of their own moral integrity, to make clear how their use of just war categories enables them to ward off the more popular and less careful modes of holy war, "realism," and "Rambo" chauvinism. Those other modes are not mere mental constructs; they are temptations. There are real people out there, some of them in public office, who take and publicly advocate those positions. What is at stake is then the moral credibility of those who hold that their acceptance of *some* violence is not a blank check, not murder.

What then is the just war system? The system is a set of criteria by which to evaluate the concrete characteristics of a particular war. There is no one official list of these criteria, but the rough consensus of the different interpreters of the tradition is far-reaching.[9] What will it take to make credible the claim of those who say that they do in fact plan to govern their political responsibility by this tradition?

The just war tradition is a commonsensical system. Its interpreters logically assume that its primary terms have self-evident definitions. Yet every term is susceptible to more than one interpretation. What makes a cause *just,* an authority *legitimate?* It is formally characteristic of common-sense positions that they tend to assume that the meanings of their operative terms are obvious to all. They thereby ignore or neglect the basic definitional tasks which philosophical analysis and cross-cultural comparison cannot help raising.

The just war tradition is, secondly, an empirical system. The other ways of justifying war — the "realistic" mode, the "holy" one, and the macho one — do not need to attend carefully to the details of the case. They make their decisions on other grounds. The same is the case for the pacifist. The justifiable war view, on the other hand, is dependent on a number of criteria, which must be applied to empirical data in the world. If that distinctive logical shape is to be honored, its prerequisites are of several kinds.

I. THE INTENTION OF THE USERS OF THE JUST WAR TRADITION

A. We need to know whether the just war ethicist does in fact intend the use of criteria to be capable of yielding a negative judgment on the admissibility of a particular war or a particular weapon. This "strict construction" is the prima facie implication of the system. It is presupposed by the accusations against the other side which provide the most current notions of "just cause." It is presupposed by the modern concept of selective conscientious objection. It is presupposed by the use which both groups of bishops make of the criteria of discrimination, immunity, and proportion, as they condemn our present national policy of nuclear deterrence. It is presupposed by prosecuting "war crimes." Yet there are points in the argument where that possibility of negation is not affirmed.[10]

B. If there is a verbal commitment to make actual *personal* moral choices against a given war, or a given strategy, is there a serious readiness on the part of individuals to bear the cost of the possible negative decision? For the citizen, this would mean opposition politics. For the soldier it would mean a selective refusal to use illegitimate means, and a general refusal to fight under an illegitimate authority or for an unjust cause. For a munitions factory worker it would seem to mean general refusal ever to produce weapons that could never be legitimately used, and a conditioned refusal to produce weapons that could otherwise be legitimate if a particular planned use was wrong. First of all this is a question of stated intention, of will.

C. It is secondly a question of education. For such moral accountability to be real, there must have been some kind of effective moral education, acquainting the individual with the basic notion of moral accountability, as well as with the criteria by which it must be guided. How many high schools do that kind of civics instruction? How many curricula in our war colleges and ROTC units teach the grounds, or the procedures, for disobeying an unjust order?

D. If there is a commitment to make moral *public choices*, is there public preparation for the alternative? As I have demonstrated elsewhere,[11] the alternative to a war which one cannot morally pursue is to sue for peace. This would be the duty of a field commander on tactical grounds, of a theater commander on strategic grounds, or of a government for the war as a whole. This alternative has been clearly stated for thirty years by the most responsible nonpacifist theologians, including John Courtney Murray and Paul Ramsey, yet we have seen no contemporary prominent political spokesperson or political scientist acknowledge it. There is no evidence that our institutions of higher military education prepare accordingly the future commanders they train.[12] Neither group of bishops, writing two and a half and three decades after Murray, Ramsey, et al., has acknowledged the problem. The implication of suing for peace is that the nation's leaders would need to do contingency planning to chart and evaluate possible alternative ways of defending the nation's values.

When in 1957 Sir Stephen King-Hall, Commander of Her Majesty's Navy, instructor in military science, wrote *Defense in a Nuclear Age*,[13] he noted his technical conviction that nuclear weapons can never be rationally used and concluded that other appropriate means of defense would be needed, which he was confident an Anglo-Saxon democracy could devise.[14] But where is the national investment in planning for the cases where military means will be morally unusable? If such alternatives are conceivable and have not been investigated, the claim of "last resort" is forfeited.

II. EMPIRICAL ACCURACY

E. The just war tradition argues that the decision about a war or a weapon must be based upon the facts of the case. These facts are however not easily agreed upon. In all important cases they are in fact the object of purposive disinformation. If then the agents of moral discernment are to make responsible decisions, the information on which they are to base their evaluations must be provided by objective and competent sources. That must mean independent sources. By definition they cannot count on the political and military authorities themselves, or on the information channels which those authorities control in times of crisis, to provide the data on which dissent can be based. Is someone in fact providing for those information sources? They would have to be for just war rigor to be thoroughly implemented.

F. But even if we were not misled by intentional disinformation from partisan sources, all empirical information is subject to uncertainty. How sure must one be of all the component factual judgments for recourse to war to be justified? If there are five different debatable readings of actual fact at stake in determining whether a given possible war meets all the criteria, and if each of these readings is 80 percent likely to be right, then the cumulative probability of the combined evaluation's being correct is 80 percent to the fifth power, or 33 percent. That means that the probability of being factually wrong in the cumulative factual reading is two-thirds. Yet in any complex and contested political decision there are more than five contested component factual readings, and the chance of error in each of them is hardly as little as 20 percent. Then we shall be launching into hostilities 100 percent sure to destroy lives and other values, on the basis of factual and predictive readings which are more likely to be wrong than right. Can moral responsibility which claims to be rational disregard this element of uncertainty?

G. The option of individual selective conscientious objection is sufficient only if individualistic decision is held to be morally adequate. But as the Roman bishops say explicitly and the Methodists implicitly, to leave decision in morally important political matters to individual conscientious integrity is not an adequate foundation for decisions that are collective in their nature. The credibility of the claim that just war discernment applies objective criteria, publicly known to natural reason, to the facts of the case, would be abandoned if it were to be argued that each decision allegedly based on the just war theory must ultimately be left to individual conscience. To conceive of moral dissent only in the form of the selective conscientious objection of courageous individuals is apolitical and undemocratic. But then there would need to be some organ of shared information and decision.

Both groups of bishops do in fact accept that role, with regard to only one kind of use of only one kind of weapon. They do it with regard to only one set of the dozen or so classical just war criteria, namely, discrimination, noncombatant immunity, and proportion. These three interlock: each depends on the others. Discrimination is a procedural criterion, without which the other two cannot be respected.[15] The immunity of the innocent is a deontological or principled imperative; proportion is a consequential one. Countercity use of nuclear weapons sins against all three. That is therefore logically the easiest case, for which the just war tradition logic can yield a firm negative conclusion. It is the only one which these pastoral letters have dared to touch.

If the *principle* of shared decision were to be seriously respected, pastoral responsibility would have to be ready to evaluate many more claims — not only the *ad bellum* criteria of last resort, intention, just cause, probable success, and the proportionality of cost and benefit; but also the *in bello* standards as they apply to other strategies and tactics than the nuclear bomb. Since writing their letters neither group of bishops has taken any further steps toward greater breadth in applying other criteria.

III. SUBSTANTIVE DEFINITION OF THE CRITERIA

H. If the claim is to be sustained that the just war tradition is capable of structuring effective moral discernment, the definition of the criteria needs to be moved from the unexceptionable self-evidence of common sense to the kind of clarity which the word *criterion* normally signifies. They have to be so defined that they can be used to measure with.

James Childress, an insightful current interpreter of the just war tradition, has argued, in a landmark article on "Just War Criteria,"[16] that whereas the tradition makes sense as a "formalist theory," the doctrine breaks down at this point because a "substantive theory" is dependent on a common cultural consensus, which no longer obtains, though it once did. All that remains is a "formalist" role as "framework for debate." For Childress the difference between form and substance is self-evident and profound. If he is right, the doctrine may provide a common vocabulary for public discourse. But discourse is ultimately vitiated by pluralism.

There is a philosophical paradox here. Childress is, on one level, presupposing and extending the notion which moral thinkers used to call "natural law"; but on another he is exploding it. He begins by applying a "natural reason" approach to the question of how one might think morally about the legitimacy of harming people toward whom one recognizes a prima facie duty not to harm them. That is as far as one can go in abstract formalism, and on that level it is convincing. He shows how the several just war criteria, as long as they are kept formal, can be explained as a check list of the kinds of questions to ask before overriding that prima facie duty of respect for the adversary's dignity. With that I agree: that is the first step toward sharable moral accountability.

But then natural reason breaks down just where we need it,

namely, when we ask it to make the criteria transculturally usable to measure with. If each party's perception of the values which justify its own belligerence is incorrigibly community-dependent, we are in the crusading mode after all.

In the face of Childress's focusing of the problem, the friends of the just war tradition can take either of two paths. They can admit the limits of the community for and to which they speak. Their documents are called "pastoral letters," after all. There would be no shame or confusion involved in granting that the *substantial* definitions which they apply are specifically those of Roman Catholic Christians, or those of Methodists, in the United States. They could still count on considerable commonality with justice notions shared with other Americans but without letting the bindingness of those notions — for Catholics, for Methodists, for others of "good will" who understand — be dependent on the assent of all others.

The other path would be to prove by some survey process that certain definitions are in fact more widely shared, that they are not in fact hopelessly community-dependent even though Childress says that in principle they might be. Either path could come up with substantial content. Neither has been taken thus far.

Space forbids my reviewing the entire spectrum of logically formulated criteria to show in detail how each is in need of definition. I noted that *The Challenge of Peace* lists seven criteria *ad bellum*, yet no effort is made by the letter to apply any of them to America's wars past or present. The bishops apparently assumed that there are no problems there. This was a singular omission at a time when the United States was involved in surrogate hot wars in Afghanistan, in Central America, and (less directly) in Angola.

The bishops' limiting themselves to the nuclear agenda lets them avoid facing it. Many who agree to reject war between modern nation-states support insurrection against unacceptable regimes. What replaces "legitimate authority" in that case? What changes in accountability follow from naming freedom or justice instead of peace as the ultimate intention?

There are those on both sides of the debate about liberation theology who see in it a great innovation, at the point where violent insurrection may be justified. To make that argument on either side is evidence of inattention to history. Legitimate insurrection as a logical possibility goes all the way back to Thomas Aquinas.[17] As the topic of a corpus of literature it goes back to the 1570s,[18] expanding themes opened up by the peasants' wars and then by Zwingli and Calvin. As concrete politics it was implemented successfully in the Puritan wars of the 1640s. It is however the case that the criteria for evaluating the legitimacy of a particular organ of military "liberation struggle," as a distinctive kind of war, with regard to probable success, authority, and means, are largely undefined and easily replaced by ideological rhetoric.

I. A subset of the challenge of defining the meaning of terms is the need to clarify the logic whereby the multiple criteria are supposed to interlock. A "strict construction" would demand, if not mathematical absoluteness, at least some kind of moral certainty that all of the criteria are met. It would hardly work to say that just intention would suffice without legitimate authority or just cause, or vice versa. But how do *ad bellum* and *in bello* criteria relate?

The tradition is quite firm in saying that you must respect *in bello* limits even when you are convinced that the adversary's *ad bellum* claims are inadequate. But what do our own *in bello* infractions do to our claims of just cause or legitimate authority? In American experience, the most pertinent case was one where reports of *in bello* infractions being committed in Vietnam convinced a few thousand of our young men that the cause could not be just. At that time, ethicists and pastors certified that selective conscientious objection, based on *in bello* criteria, was morally acceptable. Since the recent pastoral letters attend only to *in bello* limits, the bishops must believe that too, but they give no explicit attention to how much *in bello* infraction it would take to reject how much *ad bellum* legitimacy. We quickly apply this criterion to the adversary, whose cause we claim is unjust or authority illegitimate on the ground of *in bello* infractions, which in that case we call "atrocities."

The appeal to *necessity* is a frequent cover for this gap. In standard military doctrine, necessity is a criterion for further restraint *within in bello* limits. Even means that are licit on the books may be used only when there is no other way. This is stated firmly as early as Francis Lieber's 1863 code and still stands in the most recent redaction of the 1956 U.S. Army *Field Manual FM 27 10.*

Some have tried to structure the evaluation of necessity through the Catholic casuistic scheme of "double effect" reasoning. That grid justifies only actions which are "not intrinsically evil." Then a clear negative ruling on *in bello* infractions would be possible. Yet the lay notion of "military necessity," as Telford Taylor and Richard Wasserstrom have indicated, tends to justify any means which is militarily useful.[19]

J. How is proportional calculation done? To determine which evil is "lesser," all of the projected costs of a war or a strategic option must be somehow calculated against one another. The very term *proportion* presupposes measurement against some common scale. How are these values to be quantified? What can be the common denominator? The criterion of proportion applies on several levels: in *ad bellum* it applies in determining just cause; in *in bello* it is part of the evaluation of intention in issues of "double effect." *The Challenge of Peace* applies *proportion* consideration to particular weapons or tactics, without discussion, as if its concrete criteria were self-evident. They come closest to being self-evident in the most obvious case, where one can claim to save many innocent lives at the cost of fewer innocent lives, although some of the purest hypothetical forms of that ideal case do not convince everyone. It however begins to need a qualitatively different argument, which the ethicists do not seriously provide, when one begins to count enemy innocent lives against friendly ones, or noncombatant against combatant. The confusion grows into a qualitatively different range when one counts lives against strategic values like holding a piece of territory, or against political ones like the survival of a particular regime. The discrepancy grows even greater when the survival of a particular regime is equated with abstractions like *freedom* or *justice*.

The first problem with proportion is thus whether the values we are talking about can be quantified at all and measured against one another on some common scale. If not, the very notion of proportion is nonsense.

A second problem is consequential cost/benefit calculation. It is hard enough, in a realm of intense value conflict, to be sure of the accuracy of readings about present procedures and states of affairs. The uncertainty increases by several orders of magnitude when the quantities being weighed against each other are the future outcomes predicted as likely to result from the complex causal sequences triggered by a specific military choice, in a system where many actors are making and implementing decisions at cross purposes. Third, this is the sector of the problem where the difficulty in defining all of the values at stake and reducing them to a common denominator is the greatest.

IV. NEW NUANCES

K. The above considerations all arise from considering the just war tradition as a classical system. One additional set of questions has arisen with new clarity in the face of the nuclear agenda. This is the point at which both groups of bishops have leapfrogged across the hard questions posed by the entire many-factored checklist of classical just war criteria, to make an apparently decisive stand at the far end of the scale. Yet even at the top of the scale the clarity is not yet total. The deed of massive annihilation must not be committed, we hear clearly. But may one morally threaten to commit it, if the objective in threatening is to avoid having to do it? May you, may a nation, morally threaten to commit an act you may not legally or morally commit?

One component of this new puzzle is its collision with classical notions of the place of *intention* in morality. If you threaten to do something immoral in order to avoid having to go through with it, which is your intention? Going through with the threat if the adversary does not back down? The Catholic bishops of France and those of Germany saw no problem in giving the NATO forces credit for "intending" not mass murder (which their equipment is made for) but peace. The French bishops say with total aplomb, "Threat is Not Use." Is a mugger who holds a pistol to my head not "using" it, as long as he does not need to pull the trigger to get what he wants?[20]

The American Catholic bishops read the same facts in the other direction. One can say that the intention of one who aims a nuclear missile at Moscow is to hit Moscow; intention is incarnate in the function for which a mechanism is made. Or one can say that the real "intention" of a threat is what you are ready to do in the worst case.

It is either assured, or it is not assured, that after a massive Soviet first strike the U.S. commander-in-chief would be able to refrain from retaliating with a similar or stronger second strike. The affirmative reading is fostered by the public theatrics of the President's always having within reach the briefcase with the codes for war. If it is assured that at that moment, after the first strike, retaliation could be stopped, deterrence is in jeopardy. If on the other hand such control is not assured,[21] the difference between "threat" and "use" is gone. There would seem to be no middle ground.[22]

L. The other side of the question of the moral viability of the notion of deterrence is its psychological practicality. Can you make the adversary believe that a threat is real, so that it can deter, without in fact being ready to carry it out? Can readiness to fire the missiles be built into the standard operating procedures of silo dwellers under the plains and submariners under the seas, and yet leave real liberty to a civilian commander-in-chief, not to use those arms in the crunch? The American Catholic bishops seemed in 1983 to believe that the nation could keep the arms, and keep (for a while) their deterrence efficacy, leave them armed in the subs and the silos, yet clearly respect the bishops' prohibition of their ever being fired. The Western European bishops agreed that the all-out nuclear war must never happen but refused to move from there to say that anyone must renounce the weapons' use. To insure deterrence, they had no qualms about credibly threatening even a disproportionate retaliatory strike (since they trust that there will be no need for the blow actually to be struck, there is nothing wrong with its being disproportionate).

The differences at work here are not contrasting readings about the facts of nuclear technology but about styles of moral rhetoric, especially about the notion traditionally labeled *intention*. The American Catholic bishops consider it possible that an executive decision by American politicians might respect their prohibition, although they do not attend critically to proving how that could be possible. It is not prima facie evident that since 1983 any federal political thinkers have been listening.

Nonetheless the bishops still do claim that it is possible to implement politically the restraint the tradition demands. The Methodist bishops, while more strongly rejecting in theory the notion of deterrence, attend even less to the question of whether anyone in public office might respect their prohibition. The French and German bishops, being more concerned for deterrent efficacy, and more confident in the virtues of their command systems, have no reason to say anything about executive decisions.

V. THE SHAPE OF THE QUESTION AS NOW POSED

My intention here has been not to conclude or to obviate a conversation, but to initiate it by identifying its agenda. I have sought only to prepare an outline for the good faith debate about whether the just war tradition is a resource for concrete political decisions.

Some may argue that it used to be that, but that with the fading of the "Christendom" consensus about substantive moral values it can no longer serve. Others can argue in the other direction, namely, that in the more distant past it did not so serve, but that now, with the advent of selective conscientious objection, international treaties, the Nuremberg principles, and the bishops' pastoral thinking, it can begin to be effective.

Or one might say, as *The Challenge of Peace* says about nonviolence, that to apply the just war tradition consistently is possible for individuals but not for communities. "Realists" will continue to argue that just war language is a screen (whether used naively or shrewdly) for behavior which in fact is "holy" or "realistic." Perhaps it can serve fruitfully as rhetoric for the political opposition but cannot be respected as morally obligatory by sovereigns. Perhaps the just war ethicist is just as utopian as the pacifist, to think that the normative system can be applied with integrity. If that is true, some will argue that an honest "realism" would be morally preferable to a self-deceiving use of just war rhetoric.

NOTES

1. Paul Ramsey, *Speak Up for Just War or Pacifism* (University Park, Pa., and London: Pennsylvania State University Press, 1988).
2. English translations of the letters from the German and French

bishops may be found in James V. Schall, S.J., ed., *Bishops' Pastoral Letters* (San Francisco: Ignatius Press, 1984).

3. That statement of what purports to be a foundational issue is deceptive and unhelpful. I made that point briefly in my *Priestly Kingdom* (Notre Dame, Ind.: University of Notre Dame Press, 1985), pp. 113ff.

4. Roland Bainton, *Christian Attitudes to War and Peace* (Nashville, Tenn.: Abingdon Press, 1960). Other historians have objected, quite accurately, that this distinction was not clearly articulated in the Middle Ages. We are speaking here not of medieval vocabulary but of types of moral discourse. On that level Bainton was surely right.

5. Michael Walzer, *Just and Unjust Wars* (New York: Basic/Harper, 1977).

6. See Arthur F. Holmes, ed., *War and Christian Ethics* (Grand Rapids, Mich.: Baker, 1975), pp. 226ff.

7. Pacifism, it is held, cannot make nuanced judgments because it rigidly rejects all war; the other three cannot because they provide no grounds for restraint.

8. The argument here partly parallels my essay in *Theology, Politics, and Peace*, ed. Theodore Runyon (Maryknoll, N.Y.: Orbis, 1989).

9. Beginning with Paris 1856 on maritime law and Geneva 1864 on the treatment of the wounded, peaking 1899 and 1906 with the Hague conventions, continuing since 1949 under the auspices of the United Nations, these texts are accessible in Leon Friedman, *The Law of War: A Documentary History* (New York: Random House, 1972); in Morris Greenspan, *The Modern Law of Land Warfare* (Berkeley, Calif.: University of California Press, 1959); and in Adam Roberts and Richard Guelff, *Documents on the Laws of War* (Oxford: Oxford University Press, 1982). *The Challenge of Peace* does not take any account of this component of the tradition.

10. Briefly specified in John Howard Yoder, *When War Is Unjust* (Minneapolis, Minn.: Augsburg, 1984), pp. 68ff. James Childress, as we shall see later, says it cannot "work" because its working would depend on universal consensus about concepts of justice.

11. John Howard Yoder, "Surrender: A Moral Imperative," *The Review of Politics* 48, no. 4 (Fall 1986): 576–95; more briefly argued in Yoder, *When War Is Unjust*, pp. 64ff.

12. "To whom should a soldier report a war crime when his immediate commander was personally involved in the conduct of the crime?" (W. R. Peers, *The My Lai Inquiry* [New York: Norton, 1979], p. 33). Since Vietnam, military educators are more concerned about these matters. It is however not easy for a vertically structured institution to teach civil courage.

13. Stephen King-Hall, *Defense in a Nuclear Age* (Nyack, N.Y.: Fellowship Publications, 1959).

14. Examples of some alternatives can be found in American Friends Service Committee, *In Place of War: An Inquiry into Nonviolent National Defense* (New York: Grossman, 1962), and Anders Boserup and Andrew Mack, *War without Weapons* (New York: Schocken, 1975), among others. These are briefly alluded to in *The Challenge of Peace* and in the Methodist letter.

15. In *Nuclear War, Deterrence, and Morality* (Westminster, Md.: Newman Press, 1967), pp. 46ff., William V. O'Brien pretends puzzlement at Pius XII's judgment on any weapon which "entirely escapes from the control of man," as if that idea were new. Obviously every common-sense criterion is in need of further definition, but the logic of the Pope's condemnation is clear. If a weapon cannot be controlled ("discrimination") it is by definition impossible either to respect noncombatant immunity or to measure proportionality. Thus discrimination, proportion, and immunity form a threefold cord, each strand dependent upon the others.

16. James Childress, "Just War Criteria," in *War or Peace?* ed. Thomas Shannon (Maryknoll, N.Y.: Orbis, 1980), pp. 40ff.

17. Thomas Aquinas, "Whether Sedition Is a Special Sin," *Summa Theologica*, 2.2., quest. 42, in Holmes, *War and Christian Ethics*, pp. 114ff.

18. Hubert Languet, *Vindiciae contra tyrannos* (1579); see also Duplessis-Mornay, Hotman, Philip Marnix; for recent interpretation see Michael Walzer, *The Revolution of the Saints* (London: Weidenfeld & Nicolson, 1965).

19. See Yoder, *When War Is Unjust*, pp. 58ff.

20. Daniel Ellsberg itemizes at least eight times when the formal threat of nuclear attack by the U.S. has entered into negotiations, to say nothing of the low-level way in which the prospect of escalation is always part of the picture. See his "New Weapons: Will We Use Them?" *Current* (June 1981): 41ff.

21. For a fuller analysis of the themes of menace (deterrence) and "intention," see John Howard Yoder, "Bluff or Revenge: The Watershed in Democratic Deterrence Awareness," in *Ethics in the Nuclear Age: Strategy, Religious Studies, and the Churches*, ed. Todd Whitmore (Dallas: SMU Press, 1989).

22. Standard operating procedures for nuclear-armed submarines are reputed to provide for retaliation even as late as a month after a Soviet first strike against the U.S. The certainty of retaliation is held by strategic thinkers to be more important for deterrent effectiveness than its promptness. But then in case of command/communication breakdown

there might be no way to stop the second strike. How can we know that the Trident commander under the Arctic Sea does not already have on board the orders to fire back in the case of a communications breakdown with the command post? That is what the Soviets are supposed to think.

3

Early Advocates of Lasting World Peace: Utopians or Realists?[1]

SISSELA BOK

THE PLANS THAT Erasmus, the Abbé de Saint-Pierre, Kant, and others offered for moving toward a universal and perpetual peace have long been dismissed as utopian or hypocritical, at times even suppressed as dangerously heretical. These thinkers challenged the common perception of war as an immutable aspect of the human condition and of lasting peace as possible, if at all, only in the hereafter — a perception that has seemed self-evident to most commentators from antiquity onwards, whether they espouse what has come to be called a realist, a pacifist, or a just war perspective.

In the nuclear age, however, nations can no longer afford to leave that perception unchallenged. They cannot run the risk of yet another world war, even in the unlikely event that such a war could be kept nonnuclear. Today's conventional weapons would bring devastation beyond anything that humanity has experienced. Likewise, prolonged regional conflicts are increasingly seen as intolerable, given the levels of impoverishment, homelessness, and suffering that they inflict, as well as the risk that they will ignite large-scale war. The social and environmental threats that nations now face collectively, moreover, call for unprecedented levels of cooperation that will be unattainable except under conditions of lasting peace.

If, therefore, self-preservation now dictates collective efforts toward a lasting world peace, no matter how difficult to achieve, it is worth reexamining the writings of those who once pioneered such an approach. To be sure, they had more than their share of

quick-fix solutions; and the particulars of even the most sophis-
ticated of their plans can hardly be adequate for today's international relations. But two aspects of the best among their writings
are as relevant today as in the past: first, their intrepid challenges
to the common assumption that war will always be with us; and
second, their suggestions for how to create a social climate conducive to the forging of a stable peace.

In the works of Desiderius Erasmus and Immanuel Kant, these
lines of reasoning are pursued with special subtlety and force. They
are as relevant to practical choice by contemporary governments,
organizations, and individuals as to theories of war and peace.
By now, many proponents of realist, just war, and pacifist theories
have come to agree on the necessity of working toward the goal
of lasting peace, while continuing to differ about the means. It
will help, in debating the means, to consider the coordinated,
practical measures explored by these two thinkers in the light of
all that we have later learned about which ones work best and
why. In turn, such a study will require a rethinking, from within
each of the three theoretical perspectives, of the role and the demands of morality in international relations.

I

> It will be enough for me, however, if these words of mine
> are judged useful by those who want to understand
> clearly the events which took place in the past and which
> (human nature being what it is) will, at some time or
> other and in much the same ways, be repeated in the
> future.
>
> Thucydides, *The Peloponnesian Wars*

The conflict between Athens and Sparta depicted by Thucydides has been reenacted time and again over the centuries. Most
thinkers since his time, whether they have gloried in war, tolerated it, or denounced it, have taken for granted that it will remain a constant in the human condition. To be sure, they have
argued, it can be staved off for a time or fenced away from one
or more regions of the world; but experience shows that it cannot

be eradicated for good. To think otherwise is to be caught in an illusion.

They have explained the perennial nature of war by referring, as did Thucydides in the passage cited above, to incorrigible traits in human nature such as pugnacity, vindictiveness, partisanship, and the lust for conquest and power. They have also invoked the external circumstances of scarcity and hardship that drive communities to fight one another in order to survive. These traits and circumstances have in turn often been seen as inflicted on human beings by fate or some supernatural power. Thus Homer portrays the gods as prolonging the Trojan War by using participants for purposes of sport or intrigue or amusement. And the biblical God has been interpreted as imposing hardship and tribulation to punish human beings, to test them, or to separate the just from the unjust.

The debate about how to respond to such a predicament was, for centuries, largely three-cornered. Against the common background of war as a constant in the human condition, the responses accorded with one or the other of what we now call the realist, pacifist, and just war traditions.

Realists, often invoking Thucydides, held that it was useless and perhaps even dangerous to rail against the cruelty and immorality of anything as perennial as war. What mattered, rather, was to act according to the best available strategic estimates of what would serve a ruler's or nation's self-interest. In this way, engaging in wars for the sake of preserving or increasing a nation's independence, wealth, or power was acceptable, even commendable. Moral judgments about the rights and wrongs committed in starting any particular war or in its conduct were, according to such a view, at best beside the point.

Tertullian, Origen, and other early Christian pacifists argued, on the contrary, that morality and religion commanded human beings to renounce war and all killing. No matter how prevalent war might be and no matter what interests any one war might serve, the Christian's duty was to refuse all participation. Otherwise the biblical injunctions to love one's enemy and to turn the other cheek would lose all meaning.

Just war theorists, from Augustine and Thomas Aquinas on, advocated, on similarly religious and moral grounds, limiting rather

than renouncing the recourse to war. Among the causes these thinkers regarded as justifying going to war were, variously, wars fought
in self-defense, wars in defense of an ally, and wars of conquest
and crusade to punish wrongdoing and to convert unbelievers. But
justice also required careful scrutiny of the conduct of the warring forces, no matter how just the cause to which they laid claim.

Beginning in the sixteenth century, a fourth pattern emerged
among the responses to the prevalence of war — that of Erasmus
and other advocates of specific, practical steps toward what they
called "perpetual peace." They challenged, not only the commonly
accepted thesis regarding war's perennial nature, but also the specific claims of thinkers in the existing three traditions regarding
when, if ever, war was legitimate. Because the proposals for a lasting peace were often summarily dismissed or even suppressed, they
did not constitute a lineage of well-known fundamental texts, nor
give rise to the wealth of commentary generated by the other traditions. As a result, advocates of perpetual peace were rarely seen
as contributing to a tradition separate from that of pacifism. By
now, however, it is becoming increasingly clear that they were
shaping a new tradition of thinking about war and peace fully
as worthy of study as the three others. To this tradition belong,
among others, Erasmus, William Penn, the Abbé de Saint-Pierre,
Immanuel Kant, and Jeremy Bentham.[2] Among its interpreters
and critics are Leibniz, Rousseau, and Hegel.[3]

Thinkers in this fourth tradition had no illusions that peace
was somehow a natural state for the human species. And they could
hardly quarrel with the historical record of recurrent aggression,
injustice, and warfare. They meant, rather, to challenge what they
saw as the unthinking extrapolation from that past experience to
the future, the unwarranted inference from what has been to what
must always be. Over time, they argued, nations could break away
from the destructive patterns of the past. But they had little faith,
unlike a number of utopians, in some convulsive political or religious transformation that would bring permanent harmony — the
more so as they had seen at close hand the corrupting and brutalizing effects of unrestrained violence both on perpetrators and on
victims, no matter how humane the original motives.

The synthesis arrived at by these thinkers was eloquently
voiced by Erasmus and formulated with greater precision, clarity,

and scope by Kant. It employs both the realist language of strategy and the normative language common to pacifists and just war theorists. According to this view, nations can only achieve lasting strategic benefits by respecting fundamental moral constraints. But it does little good merely to stress these constraints without setting forth concerted, practical steps to facilitate and reinforce their observance. War may indeed continue to be our lot, they admit; but we are free to choose differently. Each generation, far from being condemned to reenact the errors of the past, has the opportunity to learn from the mistakes and disasters of previous generations, and thus the capacity to move toward a state of perpetual peace.

II

> What is more brittle than the life of man? How short its natural duration! How liable to disease, how exposed to momentary accidents! Yet though natural and inevitable evils are more than can be borne with patience, man, fool that he is, brings the greatest and worst calamities upon his own head. . . . To arms he rushes at all times and in all places; no bounds to his fury, no end to his destructive vengeance.
>
> Erasmus, *The Complaint of Peace*, 1517

Few have spoken out more forcefully than Erasmus about the folly and cruelty of war. Already in his *Adages*, published in 1500 and reportedly more widely circulated at the time than any other book save the Bible, he had inveighed against war in an essay entitled "Dulce bellum inexpertis," or "War Is Sweet to Those Who Have Not Experienced It."[4] Between 1514 and 1517, when a brief interval in the near-constant wars between European powers made a more lasting peace seem at least possible, Erasmus devoted himself wholeheartedly to helping bring it about.[5] He suggested summoning a *congress of kings* — a *summit meeting* among the kings of Europe — for the purpose of signing an indissoluble peace agreement. He revised and expanded his essay on the sweetness of war to the inexperienced for the latest edition of the *Adages*. And he wrote a manual for princes — *The Education of the Christian Prince* — to guide the young Prince Charles of Spain who was shortly to become Charles V.[6]

This book presents a striking contrast to Machiavelli's *Prince*, written a few years earlier but still unpublished.[7] Where Machiavelli had broken away from the stress on virtues so common in previous books of advice for princes, and urged the prince to resort to violence, deceit, and betrayal whenever necessary to gain or retain power, Erasmus emphasized moral virtues as prerequisites to a good reign. And whereas Machiavelli had urged the prince to study war above all else, Erasmus gave precedence to learning "the arts of peace": how to establish and preserve a rule of just laws, improve the public's health, ensure an adequate food supply, beautify cities and their surroundings, and master the diplomatic alternatives to war. A last, brief chapter, entitled "On Beginning War," counsels the prince never to go to war at all, save as a last resort; but "if so ruinous an occurrence cannot be avoided," then the prince should wage it with a minimum of bloodshed and conclude the struggle as soon as possible.[8]

A year after publishing his *Education*, Erasmus returned to the charge with *The Complaint of Peace*.[9] This time he sent his book to all the rulers of Europe rather than addressing it to one prince alone. Peace, speaking "in her own person, rejected from all countries," is the protagonist of this book. Her complaint addresses the irrationality and inhumanity of war. Of all the evils that beset humanity, she argues, surely war is the most puzzling, because it is self-chosen. If the insults and indignities heaped upon her went along with advantages to mortals, she could at least understand why they might persecute her. But since they unleashed a deluge of calamities upon themselves through engaging in war, she has to speak to them of their misfortune even more than complain of her own.

In these several works, Erasmus gives short shrift to the realist and just war schools of thinking that ruled the day at the courts of Spain and other European powers. At the same time he distances himself from pacifist calls for nonresistance at all times. However attractive a war may seem at the outset, first of all, Erasmus argues, it appeals to dreamers, not to realists. From war "comes the shipwreck of all that is good and from it the sea of all calamities."[10] Claims about the benefits of war result, he argues, from inexperience. Those who have had to live through war are too rarely consulted. As a result, each generation foolishly undertakes to learn about war's costs from scratch. Even on the strictest strategic grounds of national self-interest, Erasmus insists, a truly realistic look at the costs of war should dissuade a prince from just about all recourse to arms.

Second, Erasmus is skeptical about claims that particular crusades and wars are just. He writes scornfully of the spectacle of clergy on both sides of so many wars declaiming the just cause of their own rulers. When does one not think one's own cause just? he asks, warning that the likelihood of bias and corruption is so great in seeking reasons for going to war that "the good Christian Prince should hold under suspicion every war, no matter how just."[11] This suspicion, he held, was the more necessary since so many conquests and crusades were being fought in the name of the Christian Church, even though "the whole philosophy of Christ teaches against it."[12]

Third, Erasmus addresses pacifist concerns by holding that wars in self-defense are, indeed, legitimate, but only after all other alternatives, including arbitration, have been exhausted; and only after obtaining the consent of the people, who will, after all, suffer so much more directly from any war than their rulers. If such procedures were taken seriously, it is doubtful whether any war would remain to be fought. But the decision to avoid going to war would then be made on pragmatic as well as religious and moral grounds, rather than constituting an absolutist rejection of all war no matter what the costs.

In *The Complaint of Peace*, Erasmus advances a carefully reasoned attack on the underlying assumption widely shared in his day as in our own: that violent conflict and organized war are somehow inherent in the human condition. He discusses each of the three most common explanations for why human existence should be so burdened with the ravages and deaths that war brings: that war will always be with us because of indelible deficiencies in human nature, unrelenting outside pressures, or divine intention — perhaps because of all three.

To those who embrace the first explanation and point to aggression and vindictiveness as human traits so pervasive that they eliminate all chances of a lasting peace, Erasmus responds by asking, What is it in human beings that predisposes them to war? Are they saddled with indelible personality traits that preclude all chances of a lasting peace? How do we have to envisage human nature for this to be true? If it carries with it traits that make wars inevitable, Erasmus begins, they cannot be traits shared with animals, since animals show no organized hostility to members of their own species. The conduct of human beings can be so much baser than that of animals that the word *bestiality* bestowed upon the worst forms of human conduct is unfair to animals.[13] Neither the viciousness that human beings can show one another nor the increasingly destructive machinery they were coming to employ in combat had equivalents elsewhere in nature.

What about the traits which distinguish persons from animals? Surely they are not such as to predispose us to war. Our human capacity to reason, our inability to survive alone that makes us dependent on family and society, and our "power of speech, the most conciliating instrument of social connexion and cordial love"—these traits, he argues, need hardly be conducive to war. On the contrary, they should predispose human beings to living with one another in peace, not war. It is only our familiarity with everlasting feuds, litigation, and murder, that produces the conduct that we mistake for a natural predisposition to war — the more readily so if leadership, education, and social reforms offer no counterbalance.

To the second standard explanation — that outside pressures of scarcity and hardship and natural calamities inevitably cause recurrent conflicts — Erasmus answers that it is surely madness to add to these undoubted outside pressures all the suffering that wars bring. The corruption into which human societies have fallen has rendered them unable to deal in the most reasonable way with conflicts engendered by such hardships. For the state of affairs in his own period, Erasmus holds rulers responsible above all others. In their greed and folly, they repeatedly and mindlessly drag their peoples into the tragedy of war. But rulers cannot wreak this havoc by themselves. Hatred and conflict have become endemic. Erasmus catalogues the groups which harbor such traits. There are citizens given to strife and dissension; courtiers poisoning the climate with their intrigues and grudges; scholars and theologians at daggerheads with one another; clergy and monastics tearing one another to pieces through their partisan disputes; mercenary soldiers feeding as vermin on the miseries they inflict on human communities.

The third explanation common since antiquity — that the human predisposition to war is due to divine intention — could in principle account for the first two and undercut all proposals for reform. While human nature may not by itself be destined for perennial warfare and while outside pressures might not of their own precipitate it, God may have seen to it that these conditions would nevertheless persist. In response to such theological claims, Erasmus invokes Scripture. Christ's central message is one of peace, forgiveness, and nonviolence. If anyone has intended the brutal, near-constant warfare which admittedly beset Europe in his time, he suggests, it must rather be Satan.

Having countered the three explanations most often brought forth to buttress ancient dogmas about the inevitability of war, Erasmus turns to the future. Though a lasting peace is possible, great changes are needed to bring it about. Peace cannot simply be ordained by religious or political authorities, nor can it be mandated merely through treaties and alliances alone. Rather, it has to be undertaken at every level of society. Kings must work together for the good of their citizens and consult them before embarking on any war. And citizens must grant kings "just so many privileges and prerogatives as are for the public good and no more."[14] Erasmus, who never ceased criticizing kings for their exploitative and brutal schemings at the expense of their peoples, here hints at the alternative of government limited by democratic consent — hard to envisage in his time and dangerous for anyone to promote. If nations submitted, further, to an international court of arbitration, they could avert many wars; if need be, peace should be purchased to prevent still others.

Bishops and priests must likewise unite against war and cease appealing to just war theory to excuse every war their king or the pope undertakes. The nobility and all magistrates must also collaborate in the work of peace. To each of these groups, and to "all who call themselves Christians," Erasmus pleads: "unite with one heart and one soul, in the abolition of war, and the establishment of perpetual and universal peace."[15] But beyond Christianity, Erasmus also wishes to suggest that the hostilities between faiths and nationalities could be tempered if only people reflected that they are, above all, members of the same human race: "If name of country is of such a nature as to create bonds between those who have a common country, why do not men resolve that the universe should become the country of all?"[16]

During the remaining decades of his life, Erasmus saw the world move relentlessly in the opposite direction. Wars of conquest succeeded one another, religious and ideological persecution spread, and the religious conflicts that would later culminate in the Thirty Years' War intensified. Though frequently reprinted, Erasmus's writings on war and peace fell out of favor in many quarters. To militants of every persuasion, his insistence on arbitration and other peaceful means of resolving conflicts seemed an endorsement of cowardice and vacillation. Over time, his work was deprecated, even outlawed. As a result, later advocates of perpetual peace too often ignored the depth and scope of his proposals. They tended, rather, to stress purely diplomatic methods for achieving lasting peace. Thus the Abbé de Saint-Pierre proposed, in 1712, a permanent league of European rulers under common laws.[17] Even today, most texts dealing with issues of war and peace mention Erasmus only in passing, if at all.

III

Wars, tense and unremitting military preparations, and the resultant distress which every state must eventually feel within itself, even in the midst of peace — these are the means by which nature drives nations to make initially imperfect attempts, but finally, after many devastations, upheavals, and even complete inner exhaustion of their powers, to take the step which reason could have suggested to them even without so many sad experiences — that of abandoning a lawless state of nature and entering a federation of peoples in which every state, even the smallest, could expect to derive its security and rights. . . .

Immanuel Kant, "Idea for a Universal History with a Cosmopolitan Purpose"

It was not until Kant published his essay on "Perpetual Peace" in 1795, building on earlier works such as his article on "Universal History," that individual and institutional change were once again brought into public debate as prerequisites for arriving at a lasting peace.[18] Like Erasmus, Kant argues that such a state of peace is fully achievable, even though war, thus far, has been a constant factor in the human condition. But Kant sees greater obstacles to achieving such a peace than Erasmus ever conceded.

Kant shares, first of all, the Hobbesian view of international relations as anarchic. Nations exist in a "lawless state of nature" where "the depravity of human nature is displayed without disguise," whereas, within civil societies, it is at least controlled by governmental constraints.[19] Unlike Erasmus, Kant also agreed with those who held that wars had served important purposes throughout history and had most likely even been intended for such purposes by nature. Without the incentives provided by competition, lust for power, and conflict, human beings might never have developed their talents or their technology much beyond the animal stage. But wars had become increasingly destructive and risked becoming even more so, to the point where a war of extermination could bring about "perpetual peace only on the vast graveyard of the human race."[20] As a result, the time had come when nations would have to break out of the state of nature or perish.

Given Kant's concessions to the holders of the majority thesis, how did he envisage that such a change might be brought about? To begin with, he saw grounds for hope that nature has intended such a shift for human beings. We cannot prove that this is so, nor even infer it, but it is "more than an empty chimera."[21] Each individual life is brief and flawed, but through experience, human beings may eventually achieve a sufficient degree of rationality and the capacity to cooperate in achieving security for themselves and their descendants. That it is *possible* for human beings, thus equipped, to change is clear. Kant acknowledges that human beings do exhibit a propensity to evil and to war, but they also possess a predisposition to good. They are at all times free to choose to act according to what they recognize as right and to guide their lives differently. Though peace will not come of its own accord nor from some oversupply of human goodness, it can be instituted, if chosen.

But bringing peace about will require far more than the piece-meal reforms too often advocated. Plans such as those of the Abbé de Saint-Pierre have been ridiculed as wild and fanciful, Kant suggests, in part because their proponents took for granted that the necessary changes were imminent, easy to institute, and unproblematic. Any realistic approach would have to be based on the recognition that change would be slow to come, that it would require reforms at every level of national and international society, and that such reforms would be bound to fail over and over again unless measures were first taken to change the very atmosphere in which negotiations are carried out.

Accordingly, Kant began his essay on "Perpetual Peace" by proposing a set of "preliminary articles" to help prepare the social climate for the larger institutional reforms. Some of these preliminary articles set forth steps that governments could take right away to reduce the distrust standing in the way of all meaningful cooperation. If governments could negotiate peace agreements without secret reservations concerning future wars; if they could abstain from forcible interference in the affairs of other nations; and if they could, even when at war, discontinue what he called "dishonorable stratagems" such as the breach of agreements or treaties, the employment of assassins, and the instigation of treason within one another's states, then they would, at the very least, not be poisoning the atmosphere for peace negotiations.[22]

By stressing basic moral constraints not only within but also between nations Kant does not mean to say that these constraints, by themselves, will provide all that is needed to ensure a lasting peace.[23] He merely insists that so long as they are not taken into account, there can be no chance whatsoever of instituting such a peace. Distrust, as Hobbes had pointed out before him, undermines the incentive to cooperate. Little wonder, then, Kant argues, that a lasting peace has been out of reach. The *reasons* for such debilitating distrust have never been carefully addressed. But at the same time, we need not imagine that peace will continue to elude humankind, once the constraints are taken seriously and once it becomes clear that they are indispensable to long-term collective survival.

Along with creating a climate that allows for institutional reform, Kant sees three "definitive articles" as necessary for a perpetual peace among nations. The first calls for the achievement, over time, of a world in which more and more states have representative governments elected by free citizens equal before the law. Such a form of government will do much to cut back on the wars of any state, since citizens tend to be far less enthusiastic about wars they know they will have to pay for and fight in than autocratic leaders who impose taxes and give orders from the sidelines. But of course, citizens in such states can still be persuaded to concur in wars of conquest by skillful propaganda. As a result, additional international measures are necessary. The second article proposed by Kant calls for the joining together of states in a federation capable of keeping a just peace. The third calls for respecting the human rights of visitors or outsiders to such states so as not to enslave or conquer them.

Kant may well have been thought utopian to speak of the spread of representative government as conducive to lasting peace at a time when only the young American republic could lay claim to a stable form of such governance, and to invoke "a universal right of humanity" in condemning slavery and imperialistic conquests in a period when these practices were so widespread. But he insisted that such an idea was not "fantastic and overstrained." "Only under this condition can we flatter ourselves that we are continually advancing toward a perpetual peace."[24]

IV

In your hands rests our future. By your labors at this conference we shall know if suffering humanity is to achieve a just and lasting peace.

President Harry S. Truman, speaking to delegates
at the opening session of the UN Conference
in San Francisco, April 23, 1945

In 1953, President Dwight D. Eisenhower spoke of the change that the Cold War had brought since that "hopeful spring of 1945." At that time, "the hope of all just men . . . was for a just and lasting peace. The eight years that have passed have seen that hope waver, grow dim, and almost die. And the shadow of fear again has darkly lengthened across the world."[25] That shadow has continued to lengthen. By now, over seventeen million people, most of them civilians, have died in wars since the end of the Second World War, and many more have been driven from their homes. The great powers have built up vast stockpiles of nuclear weapons with unprecedented destructive potential, and still more nations stand poised to follow suit. As a result, Kant's warning that a war of extermination could bring perpetual peace on the vast graveyard of humanity has taken on a directness in the nuclear age that even he could hardly have predicted.

The full horror of such a prospect has decisively shifted the incentives with respect to war. It has become a commonplace for world leaders to speak of the necessity of lasting peace. In principle, if not yet when it comes to implementation, they have agreed to make every effort to avoid unleashing, even accidentally, another major war.

So it is no wonder that we are also witnessing a realignment within the several traditions of thinking about war and peace. Their exponents are moving closer to one another, and in turn — often without knowing it — to the principled yet practical stance by which thinkers in the perpetual peace tradition combined moral and strategic considerations.

Already during the nineteenth century, many pacifists adopted the language of the perpetual peace tradition, its stress on step-by-step efforts to strengthen conditions for lasting peace, and its support for international organizations. Thus British Quakers founded a "Society for the Promotion of Permanent and Universal Peace" in 1816.[26] They disagreed among themselves, as did other pacifists, about whether to endorse complete nonresistance in all wars or to accept resistance in clear cases of self-defense when all other methods have failed. This disagreement still persists among pacifists today. Many who, like Tolstoy, were once in favor of unilateral disarmament and noncooperation with all military activities, including strictly defensive ones, have had to weigh whether such a stance with respect to nuclear weapons might not increase, rather than decrease, the risks to humanity. "Do what is right though the earth should perish" has taken on an entirely new and more literal meaning since Hiroshima and Nagasaki.[27]

Only a minority of those active in contemporary peace movements adopt such an absolutist stance. But the threat to collective survival posed by nuclear weapons has induced many to focus their attention on weapons systems and government military strategy. Their research and advocacy has at times reflected back, as in a mirror, the priorities of their opponents; and the underlying moral debate has centered on issues of violence and nonviolence. But as the events beginning in the late 1980s continue to unfold, it is becoming increasingly clear that the chances for peace depend on a complex linkage of individual, domestic, and international policies. Shifts in military strategy do not lead but rather follow upon a restructuring of such policies, as seen in the present thawing of the Cold War. A more comprehensive moral framework is needed, in which nonviolence plays a central but not exclusive role. In the Philippines, in East Germany, in Czechoslovakia, and in Hungary, "people power" has shown itself victorious in the face of massively armed governments. As Václav Havel long continued to insist at great personal risk, citizens who are "living in truth" can overthrow dictatorships by nonviolent means.

Realists, whether of a practical or a theoretical bent, are increasingly driven to reconsider their most fundamental presuppositions in the face of the present predicament. Many among them once argued that strict national self-interest should dictate foreign policy, quite apart from what might be desirable for other nations, and that morality was beside the point in international relations. By now, the first argument has had to be sharply modified and the second abandoned. National self-interest now clearly mandates a concern for comprehensive international security. International security, in turn, is affected by such factors as hunger, deforestation, and population growth the world over.

Even from a strictly strategic point of view, therefore, it matters to attend to these factors. Doing so necessitates being alert to the role of moral claims, such as those voiced the world over regarding fundamental human rights. References to human rights abroad were once dismissed by many realists as sentimental, given political realities in most nations, and as potentially counterproductive efforts to interfere with sovereign states. But the political power of calls for human rights can no longer be denied, nor their importance to foreign relations. The same is true with respect to the action or inaction on the part of governments in matters of environmental or nuclear strategy. It is not surprising, therefore, that George Kennan, who has long argued against the assumption "that state behavior is a fit subject for moral judgment," does not hesitate to express such moral judgments when it comes to nuclear weapons. In *The Nuclear Delusion*, he cries out, in a tone that Erasmus would not have disowned, against the readiness to use nuclear weapons against other human beings, thus placing in jeopardy all of civilization, calling it a blasphemy and "an indignity of monstrous proportions."[28]

Contemporary just war theorists, unlike those in the realist tradition, have consistently advanced moral claims in the context of war and peace. If the nuclear balance of terror has accelerated a shift, on their part, in the direction of Erasmus and Kant, it has been in reducing the range of wars seen as potentially just ones. It is hard, at present, to see many wars as likely to serve the cause of justice. Whereas Augustine and Thomas Aquinas argued in favor of certain wars to avenge wrongs, the U.S. Catholic Bishops stated, in 1983, that "if war of retribution was ever justifiable, the risks of modern war negate such a claim today."[29] They restate the just war position so as to exclude, in the contemporary world, nearly all wars as unjust except those of strict self-defense or defense of others under attack, and only then as a last resort. And, like Erasmus and Kant, they emphasize the monumental injustice of governments in channeling such a vast proportion of the world's scarce resources into armaments, calling it "an act of aggression upon the poor."[30]

Marxists have also been narrowing the very different criteria that V. I. Lenin and Mao-tse Tung elaborated for when wars are just. Lenin held that wars against oppressors by wage earners and enslaved or colonized peoples were fully legitimate, progressive, and necessary. "Whosoever wants a lasting and democratic peace must stand for civil war against the government and the bourgeoisie."[31] Mao likewise argued that the only just wars are nonpredatory wars, wars of liberation. "Communists will support every just and nonpredatory war for liberation, and they will stand in the forefront of the struggle."[32] But it has become increasingly difficult to maintain that the fanning of regional wars has promoted justice. The faith that a lasting peace is bound to result from such warfare is faltering even among many committed Marxists. Similarly, Marx's castigation of moral claims as "ideological non-sense" is undergoing impassioned rejection throughout much of the Communist world.[33]

In all these respects, Kant's essay on "Perpetual Peace" bears rereading. Nearly two centuries after its publication, and especially after the events of 1989, it no longer seems fantastic or overstrained to link the chances for peace with the respect for human rights and with the growing cooperation between nations in which those rights are protected by representative forms of government.

Just as contemporary thinkers who once rejected fundamental moral claims as irrelevant or postponed them as premature have been led to take them into consideration on strict realist grounds, so, too, have many who once based their position on strictly normative claims had to acknowledge that strategic realities affect their choices. While the goal of lasting peace may still seem out of reach, it no longer makes either strategic or moral sense for governments, policy advisers, or theorists to fail to move in the direction of that goal.

But if so many have come to take such a goal seriously as at least worth striving for, however utopian it seemed when first advocated by thinkers in the perpetual peace tradition, then there is reason to take equally seriously the ways of moving closer to that goal that they suggested. Clearly they could not have foreseen the kinds of negotiations required by today's weapons and international alignments, nor the present social and environmental threats to humanity. These developments call for responses of a complexity that no one could have predicted centuries ago. But the tradition of perpetual peace may be much more helpful when it comes to exploring the crucial role of the social climate that determines whether or not adequate levels of cooperation will be possible, and the framework of moral constraints needed at every level of society to keep that climate from deteriorating.[34]

Our century has seen the development of new strategies for bringing about change in ways that respect the social climate. The tradition of nonviolent resistance to oppression that began with Mohandas Gandhi in India and continued in the civil rights struggle led by Martin Luther King, Jr., in the United States has influenced political change in countries as different as South Korea and East Germany. During the past year, we have witnessed a striking contrast. While peaceful revolutions produced astounding successes in one country after another in Eastern Europe, fighting dragged on with no end in sight in Lebanon, Ethiopia, El Salvador, and too many other nations, producing only further suffering. Few have doubted that nonviolent resistance is more respectful of human rights and less likely to brutalize and corrupt its participants. What is becoming increasingly clear is that, with the help of modern communications media, such resistance can also bring speedier and more far-reaching results. Being more protective of the social climate, it is also more conducive to the cooperation that is so desperately needed once the struggle is over.

To be sure, nothing guarantees that those who lead such movements to victory can govern well, or that changes wrought with nonviolent means will not once again succumb to violence. Nor do all efforts at nonviolent resistance succeed, as Tiananmen Square and too many other examples demonstrate. But even when the latter efforts meet with repression, as did Solidarity for years, nonviolent movements have a better chance of ultimately succeeding than groups that resort to a violent uprising.

Only time will tell whether a cumulative process of nonviolent and principled efforts at domestic and international change can, in the long run, disprove the age-old assumption that war will always be with us. Much that Erasmus, Kant, and others suggested, such as giving citizens a voice with respect to whether or not to undertake a war, convening international parleys and federations, and submitting disputes to arbitration, must have seemed highly improbable — indeed utopian — at the time. The word *utopia* can have two meanings. One indicates an excellent place or society that is possible but at present merely visionary; the second refers, rather, to an unattainable society advocated by impractical idealists. In arguing that it is possible for human beings to establish a lasting world peace, Erasmus and Kant may well have been utopian in the first sense; but we have everything to lose by not trying to disprove the claim that they were also utopian in the second.

NOTES

1. This essay was published in *Ethics and International Relations* 4 (April 1990): 145–61.

2. For the works by Erasmus that contributed most to this tradition, see notes 3, 5, and 7 below. See also Edwin D. Mead., ed., *The Great Design of Henry IV from the Memoirs of the Duke of Sully* (1559–1641) (Boston: Ginn & Co., 1909); William Penn, "An Essay Towards the Present and Future Peace of Europe" (1693) in *The Witness of William Penn*, ed. Frederick B. Tolles and E. Gordon Alderfer (New York: Macmillan & Co., 1957), pp. 140–59; Abbé de Saint-Pierre, *Selections from the Second Edition of the Abrégé du Projet de Paix Perpétuelle* (1712) (London: Sweet & Maxwell, 1927); Immanuel Kant, "Perpetual Peace: A Philosophical Sketch" (1795) in *Kant's Political Writings*, ed. Hans Reiss (Cambridge: At the University Press, 1970), pp. 93–130; Jeremy Bentham, "Essay on Universal Peace: Essay IV: A Plan for an Universal and Perpetual Peace," (written in 1789; first published in 1843), reprinted in *Jeremy Bentham*, ed. Charles W. Everett (London: Weidenfeld & Nicolson, 1966), pp. 195–229.

3. Gottfried Wilhelm Leibniz, "Observation sur le projet d'une paix perpétuelle de M. l'abbé de St. Pierre," in *Opera Omnia*, ed. L. Dutens (Geneva, 1768), vol. 5; Jean-Jacques Rousseau (editing and commenting upon the work of the Abbé de Saint-Pierre), *A Project of Perpetual Peace*, trans. Edith M. Nuttall (London: Richard Cobden-Sanderson, 1927); Friedrich Hegel, *Philosophy of Right* (1821), trans. T. M. Knox (Oxford: Clarendon Press, 1958), pp. 208–16.

4. *The Adages* were first published in 1500. A later edition, published in 1515, contained a greatly expanded version of "Dulce bellum inexpertis." See Margaret Mann Phillips, ed., *The Adages of Erasmus: A Study with Interpretations* (Cambridge: At the University Press, 1964), pp. 308–53.

5. In 1516, France and Switzerland concluded the Treaty of Fribourg, known as "La paix perpétuelle," which lasted until the French Revolution. The year before, Henry VIII had concluded a "permanent" but much more short-lived peace with France. For a few years, nevertheless, Erasmus, Thomas More, and other humanists had hopes for a flowering of peace that would permit the shaping of a new political and cultural order.

6. Erasmus, *The Education of a Christian Prince*, trans. Lester K. Born (New York: Octagon Books, 1973).

7. Niccolo Machiavelli, *The Prince and the Discourses* (New York: Random House, 1950).

8. Erasmus, *Education of a Christian Prince*, p. 249.

9. Erasmus, *The Complaint of Peace* (Boston: Charles Williams, 1813). For a more recent translation, though not entirely complete, see Jose Chapiro, *Erasmus and Our Struggle for Peace* (Boston: Beacon Press,

1950), pp. 131–84, "Peace Protests!" In a letter from 1523, Erasmus comments bitterly in a letter to a friend that he must "soon compose the Epitaph, rather than the Complaint, of Peace, as she seems to be dead and buried and not very likely to revive" (cited in the translator's preface, 1813 edition of *The Complaint of Peace*, p. iv).

10. Erasmus, *Education of a Christian Prince*, p. 249.

11. Ibid., p. 250.

12. Ibid., p. 251.

13. Comparisons between animals and human beings traditionally placed humans above animals in the chain of being. Cicero, among many others, had argued that the two ways of doing wrong—by force or by fraud—were both bestial: "fraud seems to belong to the cunning fox, force to the lion: both are wholly unworthy of man, but fraud is the more contemptible" (Cicero *Of Duties* 1.13.41). Machiavelli had accepted the comparison only to argue that human beings ought to learn from the fox and the lion in those respects. Erasmus intended to show, on the contrary, that force and fraud on the scale practiced by humans and with the means at their disposal were of an entirely different order, and that to attribute such aspects of human conduct to animals was merely to calumniate them.

14. Erasmus, *Complaint of Peace*, p. 51.

15. Ibid., p. 79.

16. Erasmus, "Peace Protests!" in Chapiro, *Erasmus and Our Struggle for Peace*, p. 173.

17. Saint-Pierre, *Selections from the Second Edition of the Abrégé*. See also Rousseau, *Project of Perpetual Peace*.

18. Kant, "Perpetual Peace," and "Idea for a Universal History with a Cosmopolitan Purpose," in *Kant's Political Writings*, ed. Reiss, pp. 93–130 and 41–53.

19. Kant, "Perpetual Peace," p. 103.

20. Ibid., p. 96.

21. Ibid., p. 114.

22. Ibid., p. 96.

23. For a discussion of these constraints in Kant's writings and of their role in international relations, see Sissela Bok, *A Strategy for Peace* (New York: Pantheon Books, 1989).

24. Kant, "Perpetual Peace," p. 108.

25. Dwight D. Eisenhower, "The Chance for Peace," (Address delivered before the American Society of Newspaper Editors, April 16, 1953), reprinted in *War and Peace*, ed. Kenneth E. Alrutz et al., Lynchburg College Symposium Readings, vol. 5 (New York: University Press of America, 1982), p. 621.

26. See F. H. Hinsley, *Power and the Pursuit of Peace* (Cambridge: At the University Press, 1963), pp. 93–97.

27. Kant explicitly defended this motto; but while it committed him to absolutism with respect to lying, it did not do so when it came to violence, since he regarded violence in self-defense as legitimate. See Sissela Bok, "Kant's Arguments in Support of the Maxim 'Do What Is Right Though the Earth Should Perish'," *Argumentation* 2 (1988): 7–25; reprinted in *Applied Ethics and Ethical Theory*, ed. David M. Rosenthal and Fadlou Shehadi (Salt Lake City: University of Utah Press, 1988), pp. 191–212.

28. George Kennan, *The Nuclear Delusion* (New York: Pantheon Books, 1982).

29. *The Challenge of Peace: God's Promise and Our Response* (Washington, D.C.: U.S. Catholic Conference Office of Publishing Services, 1983), p. 39. For a secular interpretation of just war doctrine that similarly restricts the causes for just war, see Robert W. Tucker, *The Just War: A Study in Contemporary American Doctrine* (Baltimore: Johns Hopkins Press, 1960).

30. *The Challenge of Peace*, p. v.

31. V. I. Lenin, "Socialism and War," in *Collected Works* (Moscow: Progress Publishers, 1968), p. 316. See also "The Question of Peace," vol. 21, pp. 290–94, and "April Theses, 1917," vol. 24, pp. 21–26.

32. Mao Tse-tung, *On Revolution and War*, ed. M. Rejai (Garden City, N.Y.: Doubleday, 1970), p. 67.

33. Karl Marx, *Selected Writings*, ed. D. McLellan (Oxford: Oxford University Press, 1977), pp. 568–69.

34. See Bok, *Strategy for Peace*, chap. 4.

4

From Leviathan to Lilliput[1]

STEPHEN TOULMIN

THE CLAIMS of the modern nation-state to unfettered sovereignty upset the conditions under which individuals and communities are able to live at peace with one another. Yet these claims have not always been made, let alone always conceded. They are features of a particular set of historical circumstances, which had a beginning and which may now be coming to an end. So let me propose a general historical characterization of the epoch in which these claims about the absolute nature of national sovereignty were first made, then sustained, and finally hopefully are in the course of being discredited.

In order to understand those claims and their limits, we need to ask how they originated. Historians regularly refer to these claims as a form of "absolutism." By this they simply mean that each sovereign nation-state was entitled to run its own affairs as it thought best, and that nobody outside it was really entitled to pass any kind of judgment on that process. This is a central issue for the maintenance of peace, because it meant that the individual nation-state was no longer morally and politically accountable to a larger community beyond its borders.

Throughout the High Middle Ages, states and rulers were subject to outside criticism, and they took this criticism seriously. There was, for example, an active debate about the conditions under which states and rulers could justly wage wars as a means of achieving their legitimate goals. The debate was limited in time, and the last major treatise on this subject which attracted universal concern in European culture was *De jure belli et pacis*, published by Hugo Grotius in 1625. Nevertheless, while it lasted, it

73

was a continual reminder of the extent to which nations were necessarily attentive to outside voices. At a certain point in the seventeenth century the debate shifted, and states were no longer seen as subject to public, transnational moral criticism in the way they had always been hitherto. In the last few years, however, people have returned to the issue of the just war, criticizing the exercise of sovereignty by the rulers of nation-states. In the United States this is illustrated most prominently by the well-deserved success of Michael Walzer's book *Just and Unjust Wars.* It is also apparent in the letter from the U.S. Catholic bishops on nuclear war, which brings to bear some of the traditional debate on just and unjust wars to questions about nuclear weapons.

Both of these publications illustrate the return to respectability of a tradition which discussed ethics in terms of cases rather than principles. This "casuistry" had been repudiated in the mid-seventeenth century after Pascal published anonymously his *Provincial Letters,* and has only recently come to be taken seriously again in the intellectual world of Europe and North America. The idea that ethics is a field in which one should proceed in a manner more like that of the Anglo-American common law, and less in terms of some kind of abstract geometry — *more geometrico,* as Spinoza puts it — is an interesting and important change in the way in which the subject has been discussed in recent years.

This interregnum, during which the just war controversy was set aside, was the period between the mid-seventeenth and the mid-twentieth centuries, which many now refer to as "modernity," or the "modern" age. The political absolutism that developed in this period — the unqualified sovereignty of systemically, stably organized nation-states, not open to criticism from outside — was part of a larger theory of human affairs, which concerned not only political issues but also other serious intellectual matters. Originally, from 1650 on, this move toward nation-states had considerable utility; but, I shall argue, in the course of the twentieth century this utility has been exhausted.

There is a discrepancy here, between the received wisdom about the nature of modernity and what we now have reason to believe. The received doctrine of forty years ago can be summarized in three propositions.

(1) Modern science and modern philosophy began because

people in the seventeenth century were at last prosperous enough and free enough to explore new intellectual possibilities. The assumption was that Europe in the seventeenth century was newly prosperous, newly comfortable, and newly leisured.

(2) We were taught to believe that, in the seventeenth century, there was less constraint than before on people to believe what their church wanted them to believe, and that therefore a new kind of intellectual freedom emerged.

(3) Finally, the invention of printing and the distribution of printed books created a situation in which "modern" culture was essentially a lay culture, and this lay modern culture rapidly superseded the ecclesiastical culture which had been the heart of the Middle Ages.

Over the last twenty or thirty years historians have come to recognize that the first two of these three propositions are simply false.

(1) It is just not the case that the first half of the seventeenth century was a time of new prosperity and comfort. The sixteenth century had indeed been a period of prosperity, during which economic activity in Europe continuously expanded, capitalized by the imports of silver from South America in Spanish treasure ships. But shortly after 1600 there began a series of economic depressions, recessions, and stagnations, as a result of which general historians these days refer to the first half of the century as "the general crisis" of the early seventeenth century.

(2) As for the idea that the church ceased to put constraints on intellectual freedom, we have to admit that Galileo had much more trouble with the church than Copernicus had had in the 1530s and '40s. It was much easier for Copernicus to entertain heterodox ideas about the nature of the natural world in the middle of the sixteenth century than it was for Galileo to present similar ideas a hundred years later. On both sides of the doctrinal fence in Europe, whether you were a Protestant or a Catholic, the ecclesiastical pressures were worse, not better, after the Council of Trent in the late sixteenth century than they had been before.

(3) The creation of a lay culture that followed the invention of printing was already far advanced during the first quarter of the sixteenth century. It is well represented by late Renaissance humanists from Erasmus, by way of Rabelais, to Montaigne and

Shakespeare. We did not have to wait until the seventeenth century for a lay culture to develop as a rival to the earlier ecclesiastical culture.

I underline these things because they illustrate an incongruity between the way in which history of philosophy and history of science still tend to be written, and the way in which general economic and social history are written these days. Look up, for instance, the volume of the *New Cambridge History of Europe* for the period in question. This book comprises a series of essays about the early seventeenth century in Spain, France, England, Germany, and Italy, in science, industry, economics, social change, military techniques, international relations, church doctrine, and so on. In every essay except one, great emphasis is placed on the disruptive effects of the early seventeenth-century crisis on the events of the time. The one exception is the essay by Alistair Crombie and Michael Hoskin on the history of science. One can read their essay without realizing that there ever were any religious wars, let alone that bloody, brutal, and intolerable war known as the Thirty Years' War, from 1618 to 1648, in which one-third of the population of Germany, and three-fifths of the cities of central Europe, were destroyed in the name of a religious belief without anybody being able to see how on earth to bring the conflict to an end.

So much for the history of science. In the history of philosophy, pick up the *Grande Encyclopédie* (the French counterpart of the *Encyclopedia Britannica*) and turn to the biography of Descartes; you will be told in the opening paragraph that, if you want to know about the life of Descartes, all you really need to know are two dates and two place names: where and when he was born and died. The entry goes on to say, "The whole development of Descartes's thought is the interior unfolding of an *ésprit* (intellect): the *événements extérieurs*, or external events of his life, are of relevance only to the extent that they happen to throw some fleeting light on the unfolding of his genius." The authors are delighted to think of philosophy as a subject in which people of a reflective nature — wherever they come from, at whatever time — can sit back and develop for themselves a picture of the world that is entirely independent of anything else that is happening at the time.

People in the early seventeenth century (on this account) believed that all matters of serious philosophical and scientific interest could be *decontextualized*, that is, stated in ways that were totally independent of the situation in which they were presented. The general crisis of the early seventeenth century was, thus, not just an economic and social crisis, but also an intellectual and spiritual crisis; and people responded to it by arguing that the rational way of dealing with this crisis was by cleaning the slate and making a fresh start. This move was particularly attractive because the schism within Christianity, which Luther had not intended to inaugurate, carried with it a wider cultural confusion about whose beliefs were right and whose were wrong. People no more knew whether to be Ptolemaic or Copernican in their astronomy than they knew whether to be Catholic or Protestant in their theology. One way or another, it seemed, there was no longer any ground after 1600 on which a consensus for debate was possible for serious-minded people on different sides of the ideological fence.

All that kept European culture and society together at this point was the determination of a few people to keep alive a sense of the need for religious toleration; and this last hope was destroyed with the murder of Henry IV of France, on May 14, 1610. Henry IV was the only ruler in early seventeenth-century Europe who was determined to make religious toleration a serious matter of state policy, and his murder led most people in Europe to conclude that a policy of religious toleration had been tried and had failed. So when, in 1618, a general war broke out in central Europe, it was even more interminable and even more irresoluble than the recent war between Iran and Iraq. In this situation, there was no ground on which people could sit down and argue together about the rights and wrongs of the war. Serious-minded intellectuals sought for common foundations of argument on which people could talk together, regardless of their original doctrinal, national, or cultural backgrounds.

The move to what we now know as foundationalism — Descartes's program of rejecting all merely inherited beliefs, taking a clean slate, and writing on it a fresh text, whose foundations were acceptable to people of intellectual honesty and reflective candor from any background — thus had a charm, an appeal, and carried conviction, in a way that was very much *of its time*. The charm of certainty, which was central to this foundationalism, was not just a matter of intellectual aesthetics; rather, it promised a way to escape from a situation in which consensus and dialogue had collapsed and the only way ahead was to find a new vocabulary on which people of different backgrounds could agree.

Before 1630, western Europeans really had nothing that we would now call a "political theory," in the sense in which, for example, Thomas Hobbes wrote about political theory. Before 1600, politics was a matter of practice, like law and medicine. You looked to see how human affairs had been organized in earlier times, what had been the merits and defects of organizing human affairs in different ways, and what problems had arisen. It was a matter of what Aristotle called *phronēsis* — practical wisdom developed on the basis of human experience — not *epistēmē* — developing an abstract, general, universal, and timeless axiomatic theory, which was supposed to make matters of this kind clear, distinct, self-evident and inevitable. In the best political writers of earlier times you find maxims of great penetration and casuistic discussions of the rights and wrongs of this or that political way of dealing with political problems. But you do not find the kind of abstract, general account of what it is for a state to be composed of atomic, social individuals that you find in the work of Hobbes, and that is the starting point for so much subsequent political theory. Read Machiavelli, Guicciardini, or the other political writers of the Italian Renaissance, and you will find reflections about actual historical episodes. They encourage us to see what can be learned by studying the different ways in which people have attempted to deal with political problems: they do not produce a general, abstract theory of the state but offer reflections on how a prince or a democracy or an oligarchy can best run the operations of the state in one set of circumstances or another. Only with Hobbes, who had learned from Descartes the necessity of cleaning the slate and making a fresh start, do we find political theory presented as an entirely general problem of how, at any time and place, a state is to be seen as related to its individual citizens.

The Thirty Years' War came to an end more out of exhaustion than because anything had been proved; and Europe was faced with the task of reconstructing itself. In the context of the reconstruction of Europe after the Thirty Years' War one can understand why the *nation* became a new focus of state organization. This had not been the case in the Middle Ages. The rulers of the European states in the Middle Ages were much more like property developers. The whole clan of Hapsburgs, for instance, eventually established itself as the owners of a lot of territory, in which there were people of many different nations, cultures, and religions. The fact that some of these inhabitants spoke French, some Flemish, some Spanish, some German, some various other Slavic or east European languages, isn't the point. The point is that the stability of the resulting political system was an expression of their primary ownership.

So the condition of Europe after 1648 was really quite a new thing. The medieval sovereigns had holdings that were heterogeneous in culture, language, religion, and customary law, but they were also subject to the oversight of a transnational church which could subject them to moral censure. The medieval church was indeed a transnational institution: it had something like a monopoly on learning; it spoke for the common law; and it could criticize the positive legal codes of one place or another in the light of shared principles. It spoke also for the conscience of humanity; it spoke for what Aquinas called the *ratio naturalis* — the ability of human beings, whatever their background, to recognize certain things as basically acceptable or unacceptable from a moral point of view. Only after 1650, with the reconstruction of Europe during the late seventeenth century, did the modern nation-state begin to take shape clearly and irreversibly.

The modern nation-state developed in part, then, as a theoretical construct, within which the will of the sovereign was something against which there was no appeal. There were no institutions to which one could appeal against the will of the sovereign, so Europeans got into the situation described by Hobbes, which he perceived as one in which Leviathan makes Leviathan's own laws. To recall one crucial example: in the last decades of the sixteenth century, the cities and provinces of what we now call Holland threw out their Spanish rulers and created a new state, which was known at the time as the United Provinces of the Netherlands. It is helpful to contrast the manner in which the United Provinces came into existence in the 1580s and the manner in which the United States came into existence in the 1770s. The United Provinces came into existence because, in the common interest of throwing out the Spaniards, the cities and the provinces of Holland got together and established a kind of committee. This committee was created with certain limited functions of governance. The whole operation was highly pragmatic, and there was no theory behind it of a Hobbesian or post-Cartesian kind; it took place before the great watershed of the 1630s.

So Holland was created pragmatically, by an alliance of cities and provinces that shared a practical interest in throwing the Spanish monarchy out. By contrast, the United States was defined by founding fathers who had read their Hobbes and Locke and Rousseau and felt bound to give a theoretical justification of their design. Because the political theories of Hobbes and his successors treated individual human beings as willful, independent social atoms, the crucial issue for them was to explain what would be the relationship within the United States between the individual citizens and the central power. As a result, the indispensability of intermediate institutions between individual and state was taken for granted in Holland, but in the United States these intermediate institutions were disregarded. For the first time, there were no recognized institutions, independent of the state, by which the exercise of sovereign authority by the state or its rulers could be challenged on moral grounds: the Hobbesian state is the nine-hundred-pound gorilla who sleeps wherever it wants to sleep.

To that extent, the just war debate was not discredited; it simply lapsed. This was no longer a question which people could seriously raise. The churches had split up, and there was nobody who spoke with the kind of moral unanimity that people would take seriously. So political power was exercised in the way in which unfettered sovereign political power is liable to be exercised: rulers got away with whatever they could get away with. Political theory thus became an analysis of political obligation manifested within the nation-state, which was accepted as a datum. In this situation the churches were less and less effective. Established churches were by and large toothless churches. Once they had split up and had been redefined as "the Church of England" or the Gallican Church, say, they could not be expected to bite the sovereign hand that had given them their established institutional status.

From the late seventeenth century to the twentieth century, the nation-state remained the commonly accepted unit of political and diplomatic organization. The total independence and autonomy of sovereign states remained a feasible, if not the most admirable, common policy. At the time of the First World War, Norman Angell and Woodrow Wilson dreamed of a new transnational League of Nations; but it was really only after 1945 that the limits to the autonomy of sovereign nation-states were truly acknowledged, and only from the 1960s on that the force of transnational interdependence imposed itself on states. This happened, in part, as a result of the new concern with ecology and environmental protection, in part for a dozen other reasons; but only after 1960 did more people come to recognize the involuntary constraints to which all state power is inevitably subject. The President of Brazil may criticize the international environmental movement for objecting to the way in which the rain forest is being cut down, claiming that it is *Brazil's* rain forest, that *they* are entitled to do with it as *they* please; the government of China may reject external criticisms about political prisoners in China on the ground that these criticisms are unacceptable interference in China's internal affairs. But arguments of this kind lose more and more rhetorical force with every month that passes, and the plain fact is that more and more sovereign rulers are going to have their arms twisted from outside.

For three hundred years, then, Europe and the countries that it strongly influenced learned the lessons of nationhood well. In some respects they must now unlearn them. The task is not to build new, larger, and more powerful powers, let alone a world state with absolute worldwide sovereignty; rather, it is to check and limit the absolute sovereignty of even the best-administered states, and to fight against all the inequalities that were entrenched during the ascendancy of the nation-state. In their place, the problems that really face us are problems on subnational, transnational, and multinational levels, which require the development of procedures that are better adapted to the political, economic, and social functions to be served in the years ahead.

In the "modern" era, the basic question of political theory was always: "How does state power and authority come to be binding on the subjects of a particular state?" Political theorists gave little attention to the question of how moral judgment can be passed on the exercise of state power and authority. True, flagrant malefactors became objects of ridicule throughout Europe, so that William Ewart Gladstone could thunder in the House of Commons against atrocities in Bulgaria; but these isolated rhetorical episodes created no precedents and developed no institutional basis.

We live today in a different age. After the First World War, in response to Woodrow Wilson, the Allied powers sponsored the establishment of the League of Nations, and from the start, this multinational institution was intended to have a moral authority capable on occasion of overriding the authority of any single power. That same limitation on moral authority is implicit in the United Nations charter. In the late twentieth century, the limits on the sovereignty of individual states are implicit also in the operations of the International Court of Justice and in the founding documents of the European Community and the Treaty of Rome. Yet all these limits are still seen as *self*-limitations: the state accepts them as an outcome of entering into voluntary association with other coequal states. As such, they are not external constraints which bind nation-states willy-nilly; rather, they are internal glosses on the modern nation-state's continued exercise of its absolute sovereignty. In this respect, the moral authority of institutions like the United Nations is therefore less striking or influential than the spiritual authority of the medieval church.

Paradoxically, external moral authority belongs today to other, nongovernmental institutions. Nobody takes wholly seriously moral opinions voiced in the United Nations General Assembly or Security Council, whether in sorrow, outrage, or excuse; these opinions are always presented by official representatives of the member states, whose status has a built-in conflict of interest. The only institutions whose moral opinions command general respect and are heard as stating "the decent opinion of humankind" are the opinions of Amnesty International, the World Psychiatry Association, Greenpeace, and other bodies which are intrinsically devoid of material power or "armed forces." In a moment of cynical joviality, Josef Stalin once asked (in a question worthy of Pontius Pilate), "How many divisions has the Pope?" But in the eyes of decent human opinion, moral challenges are never answered by displays of force. The day that Amnesty International takes possession of a machine gun, let alone an atom bomb, its capacity to gain a hearing and influence events will be at an end. Here lies the effectiveness of Jonathan Swift's image of Lilliput. Josef Stalin did not see that the military triviality of the Pope's Swiss Guard increases rather than betrays his claim to a moral hearing. The moral authority of Amnesty International, similarly, is that much the greater just because Amnesty is a *Lilliputian* institution.

From 1650 on, the prototypical organization of this kind was the Society of Friends. From the beginning the Quakers embodied in practice the minority opposition to the dominance of the nation-state; and they maintained this opposition throughout the whole time when, as a matter of theory, respectable opinion in Europe was committed to the absolute sovereignty of the state. Only now, when other Lilliputian organizations like Amnesty have joined this opposition, can we see in retrospect how far, as early as the 1660s, those who had eyes to see were already aware of the hidden agenda of the modern nation-state, and adopted a way of life that emphasized human equality and was a standing reproach to the new system. Politically, to this day the patterns of our lives are shaped by the actions of state authority; morally, by contrast, the rulers of contemporary states are open to outside moral criticism of a kind that has not been widely available since before 1600. Even the most forceful superpowers can no longer ignore this fact. Mikhail Gorbachev sees, as Josef Stalin never saw, the harm that a challenge from the World Psychiatric Association does to the Soviet government; and, in fact, the Soviet government has finally invited Amnesty International to send representatives to Moscow to discuss how it can get out from under Amnesty's criticisms.

Lilliputian organizations cannot compel immoral rulers to apologize on their knees, as Henry II of England had to do after the murder of Thomas Becket. But they can expose rulers who refuse to mend their ways to damaging embarrassment in the eyes of the larger world. If the classical image of modernity from 1648 to 1945 was Leviathan, for the future the moral standing of national powers and superpowers will, if all goes well, be captured in the picture of Gulliver waking from an unthinking sleep to find himself tethered by innumerable tiny bonds.

What is the role of the churches in this situation? The answer is, sadly, mixed. Having had their teeth drawn by becoming "established," the national churches of the traditional nation-states have found it difficult to regain their earlier moral authority. In England, for instance, people are still well aware of the old wise-crack that the Anglican Church is "the Conservative Party at prayer." We need not doubt the sincerity of Anglican theologians who engage in serious moral criticism of political issues; but, in the last resort, the church as an institution is rarely able to stand up fully, look the state in the eye, and insist on taking a moral stand in the face of the "respectable" national consensus. On a local and even on a provincial level, similarly, the Catholic Church is more or less effective; but as a worldwide institution it shares many of the defects of the political superpowers. It is not for nothing, as a result, that religious groups such as the Quakers have a moral authority that is more clearly visible to other people.

From 1650 on, I have argued, it was reasonable to place one's intellectual and practical trust in the ideal of stable and self-contained systems, whether on the intellectual plane in science or on the political or institutional plane in the nation-state, simply because of the relative independence of both natural sciences and nation-states. But, by now, matters have taken us well beyond that point. In the intellectual realm, the central concern of most scientists today is no longer to develop a single comprehensive theory to explain everything; rather, it is to bring the totality of our different modes of explanation to bear on the complex phenomena of concrete experience. Scientists who cling to the traditional agenda of rationalist philosophy sidetrack their work into scientific irrelevance, like the students of so-called rational mechanics, for whom Newtonian dynamics is an object of formal elaboration and aesthetic contemplation, independent of its explanatory power as physics. Similarly, in the realm of social practice, the overriding concern of administrators and politicians can no longer be to enhance the power and the glory of the centralized nationalized institutions that took shape in the late seventeenth century, when sovereign autonomy was its own reward. Instead, it has to be finding ways of dispersing authority and adapting it more discerningly, both subnationally — to meet the needs of particular localities and communities — and transnationally — where our institutions must be capable of overriding the special interests of particular nation-states.

On the subnational level, many people like to believe that the 1960s are dead and gone, leaving no trace on our social institutions. That is an exaggeration on two levels. The events of the sixties and seventies continue to resonate in the minds and hearts of those who were actively involved in them: as the French Revolution was for Wordsworth, so for them, "bliss was it in that dawn to be alive, and to be young was very heaven!" And, furthermore, those years saw the establishment of many kinds of institutions — ranging from local consumer watchdog groups to transnational networks for monitoring the actions of national governments — which remain, today, thorns in the flesh of the establishment, whether the establishment be the power companies, the city and state authorities, or the central institutions of the nation.

The vigor and freedom of such nongovernmental organizations is itself a good index of the health of any country's democracy. In countries subject to military coups, for instance, these groups, which are out of control from the point of view of any *junta*, are the first to feel the pinch. And, until just the other day, these were the groups that the state authorities in the self-styled "people's democracies" of Eastern Europe found most alarming and most suspect.

Judged by this standard, the Leninist mode of government can be seen for what it is, namely, one more highly conservative variation on the political themes of unreconstructed modernity. Even in 1989, the Soviet Union has some difficulty in acknowledging the right of Lilliputian commentators to sit in moral judgment on the domestic policies of the Soviet state, though in this respect (it must be said) matters are changing wonderfully from week to week.

On the transnational level, meanwhile, we must never forget the message of Lilliput. Local communities and unrepresented groups stand in need of institutional means of self-expression and protection. The nonviolent methods of drawing attention to that need are typically more persuasive than murders by night. When antinuclear demonstrators march with candles through the streets of Leipzig, when prisoners of conscience bring Pinochet's torturers into public scorn, when women's organizations speak for their sisters under the yoke of fundamentalism, they challenge the legitimacy of absolute nation organizations. In this transnational resistance, mere candles, mere voices, and the other instruments of the powerless may seem little enough help. But it is important to recall, in conclusion, that the term *power* is itself ambiguous. There is power understood in the sense of "force" and there is power understood in the sense of "influence." Force, I have argued, has finally run up against its own limits. From now on, the name of the game is not force but influence; and in playing that particular game the Lilliputian institutions hold some of the best cards.

NOTES

1. This essay elaborates on a theme from my book *Cosmopolis* (New York: Free Press, 1989).

PART II

Christian Conceptions
of Peace

5

Conceptions of Peace: Political Challenge and Theological Controversy in German Protestantism

TRUTZ RENDTORFF

PEACE HAS A long-standing tradition within Christian history, but the meaning of peace has come under critical discussion in recent years. How do we understand the relation between peace as a religious concept — peace with God, God's peace — and peace as a political concept — among nations, over against war? How should religious visions and political activities be distinguished or brought together?

Controversies among religious thinkers and political theorists have become part of the general controversial public scene in recent years. Churches and theologians discovered that they were not at all unanimous when making use of the concept of peace. I shall report, first, on the controversy which took place among German Protestants. In the light of this controversy, I shall then develop an argument for a concept of peace in terms of political ethics.

I. THE DEBATE WITHIN THE CHURCHES

A report on the state of the discussion in West Germany between theological ethicists and churches on the one hand and strategists and politicians on the other hand has to take into account at least three different realms of debate: the general political context of the debate, the theological context of the debate, and the specific situations of Christians in Germany, living in a divided nation between East and West.

As to the general political context, the debate on nuclear weapons, nuclear deterrence, and the nuclear dilemma has taken place in two phases. The central issue in the late fifties was whether the Federal Republic of Germany should have nuclear weapons. What would be the consequences of rearmament for reunification of Germany? Which decision would help the prospect of a future reunification?

The debate in the late fifties in the discussion of the General Synod of the Evangelical Church in Germany was crucial. The synod did not reach a consensus but had to state that there was a deep split among the Protestants. The only way out was to confess that "we stay together" under the gospel in spite of deep differences in political ethics. Already a small but theologically powerful group of theologians and laypeople had decided that the question of rearmament was leading to a new *status confessionis*. They approached all questions within the context of a belief that the confessing church, which had been formed to defend the church against the Nazis, had to be continued in the changed postwar situation. To them, the problem of the A-bomb was not only a challenge to political decisions. It was much more a question of the identity of the church. The majority, however, did not follow this theological judgment and preferred to look at these problems as worldly affairs which have to be judged according to criteria of human reasoning.

Because the synod of the Evangelical Church in Germany did not come to a consensus, a small group of theologians and laypeople outside the synod issued a document which has become known as the "Heidelberg Theses" of 1959.[1] In this statement the central idea of *complementarity* paved the way for a compromise within the churches. In analogy to physics (and in quoting a concept of Niels Bohr), the statement formulated a complementarity of positions which seem to be antagonistic. In the same way as a physicist may identify light as waves or as small particles, two Christians could have different perspectives on the same issue; but the different views do not exclude each other. They are both possible and each view represents a part of the whole truth. In that sense they are complementary.

This concept of complementarity was applied to the controversy within the church and among Christians. Both attitudes, condemning nuclear weapons and tolerating them, are possible, and therefore Christians can either be against participation in nuclear politics or for it. They are bound to each other.

Complementarity makes sense only in an eschatological perspective. In a sinful world, which is "not yet" redeemed, it may "yet" be possible, or even necessary, for Christians to participate in military activities. At the same time, however, those who object to participation "already" witness to the coming world. The complementarity of decisions exemplifies the eschatological tension.

This concept of complementarity was very popular. For the churches it had a great pacifying function, although they could not agree when it "yet" should be possible for Christians to be part of military affairs, and when this period would be over. On the one hand, this period was identified with the history of a sinful world until the Second Coming of Christ. On the other hand, this period was conceived of as a period of transition in which the abolition of nuclear weapons had to be achieved. So there remained a latent conflict which came to a new outbreak in the early eighties in the second phase.

At the beginning of the INF debate, the Council of the Evangelical Church in Germany decided to ask their Commission for Public Responsibility to prepare a memorandum on the peace issue. The Commission drafted "The Preservation, Promotion, and Renewal of Peace," which took its start from an analysis of the situation of world politics and aimed at the political task of peacemaking as the primary ethical issue. It warned that military strategies and advanced military technology were not the main dangers. The memorandum called for a new perspective on the political dimension of the present conflict. The ethical question had to be reformulated. It challenged the churches to develop concepts of cooperation which might have a better chance against the language of weapons. Within this context the memorandum reaffirmed, without particularly stressing, the concept of complementarity of 1959.

This document has found wide reception within the churches and represents the mainline position of the Protestant churches in West Germany today. For the churches it serves as a platform to cope with the exploding controversies which came out of the forming of the peace movement.

In 1983 the German Bishops Conference of the Roman Catholic Church in West Germany published a "Word" to its members under the title *Gerechtigkeit schafft Frieden* ("Justice Creates Peace").[2] This statement was influenced by the memorandum of the Evangelical Church and was also a response to the 1983 pastoral letter of the American bishops. The position taken by the German bishops differed from the pastoral letter insofar as it concentrated on the ethical concept of justice and discussed the political responsibility for an international order of peace. The statement took the same line which the memorandum already had taken. The primary problem is not one of nuclear weapons as such but a problem of political order under conditions of antagonistic political systems. The political situation creates the tensions which find their expression in the nuclear scene. The main churches of West Germany therefore took a rather similar position in the general controversy regardless of differences in theological traditions and ethical language.

A different approach was taken in a statement of the Reformed Convention, an association of congregations and individual Protestants of the Reformed confession, in 1982.[3] This statement proclaimed a *status confessionis* for a position of the church against nuclear weapons. Under the title "The Confession to Jesus Christ and the Responsibility of the Church for Peace," this group argued that for the church the nuclear question is not a political question but a question of faith and confession, on the same level as the confession to Jesus Christ. Starting from the Christian confession of God's reconciliation with the world in the death and resurrection of Jesus Christ, the statement drew direct political and ethical consequences from church dogmas, which led to an uncompromising "No!" to nuclear weapons together with all military force. In the judgment of the Reformed Church, nuclear pacifism became a dividing line between true and false theology. In the given situation of the INF debate, this statement gained broad public recognition and reopened the discussion of the late fifties. Various proposals were brought forward to associate the *status confessionis* with different strategic options for nuclear-free zones in Europe, or for alternative concepts of defense. But there was no consensus with regard to the theological presuppositions made by the Reformed Church. The theological debate tended to function as a cover for political positions. The controversy was whether the nuclear weapons were to be taken in their political function, as political weapons bound up in the concept of deterrence, or whether nuclear weapons had to be negated on ethical and theological grounds without respect to the political function they might have.

The churches in the German Democratic Republic took a different route.[4] In a number of resolutions by the General Synod of the Churches in East Germany this formula developed into a kind of confession: "The Renunciation of the Spirit and Logic of Deterrence." The churches in East Germany were at first not aware of the fact that "deterrence," particularly "nuclear deterrence," was a strategic concept which had been developed by the West and which had never been official Soviet military doctrine. Therefore the renunciation of deterrence could be supported by the state authorities since it moved in the same direction as the official opposition to NATO. The churches therefore added to their formula the word *practice*, so that the position now reads "The Renunciation of the Spirit, Logic, and Practice of Deterrence." Although this put the churches in East Germany in line with government opposition to the deployment of INF weapons by NATO, their main point was to strengthen their position as churches within a socialist state.

The East German church also proposed a worldwide peace council at the World Council of Churches meeting in Vancouver. This marked the last stage of the church debate on peace and nuclear weapons. In 1985, at the *Kirchentag* in Düsseldorf, a proclamation was published asking the churches of the world to call a "council of peace." The promoter of this idea, Carl Friedrich von Weizsäcker, had been the author of the "Heidelberg Theses" of 1959. He confessed publicly that he had lost confidence in the politicians, but he felt encouraged by the peace movement. A conversion of consciousness among people might now be possible, providing an adequate way to promote a general change of peace politics. But when this idea emerged it became clear that the peace issue had already become secondary to ecological problems and economic justice in the Third World. The nuclear question is no longer the central point of controversy, but one topic among others.

The periodic dramatization of the nuclear dilemma shows clearly that the churches and the theologians have great difficulties grasping the political and ethical problems which cannot be identified along the lines of the distinction of church and state, Christian faith and the world, but which result from the involvement of Christians in political areas of universal dimensions. One enduring topic of major importance has been that of the just war. In the next section I will suggest how this teaching may be reformulated for a nuclear age.

II. ETHICAL PROBLEMS OF THE DOCTRINE OF JUST WAR

Two problems prevent a simple continuation of the doctrine of just war in peace ethics today. One is the relation of means and ends in the nuclear age. The other is the crisis in the concept of peace.

A. *The Proportionality of Means and Ends in the Nuclear Age*

In the Second World War the distinction between combatants and noncombatants, important for the just war concept of *jus in bello*, was effectively undermined. Wars of mass destruction which aim at total victory do not assess the relationship between means and ends. In the present debate on nuclear armaments this problem has become more acute. A major nuclear war would destroy friend and foe alike, and the long-term consequences for life on earth are both unforeseeable and incalculable. So there is no possible way for a "responsible" balancing of ends and means.

As a result, the discussion seeks ways to limit war and keep it in bounds. Hence it is argued that purely defensive weapons are the only justifiable *iusta causa*, and that we should lessen our dependence on nuclear weapons or get rid of them completely in favor of conventional weapons, which would then allow for "conventional" war. This ethical constraint would be real, and the argument is certainly based on experience. However, in renewing the old concept of a "just" war (that is, the revival of the *jus ad bellum* and *jus in bello* purely by means of a change of weapons), this ethical constraint is pointing in the wrong direction — namely, into the past, which tried to include war in the calculation of peace.

A further issue is the just war argument that those who deploy nuclear weapons must also be prepared, if necessary, to use them. In the context of the just war doctrine, the *intentio recta* involves the distinction between deployment and morally legitimate use. Although deployment is primarily intended (*intentio recta*) to prevent war, it does allow for potential use. The American bishops have argued that this is a legitimate distinction according to just war doctrine.[5] It is quite plainly an ethical dilemma, however, which has, in principle, no solution. Furthermore, upon that basis, can an ethical demand for peace be made? What are the actual "conditions of peace"?

B. The Crisis of the Concept of Peace

The traditional doctrine of just war arose from the framework of a "Peace Order Concept" obliging all partners in a conflict and relating them to each other. The criteria of a "just war" referred to this concept of peace. The idea of the "peace of God" and the idea of justice, which was equally binding for all parties, served as a fundamental basis for all the parties in a conflict. That was also true for the modern community of sovereign states founded on common principles of law. As a result of eighteenth-century revolutionary movements, the concept of peace has suffered a severe crisis. Most significantly, the previously unknown concept of the "war against the state," the revolutionary struggle against a certain form of government, has become a new reason for war. Such a war seeks to destroy the false, antiquated, unlawful, or oppressive political order. It is no longer regulated by an order of peace which is already given. Rather, the aim of war is to establish afresh the true and new order of peace. However, when the aim of war and the aim of peace are one and the same, then war itself can be construed as a promoter and source of future peace. To this extent, peace loses its normative regulatory power.

This leads us to a second consequence, namely, that war in this sense can appear to be absolutely just because it is in principle a "war against war," that is, a war against the real cause of previous wars, which lies in the oppressive order to be overthrown. The war to end all wars has then on its side the pathos of the last war. Secular messianic claims to "real peace" are brought into play, and a claim of final peace takes precedence over any idea of an order of peace which embraces other conflicts going on in the world.

The consequences of this development are all too easily recognizable: destruction followed by re-creation, but on a different basis. Peace is threatened by unreconciled conceptions of peace which no longer unite, but divide. This leads to the concepts of peace which have war as a necessary prerequisite before they can be realized. The concept of a uniting and obliging peace has reached a point of crisis and herein lies the decisive threat.

III. FROM THE DOCTRINE OF "JUST WAR" TO THE DOCTRINE OF "JUST PEACE"[6]

A. *Thinking toward Peace*

What are our peace aims? That is the new question with which the ethical intention of the traditional doctrine of just war faces us today. Approached constructively, the legal and ethical meaning of this doctrine was to subject war as a violent way of settling conflicts to the concepts and the rule of law and justice, which themselves are supposed to be instruments of peace. The fundamental attitude to which the doctrine of just war appealed was, in short, thinking from the basis of peace. We are living in an era in which this appeal to war as a means of peace is being questioned.

Our crisis in understanding peace did not start with the East-West conflict, nor with nuclear deterrence. The birth of modern pacifism, which has had its advocates in Europe since the last part of the nineteenth century, is itself a reaction to the power politics which now are full blown in the ideological conflict between East and West.

The profound questioning of the concept of peace itself encompasses all other peace-related criteria and thus involves political action as well as ethical consciousness. *Law, justice,* and *responsibility* only serve the precarious management of a status quo, lacking in peace. Weapons are a questionable representative of the image and concept of peace. Hopes of peace dependent on weapons hardly seem attainable, armament or disarmament. If one considers the whole spectrum of moral, legal, philosophical, and political concern, the objective lack of creative peace understanding from which this era is suffering stands out all too plainly.

B. The Concept of Peace

For Christians peace symbolizes, most importantly, the peace of God, as it appears in the Old Testament language of prophecy and promise and in the New Testament language of fulfillment and expectation. The message is that we live from peace, and not from war. The same is true of political and social life. The ethics of peace will have to ask what it means to preach universal reconciliation in a world which is not united and is not Christian.

A comparison might be helpful. The World Health Organization has defined health in a way which might also be characteristic of an exacting peace concept: health as the state of complete physical, mental, and social well-being. The formula revises the idea that health exists if one is free from bodily disturbances. Analogously, one can define peace as more than the absence of war. In the complete sense, peace is a life which satisfies all.

The logical conclusion of such a concept of peace is this: there is no peace in the world. Furthermore, peace transcends the capabilities of humankind. As a demand for what should be, such a concept of peace would be disorienting. The definition of health also leads to the conclusion that nobody is healthy. Health, however, is really the strength to cope with these disturbances independently and to live with them.[7] Transposed onto the concept of peace, we can say, therefore, that peace is not the complete absence of political conflicts but the sum of the abilities and instruments for dealing with them in something other than a violent manner. Peace is the ability to deal with conflicts politically. An active willingness for peace must live up to its political task. Peace is not the exclusive claim of one system against another system. Therefore claims that peace results from the success of the international class struggle, or can only be the victory of democracy,[8] are false. Rather, peace is a condition of the conflict of systems itself.

C. The Role of Military Force

Considering peace this way, we must question anew the role
of military force. As early as 1945 Bernard Brodie formulated the
thesis that in the future military armaments could only be used
to prevent war.[9] Taking this a step further, we can advance this
idea: "Create peace without using weapons." The renunciation of
force in international law, as formulated in the Kellogg Pact, as-
signs military power merely a role in the framework of this renunciation of force. The only rational and ethically comprehensible
function of military force when raised to the height of nuclear
weapons is to make the renunciation of force compelling and to
give this renunciation a compelling instrument. At this point,
military force steps out of the concept of a "just war." Renunciation of war is the imperative of nuclear deterrence in a world situation in which antagonistic peace aims cannot otherwise be prevented from being realized. The existence and escalation of nuclear
deterrence is not the root, but the consequence, of this antagonism. Military force has, therefore, the task of compelling an antagonistic partnership of the systems.

Nuclear deterrence takes part in the perplexity of peace. The
military guarantor against war will not necessarily be the guarantor of a new concept of peace. Discussion about more or fewer
weapons and armaments is not yet a peace debate. And the movements which owe their existence to this discussion are not yet true
peace movements.

The idea that military force can somehow help us renounce
force altogether will not solve our dilemma. To be sure, there are
many difficult questions involved in renouncing force. But military planning can have no leading role in the conversation about
peacemaking. A "just war" is no longer a means to a "just peace."[10]

D. The Problem of Peace and the Conflict of Political Ideologies

One must review the conflict of political ideologies in order
to understand our task. The East-West conflict goes back well into
the nineteenth century in its intellectual and spiritual roots. Far
from being just a military antagonism, it touches on political and
social issues, the public estimate of culture and religion, and the
relation of individual life and its rights to political society.

We cannot as yet dispense with a military backup, but the starting point for a new consideration of international justice is the recognition of interdependence. What is true of economic justice is also true of political justice. Justice opposes the domination of one over the other. Peace is therefore not a state but a process. Our question is how to change the conflict of political ideologies. Such change cannot stop at a stability guaranteed by military confrontation. This stability is inadequate for peace. One of the most significant elements of change is the conception of human rights,[11] grounded in the notion of a freedom beyond the self-preserving interests of those political ideologies which are a law unto themselves. The concept of human rights is also founded upon the idea of a law superior to every state. We have no means of compulsion available for human rights because they cannot be compelled.

Human rights do not merely exist as an idea. They are closely connected with the economic, political, legal, and cultural organization of societies. A change of political ideologies must, therefore, make it possible for human rights to be a material, economic, and organizational issue. A dogmatically oriented conception of human rights cannot determine change. Unilateralism has the best chance of pointing to the future. Offers by the West to cooperate economically with the East which are not tied to equally weighted or symmetrical performance by the East could, under certain circumstances, be a suitable investment in the process of peace building. The policies of the German Federal Republic toward East Germany which have sometimes been criticized because of their unbalanced unilateralism are a considerable contribution to such a transformation of the conflict of their political ideologies.

E. *Internal and External Peace*

It should never be forgotten that a society cannot be established on the foundation of military force alone. Protection from external force does not guarantee a just domestic peace. In a democracy there can be no mandate for self-destruction. In the long run the imperative of change must be recognized as an imperative of political self-preservation. It is not cynical to say that high aims can be achieved only when they are allied with practical political interests.

IV. THE CHURCHES AND PEACE

The churches entered this discussion in the fifth century with the doctrine of just war. Therefore, they cannot simply extricate themselves from this discussion on the basis that the discussion does not fall within church affairs; nor can they do so on the basis that the whole direction of these modern problems in science, technology, and the conflict of political ideologies is repugnant to them.

We are halfway between a doctrine of just war and a doctrine of just peace. Only if we have reason to hope that the world has not been abandoned by God and that God's peace holds sway over all that we undertake can we be encouraged to think toward peace. The churches cannot lay down a political perspective for peace, but it is their task to seek a new peace perspective in the world.

NOTES

1. "Heidelberger Thesen," in *Atomwaffen und Ethik: Der deutsche Protestantismus und die atomare Aufrüstung 1954–1961: Dokumente und Kommentare*, ed. Christian Walther (Munich: Kaiser Verlag, 1981).

2. "Gerechtigkeit schafft Frieden: Wort der deutschen Bischofskonferenz zum Frieden," in *Hirtenworte zu Krieg und Frieden* (Cologne, 1983). An English translation may be found in James V. Schall, S.J., ed., *Bishops' Pastoral Letters* (San Francisco: Ignatius Press, 1984).

3. *Das Bekenntnis zu Jesus Christus und die Friedensverantwortung der Kirche: Eine Erklärung des Moderamens des Reformierten Bundes* (Gütersloh: Gütersloher Verlagshaus Gerd Mohn, 1982).

4. Günter Baadte, Armin Boyens, and Ortwin Buchbender, eds., *Frieden stiften: Die Christen zur Abrüstung: Eine Dokumentation* (Munich: Verlag C. H. Beck, 1984); *Die Diskussion um die Friedensfrage in der Evangelischen Kirche in Deutschland: Kirkliches Jahrbuch 1983* (Gütersloh: Gütersloher Verlagshaus, 1985).

5. *The Challenge of Peace: God's Promise and Our Response* (Washington, D.C.: U.S. Catholic Conference Office of Publishing Services, 1983). For discussions see Albert Wohlstetter, "Bishops, Statesmen, and Other Strategists on the Bombing of Innocents," *Commentary* 75 (1983): 15–35; and Albert Wohlstetter, Bruce M. Russet, et al., "Morality and Deterrence," *Commentary* 76 (1983): 4ff. The German church statements make very little or no use of the just war theory. See "Gerechtig-

keit schafft Frieden"; and the German Protestant Church memorandum *Frieden wahren, fördern und erneuern* (Gütersloh, 1981).

6. This section develops the arguments that the just war theory can no longer be applied in the nuclear age. The decisive turning point is the fact that there is no convincing ethical justification for a *jus ad bellum* in the event of a nuclear war. The North American debate has therefore concerned itself merely with *jus in bello* in order to gain ethical criteria for the use of atomic weapons. This quest for ethical criteria, as justified and necessary as it is, lacks the foundation as it is expounded in the *jus ad bellum* doctrine. An ethical and political peace doctrine must take its place. The averting of nuclear war (deterrence) can provide an ethical and political foundation from which criteria for the use of nuclear weapons for deterrence or the ending of a nuclear war can be developed.

7. The argument here follows Dietrich Rössler, *Der Arzt zwischen Technik und Humanität* (Munich, 1977), pp. 60–61.

8. See Gottfried Kiessling and Wolfgang Scheler, "Friedenskampf und politisch-moralische Wertung des Krieges," *Deutsche Zeitschrift für Philosophie* 24 (1976): 37–49.

9. Bernard Brodie et al., eds., *The Absolute Weapon: Atomic Power and World Order* (New York, 1946).

10. This point incorporates ideas from Klaus Ritter, "Einige Anmerkungen zur Friedensdiskussion," in *Frieden politisch fördern: Richtungsimpulse* (Gütersloh: Evangelische Kirche in Deutschland, 1985), pp. 11–32.

11. See, for example, Jost Delbrück, "Menschenrechte: Grundlage des Friedens?" in *Im Dienst Für Entwicklung und Frieden: In memoriam Bischof Henrich Tenhumberg*, ed. Hans Thimme and Wilhelm Wöste (Mainz and Munich, 1982), pp. 89–102.

6

Political Theology and the Ethics of Peace

JÜRGEN MOLTMANN

As EARLY AS 1946 Albert Einstein wrote: "The unleashed power of the atom has changed everything except our ways of thinking. We shall require a substantially new manner of thinking, if mankind is to survive." Today, more than forty years later, the destructive power of atomic weapons has been raised to the immeasurable, but we are still looking for a "new manner of thinking" so we can escape this deadly peril to humankind. Since Hiroshima "the bomb" has abruptly changed the world, but Christian theology has only slowly become aware of the new situation in which all its traditional concepts for dealing with power, with terror, and with war are antiquated. The bombs are launched with supersonic speed, but "the spirit" apparently still goes "by foot." Human consciousness today is still limping along behind the real changes in the conditions of human existence in the nuclear age. Because we have not yet comprehended the situation realistically, we cannot see the future in convincing visions of hope. "Nuclear numbing" clouds our consciousness. Fear of the great catastrophe makes us incapable of doing what we need to do today, so our children can live tomorrow. "Where there is no vision the people will perish." That is what is happening today.

First I would like to consider the conditions of our nuclear age and the origin of a new "political theology" in Europe which in both German states is turning more and more into a "theology of peace" today. Then I shall attempt to define anew what it means to be a Christian in the midst of these apocalyptic dangers from the perspective of the Christian experience of God. Finally I want to unfold an ethics of peace in order to define finally the categorical imperative of every human ethics in this nuclear age.

My perspectives on theology, politics, and peace come from divided postwar Germany. Nowhere else in the world are so many nuclear weapons stored, so many missiles based, and so many foreign armies stationed as in West and East Germany. We are sitting on the largest powder keg in the world. Moreover, we belong to the developed industrial nations in a global economic system that destabilizes the countries of the Third World and brings them into greater and greater debt slavery. And due to our dense industrial development the ecological crisis is ever present in our dying forests, poisoned waters, and acid rain. I live in a center of these three crises, but I shall speak chiefly about the first.

I. THE NUCLEAR AGE AND THE
NEW POLITICAL THEOLOGY

Hiroshima in 1945 fundamentally changed the quality of human history. Our time has become limited time. The epoch in which we exist is the last epoch of humankind, for we live in the time in which the end of humankind can be brought to pass at any moment. The system of nuclear deterrence which we have built up and continue to make more and more perfect has made it possible to put an end to the life of humankind in a few hours. The nuclear winter which will follow a war with nuclear weapons leaves the survivors no chance. This time in which the end of humankind is possible at any time is truly the "end time." For no one can expect that this nuclear age will be superseded by another age in which this deadly threat of humankind to itself no longer exists. The dream of "a world without nuclear weapons" is only wishful thinking. We will never become incapable of doing what we can do now. Once learned, the formula cannot be forgotten. At Hiroshima, in 1945, humankind lost its "atomic innocence."

Since the nuclear age is the last age of humankind, our struggle for survival means the struggle for time. The struggle for life is the struggle against the nuclear end. We attempt to make our end time as end-less as possible by constantly granting the threat-

ened life on this earth a new temporary reprieve. This struggle
for the postponement of the end is a permanent struggle for survival. It is a struggle without victory, a struggle without end — at
best without end. We can extend this nuclear end time, but we
and all succeeding generations must again and again negotiate a
new reprieve for life in this end time under the Damoclean sword
of the bomb. The lifetime of humanity is no longer defined by nature, as it has been up to now, but must be created through a de-
liberate politics of survival.

Up to now nature has regenerated humanity after epidemics
and world wars. Up to now nature has protected humanity from
extermination by individuals. From this time on that is no longer
the case. Since Hiroshima humanity as a whole has "become mortal," as Mikhail Gorbachev correctly observed. "Immortality," as
he said, or, more modestly, "survival," has since Hiroshima inevitably become the primary task of the political culture. It means
that today all decisions must consider the life of coming generations.

The nuclear age is the first common age of all nations and
of all people. Since Hiroshima our many different national his-
tories have become one common history of one human race, even
if only negatively in regard to the common danger of extermination. The struggle among superpowers for domination of the world
produced nuclear arms. But because there was no nuclear monopoly, no one won. The nuclear superpowers neutralized one another
and became powerless, for "whoever shoots first, dies second." Nuclear deterrence has created a situation in which nothing can move
anymore. The blackmailers have become the blackmailed. The
situation of nuclear deterrence thus puts an end to all grand politics. In smaller conflicts nuclear weapons are not useful. They did
not help in Vietnam, in Iran, in Afghanistan, or in Nicaragua.
We have reached a stalemate. Is there an alternative to the nuclear Armageddon of the superpowers? America plans a new defensive system in space. But since there is a new offensive system
for every new defensive system, this development does not lead
us out of the dead end.

Ours is the first common age of humankind because we are
all possible objects of nuclear extermination. In this situation, the
survival of humankind is conceivable only when the nations organize themselves into a collective action for survival. Since Hiro-

shima the survival of humankind is inseparably bound up with the cooperation of nations for common defense against these deadly dangers. This lifesaving unification demands the relativization of individual national interests, the democratization of conflict-promoting ideologies, the tolerance of different religions, and the general subordination of all under the common interest of life. A step-by-step building up of an international network of political responsibility for peace in regional security partnerships is possible, as for example we are now beginning to see between the two German states and Western and Eastern Europe.

The system of nuclear deterrence does not secure peace, but endangers it in two important ways. First of all, the arms buildup of the Northern Hemisphere is an economic burden to the nations of the Third World, leading to the arming of the developing nations and the waging of numerous wars in these lands. Seventy-five percent of the weapons trade of the last two decades was with the developing nations. These crises are interdependent. Without disarmament in the North, no justice in the South, and vice versa. Only through building up lasting development in the South do we come to disarmament and peace. A nuclear war is a potential danger for humankind, but the North-South conflict is a present reality from which people are already dying.

An atomic war would be an ecological catastrophe. The arms build-up in the First World, however, is already fostering ecological catastrophes in the Third World through indebtedness; for exploitation creates poverty, poverty leads to indebtedness, and indebtedness forces one to sell and use up one's own natural bases for life — chopping down rain forests, overgrazing grasslands, and driving out the rural population. The arms race produces poverty and environmental destruction worldwide. We lose capital, raw materials, and workers. "Armament is theft," said President Eisenhower at the end of his presidency — rightly so, as the Brundtland Report of 1987 proves. The "spiral of mutual fear" led through mutual deterrence into the modern "weapons culture." But this is deadly both for humankind and for nature. Thus we must abolish this culture of weapons and fear and through democratization create reasonable trust.

Further, there is a human problem in nuclear technology. During the development of nuclear technology the ecological problems of nuclear waste disposal and scrapping obsolete atomic bombs were overlooked. Radioactive material cannot be returned to nature; it must be stored somewhere and watched over for centuries. In addition, nuclear technology demands perfect human beings because it is unfriendly to human error. Can this dangerous technology be controlled by fallible and corruptible human beings? The catastrophes from Windscale/Sallafield, Harrisburg, and Chernobyl, as well as the diverse international corruption scandals in the nuclear industry, say no. So we must give up nuclear technology and seek other energy sources which are ecologically more humane, since "to err is human."

A new political theology arose in Germany after the war with its dreadful shock of Auschwitz. For us young Germans who came to study theology after the war, *Auschwitz* became a turning point in our thinking and acting. We became painfully aware that we must live, inescapably, in the shadow of the Holocaust, which had been committed on the Jewish people in the name of our people. *After Auschwitz* became our concrete context for theology. With this place and crime we not only marked a political and moral crisis, but also a theological and church crisis. For us the incomprehensible thing about Auschwitz was not just the executioners and their assistants, the technical perfection of the mass extermination, or even the hiddenness of God; for us it was the silence of those who had looked on, or looked away, or closed their eyes, in handing over victims to mass murder. For us Auschwitz did not turn into a question about the meaning of suffering, as it did for the Jews. For us it was a question about guilt and shame and sorrow.

T. W. Adorno declared at that time, "After Auschwitz there are no more poems." Is theology still possible after Auschwitz? Johann Baptist Metz and I answered yes, but only because there was a "theology" in Auschwitz. In recalling the prayers that were spoken in the gas chambers, even we today can pray to God. Not until we remember the victims do we find the courage to live and hope for a different future.

With this insight we began to examine the Christian and church traditions in Germany. Why did Christians and churches largely remain silent? There was no lack of personal courage. The following patterns of behavior and prejudices can be found in the tradition.

"Faith is a private matter." Faith is concerned with saving one's soul and the inner peace of one's conscience, but not with politics. The privatization of religion in the bourgeois world of the nineteenth century had secularized politics and turned public life over to other powers. There is a modern split between "public life" on the one hand and "private life" on the other; governmental power politics without morality on the one hand and personal morality without power on the other. Many Christians who detested Hitler and lamented the fate of the Jews went into so-called "internal emigration." They tried to save their souls in accommodating themselves to political demands. But they could not save their personal innocence. They wronged their Jewish fellow citizens because they kept silent when they should have spoken.

Modern theologies with their transcendent, existential, or personalistic orientation only mirrored this modern consciousness split. They failed because the challenges of that time are no longer relevant after Auschwitz. The political theology that we developed in opposition to them starts out from public witness and the public responsibility of faith and is emphatically critical of society and power. The gospel of Christ is not about a private person but is a public proclamation. The salvation of Christ is not private salvation, but salvation of the world. That is why he ended up in deadly conflict with the godless powers of his time. Christian faith is personal conviction, but not a private matter. It is public witness to the righteousness and peace of God in this violent world.

However, the Protestant two kingdoms doctrine has taught the distinction between church and state, religion and politics, ever since the Reformation. From that doctrine follows the claim that the church must be apolitical, and the state unreligious. Thus when Hitler came to power, the church in Germany did not feel responsible for the human dignity and rights of the communists, the socialists, the democrats, and the Jews, all of whom were persecuted first. Only when Hitler wanted to subjugate the churches was there opposition by the church. Apart from individuals like Dietrich Bonhoeffer, there had been no political opposition by Christians and the churches. "The church must remain the church," it was said, whatever happens in the state and society. With this stance the churches became guilty of Auschwitz, and modern church theologies continue to mirror the separation of religion

and politics. But a church can no more exist in a society apoliti-
cally than a theology can be purely a church theology. There are
indeed politically unaware theologians, but there are in principle
no apolitical theologians. Churches and theologies who declare
themselves to be apolitical always cooperate with the powers of
the status quo and have, without exception, entered into conservative alliances. The new political theology does not want to po-
liticize the churches, but it wants to make all aware of the political relationships of the churches and Christianize the political existence of the churches. The church is "an institution of social critical freedom" (Metz). For every church that bases itself on Christ
must be reminded ultimately that Christ was not sacrificed by a
priest between two candlesticks on an altar. He was crucified by
the Roman occupation forces between two Jewish freedom fight-
ers on Golgotha, "way outside the city."

This privatization of faith and the separation of the church
from politics has had a disastrous effect on public life and politics.
In Germany it produced *Realpolitik*, the naked politics of power
without conscience. "With the Sermon on the Mount one cannot
rule the state," said the privately pious Bismarck. This German
Realpolitik has set off two world wars and destroyed our people
physically and spiritually in the long term. It is, in retrospect, not
only more responsible but also smarter to orient politics on the
standards of human rights and to regard all national politics as
a moral task in behalf of humankind. Morality and religion, conscience and responsibility will have to come back into politics after Auschwitz, if we intend to save humankind from a nuclear
holocaust.

The political theology which we began in Germany in the
1960s turned into a movement that reached far beyond the borders of Western Europe. Quite early it came to an exchange with
theologies in Latin America, at first with the theology of revolution, then with the theology of liberation. Just as early it came
to an association with the civil rights movement and black theology in the United States. Later followed the exchange with
Minjung theology in Korea and other contextual theologies in the
countries of the Third World. Today corresponding political theologies are arising all over from Christians who stand up for lib-

eration, social justice, and human rights in the specific context of their lands.

In both German states the peace movement grew on the strength of political disappointments. It reached its climax in 1981 and 1982 with mass rallies and human chains that reached for hundreds of kilometers. It strengthened the peace discussion which had already been going on in our churches. The Protestant church in East Germany was the first to reject the "spirit of the logic and practice of the system of nuclear deterrence." The Reformed church in West Germany called this system of deterrence incompatible with the Christian faith and declared the *status confessionis*. The Protestant church in West Germany and the Catholic bishops' conference reacted more cautiously because they believe that military deterrence guarantees peace.

II. BEING A CHRISTIAN IN THE NUCLEAR AGE

When Christians think about the future of this society threatened by death, they begin with the experience which makes them Christians. They intervene for the sake of the God to whom they owe their existence. Christians respond to the challenges of their times with their whole being, for these are not only questions of action, but also questions of faith and existence. The social and political involvement of Christians is the witness of Christ. The responsibility of the church comes out of the innermost core of its divine mission. But what makes a Christian a Christian, and what makes the church the church of Christ? It is the justifying and peacemaking action of God through Christ on us unjust and peaceless people.

"Christ was put to death for our trespasses and raised for our justification," says Paul (Rom. 4:25). In the letter to the Colossians (1:19–20) the same is said about peace: "And through him (Christ) to reconcile to himself all things, whether on earth or in heaven, making peace by the blood of his cross." All that determines being a Christian and all that the church is and can do is indebted to this just-making, reconciling, and peacemaking action of God. The church is therefore nothing other than the fruit of the reconciling suffering of God, the creature of God's justifying actions, and the unity of both the peacemaking and life-giving will of God. What we as believers experience as church is grace, the divine acceptance. The church of Christ cannot be anything other than a "Justice Church" and a "Peace Church."

Out of each gift, however, arises a corresponding task. If the Christians are the work of the justice-creating and peacemaking action of God, then they are also the instrument of this divine action in this world. From the justification of the unjust follows their mission as peacemakers in the injustices of this society. There can be no other answer from Christians to their experience of God. Just as humans owe their justice completely to God, so God is completely interested in the just actions of humans. God puts the hunger and the thirst for justice in the hearts of those whom God justifies. God gives us peace in order to make us peacemakers. Whoever is satisfied with the peace of God for his or her own person and does not become a peacemaker does not know the dynamics of the spirit of God.

The church exists as work and tool of God's justice. The economical, political, and social conflicts of this society are also its own conflicts. All Christians experience them in their own body. The more they believe in the justice of God, the more painfully they suffer from the injustice which they see. If there were no God, then one could come to terms with violence and injustice, because "that's just the way it is." But if there is a God, and if this God is the just God, then one can no longer come to terms with it. One can never become accustomed to injustice, but will rather contradict and resist it with all one's strength. If there is a God, then there is a justice and a judgment which no one evades.

If the Church of Christ is the work and tool of God's justice in the world, then it is also the beginning and the pledge of the coming new creation of the world in this justice. If the peace of God is experienced in the church, then the hope for peace on earth also originates here. Faith answers the experienced justice of God with thoughts, words, and works; and hope anticipates the new world of peace. Faith finds the comfort of God in all suffering, but hope looks into the future of a new creation in which there will be no more suffering, pain, or crying. Those who believe in God have hope for this earth and do not despair.

Since the 1968 conference in Uppsala we have called this life in hope "life in anticipation." Prepare the way of the Lord. The message from Uppsala is more important than ever:

> We call upon you in trust in God's renewing power: share in the anticipation of God's kingdom, and let something be visible already today of the new creation which Christ will complete on his day. . . . God renews; Christ wants his church, already, now, to be a sign and the announcement of a renewed, humane society.[1]

In fact, we live in anticipation. In fear and trembling we all put into practice today our hope for tomorrow. By virtue of their hope Christians anticipate the future of the new creation, the kingdom of justice and freedom, not because they are optimists, but because they believe in a just and faithful God. We will not realize the kingdom of justice in this world. But we can not exempt ourselves from this task, for God's sake.

III. THE ETHICS OF PEACE IN THE NUCLEAR AGE

There are ethical principles of the politics of peace in Christian perspective, which, I believe, follow stringently from the Christian experience of the nuclear age. The biblical traditions and the Christian experience of faith say unambiguously that justice alone creates a lasting *shalom*. That is why there is no other way to peace except just action and concern for worldwide justice. All church memorandums have, correctly, taken this view. But what is "justice"?

Jews and Christians will begin with God's justice. God's justice is experienced by them as a creative force. God is just because God creates rights for those without rights and sets aright those who are unjust. That is why we can pray with Psalm 31:1: "In thy righteousness deliver me!" God "executes justice for the oppressed," confesses Psalm 146:7. Through justice God creates the peace which endures. It follows from this that there is no peace where injustice and violence rule, even when law and order have been achieved by force. Peace does not bring justice. Justice brings peace. Injustice always creates inequalities and destroys balances. Unjust systems can only survive with violence. There is no peace where violence rules. Where violence rules, death reigns; not life.

We relate this biblical concept of justice to the concepts of justice in our legal culture. An early concept of the European legal culture defines justice as *justitia distributiva, suum cuique:* to each one's own. This brilliant phrase combines equality before the law ("each") with real difference between human beings ("one's own"). From each according to his or her abilities, to each according to his or her needs (Marx). Or, as the Hutterite Brethren say, "Everyone gives where he can; everyone gets where he needs it." This concept of justice is mainly technically applied to goods and services. Everyone has the human right to life, food, work, and freedom.

The personal concept of justice, through which community is established, goes beyond this technical concept. It consists in the mutual recognition and acceptance of others. Mutual recognition of human dignity creates a humane and just community. This corresponds to the Christian experience: "Accept one another, as Christ has accepted you, for the glory of God" (Rom. 15:7). This personal concept of justice also underlies modern concepts of democratic society as covenant and constitution.

But the highest form of justice is the justice of mercy through which those without rights receive justice. That is the justice of the "God of widows and orphans." In this world of injustice and violence divine justice takes on the form of the "preferential option for the poor," as the Latin American liberation theologians say. That does not mean that "mercy goes before justice," but that those deprived of their rights come to claim their rights, and the unjust person is converted to justice. This divine justice does not stand outside human justice; rather it is the justice-creating source for that system of justice which leads to lasting peace. Like the recognition of human dignity in others, so the creation and protection of the rights of the poor and weak is also the foundation of every lasting system of justice.

The biblical traditions of faith speak of a comprehensive peace because they speak of God's peace. *Shalom* means the sanctification of all life which God has created, in all its relationships. It is blessed life in communion with the life-giving God, with other people, and with all other creatures: peace with God, peace among people, peace with nature. For God's sake it is characteristic of *shalom* that it cannot be limited in a religious or individual way. *Shalom* is universal. What Jews and Christians experience of that in history are therefore beginnings and anticipations of that peace of God which will one day bring all creatures to eternal life. Judaism and Christianity are movements of concrete hope for peace for all nations and all creatures.

It follows from this that peace in history is not a state of affairs, but a process; not a possession, but a way. Peace is not the absence of violence, but the presence of justice. In peace studies one distinguishes between a negative and a positive definition of peace. The negative definition says peace is not war and thus the absence of the military use of force, of fear and oppression. This negative understanding of peace is present when it is said that the system of nuclear deterrence has "preserved peace" in the last forty years. Apart from the fact that this is not correct for all nations, peace is in this case confused with "cease-fire," and the costs of the system of nuclear deterrence are concealed.

The Christian concept of peace combines both definitions but gives the positive definition of peace preference through the emphasis on justice. It follows from this that peace in history is a continuous process, not a state of affairs. Peace in history is a common way, on which there are steps forward and steps back. On this way, the issue is the reduction of arms and violence and the building up of trust and community.

There is never lasting peace in history just for the present generation. It arises out of the responsibility for justice between the generations. Humankind is created as a series of generations. That is why every generation is the debtor of the past generations, and that is why every generation has responsibility for the life of the coming generations. Only justice in this unwritten contract of humankind between the generations promotes a lasting peace. That is why peace in history is not a state of affairs that one could come in contact with, but a way on which one must make progress to win time for humankind and to make life possible for the coming generations.

"Love of the enemy" is, according to Christ's Sermon on the Mount, the consummate, godlike form of love of the neighbor and the way to lasting peace on earth. Whoever gets involved in a dis-

agreement and has a conflict always puts himself or herself under
the law of vengeance: an eye for an eye, a tooth for a tooth. Whoever accepts the law of vengeance in regard to the enemy falls into
a vicious circle from which there is no escape. One must become
the enemy of one's enemy and is determined by this hostility. If
evil is repaid with evil, then the one evil always orients itself to
the other evil, because only then can it be justified. In the nuclear
age the arms race, which works correspondingly, leads the world
toward the abyss of universal death. There is only liberation to
life when the adversarial orientation toward the enemy ceases and
deterrence by the threat of vengeance no longer reigns. The attitude toward the enemy that Jesus puts in place of deterrence is
"love of the enemy" (Matt. 5:43 ff.). What does that mean in the
nuclear age?

Love of the enemy is not love that seeks vengeance, but creative love. Whoever repays evil with love no longer reacts, but creates something new. Love of the enemy requires great sovereignty
with regard to the enemy. The freer one becomes from fear of the
enemy, the more love of the enemy will succeed. Love of the enemy
can never mean submission to the enemy and confirmation of his
or her hostility. In love of the enemy one does not wonder anymore, "How can I protect myself against the enemy and his or her
possible attack?" but instead, "How can I take away the enemy's
hostility?" Through love of the enemy we make the enemy part
of our own responsibility. Love of the enemy is not the expression
of abstract good intentions but of concrete, realistic responsibility. Love of the enemy is only reasonable. We cannot secure peace
by eliminating or threatening to eliminate all our possible enemies, but alone by reducing our hostilities and taking responsibility for common security and a lasting development. Politics in this
first common age of humankind requires that we think with and
for each other. It demands a large amount of empathy. The first
question is not how Western Europe can protect itself against the
"Russian menace," but how we can come to a common order of
peace in Western and Eastern Europe. We must demilitarize public
consciousness and political thinking and transfer how we deal with
an opponent in a democracy to how we deal with so-called "enemies" in international relations. "With the Sermon on the Mount
one cannot rule a state," Bismarck once said to justify German

power politics. Other than the Sermon on the Mount, I maintain, there is no politics of survival in the nuclear age.

Out of the politics of love of the enemy follows the politics of the nonviolent overcoming of tyranny. Nonviolence does not mean depoliticization or the renunciation of power. For we have always distinguished between *power* and *violence*. Under *power* we understand the just use of force. Under *violence* we understand the unjust use of force. In this sense the modern state has a "monopoly on force" in society, and we speak of "naked violence," "brutality," and "tyranny" where force is exercised illegally, illegitimately, and in disregard of human rights. Christianity has not been able to abolish the culture of violence in our societies. But it has made it necessary to justify every use of violence, especially the use of violence by the state. It has broken the "innocence of violence" which Nietzsche worshiped. The law also sets limits on the state's monopoly of violence, not only in domestic politics, but also in foreign politics. Threatening humankind with a nuclear holocaust is an act of violence which nothing can justify. The use and the threat of nuclear weapons and other means of mass destruction exceed the right of every state.

The first form of overcoming violence is binding every exercise of power to law. From that follows the duty of resistance to every unjust exercise of power, be it illegal, illegitimate, or directed against human rights. The principle of nonviolence does not exclude the struggle for power when the issue in this struggle is the binding of power to law. Whoever joins the resistance to an obvious tyranny only does his or her duty as a citizen when he or she stands for the restoration of law or the rights of the oppressed.

The power of the people who suffer under tyranny is not terror but solidarity. Terror disqualifies the goals of liberation and only justifies the tyranny. Mass solidarity of the people and other peoples deprives the tyranny of every appearance of its right to exist and takes away the fear from its threats. Recently, we have had a host of examples in which a people has overcome a military dictatorship without bloodshed: Spain, Portugal, Greece, Argentina, the Philippines. Tyranny is built on sand; and when it is rejected by the people in domestic politics and at the same time is isolated in foreign politics it is thus deprived of fear as well as trust.

Overcoming violence nonviolently is possible. But it can also require martyrdom. We think of Gandhi and Martin Luther King, Jr. We think above all of Christ himself. If we think of them, then we discover that political programs are not the only way to liberating power and "success," but that suffering also has liberating power and can work convincingly in the long term.

The nuclear age is the first common age for all people and nations. Through the nuclear threat all people have been condemned to death together. Through the rapidly spreading ecological crises of the global environment all nations face the same tasks — each in its particular way, but nonetheless together. Particularistic thinking, which is oriented against other people and nations and disregards the universal community of threat and tasks, is not only morally reprehensible, but also deadly. The possibility of life on earth is dependent upon how quickly and thoroughly we recognize that we are neighbors on a vulnerable planet and that we have to provide for one another and our descendants. All the recent "state-of-the-world reports" tell us that the common environment of the world is in great danger and that humankind itself is not in good condition. We need a convincing ethics of the common life. Let me suggest some conditions for it.

First, the current crises have arisen from rivalries and power struggles. Everyone attempted to win at the expense of others. National egoism, class rule, racism, and so on arose. One assumed that in the struggle for existence only the fittest survive. Today this principle leads both the weak and the strong to death and destroys the future. Only lasting peace guarantees survival. The principle of life is: Respect for the interests of each is the condition for meeting the interests of all, just as only the mutual guarantee of security can guarantee the security of all. National egoism, class rule, and enriching oneself at the expense of others are reprehensible, because they are deadly for all. Humankind and the earth can no longer afford this power struggle and rivalry. The first question asked of all great political and economic decisions must therefore be: Does this course of action serve the common life of humankind or not?

Second, the current crises have further arisen from the egoism of humans in regard to nature. We subjugated nature and robbed it of its natural resources. In the face of the ecological crises this is no longer possible. Human egoism destroys the environment and finally even humankind itself. The first question of economic and political policies must therefore be: Does it serve the preservation of creation and the community of life on earth or not?

Third, the current crises have arisen from neglecting the contract between the generations. Every generation thought only of itself. We left the succession of the generations to nature. Today the situation is different. The contract between the generations must therefore be publicly formulated and consciously kept, so that the current generation no longer lives at the expense of the generations of the future. The first question of political, economic, and cultural decisions is therefore: Does this act serve the life of the future generations, or does it burden and destroy the future?

It follows from these three points of view that human ethics has become a task for humankind and must therefore be freed from those particularistic national, economic, and cultural interests from which it has been dominated so far. The ethical values of life, the common life, and survival of the earth have become absolute values in comparison with all only partially valid values.

It follows further that the separations of politics, economics, law, and the sciences from ethics have become untenable and can no longer be tolerated. The sad experience of the current crises is convincing proof that economics, politics, and the sciences become corrupted without ethical orientation.

It follows, finally, that the common formulation of an absolute ethical code for the community and for the life of humankind on this earth is necessary, so that the great problems of humankind can be solved today in a responsible way. It is thus time that humans remember the "eternal truths" which constitute the foundation of their humanity and subordinate everything else to these. The nuclear age has become the first common age of humanity. Let us then in all things think in the interest of all humanity!

So act that the maxims of your acting could through your will establish a universal law for all humans.

NOTE

1. N. Goodall, ed., *The Uppsala Report 1968: Official Report of the Fourth Assembly of the World Council of Churches* (Geneva: World Council of Churches, 1968).

7

The Peace of God: Conceptions of Peace in the New Testament[1]

PAUL S. MINEAR

Preface

THE UNABRIDGED RANDOM HOUSE Dictionary contains sixteen various denotations of the word *peace*, but not one of them coincides with the primary use in the New Testament. The contrast is, of course, not absolute. One can find a few instances of agreement. Random House accords first place to the definition of peace as the normal, nonwarring condition of a nation or group of nations (for example, Canada is at peace). So far as I can tell, that conception plays no role in early Christian thought. But there is greater agreement on a second Random House definition: peace as an agreement among antagonistic nations to end hostilities. The Book of Acts tells of an embassy sent from Tyre and Sidon to ask for peace, because that region was dependent on Herod for its supply of food. But why was this story told? Because when he accepted from the petitioners the reverence permissible only to a god, Herod was guilty of blasphemy and was punished by death "from worms" (Acts 12:20–23). In this story the notion of peace was present, but it was of no interest to Christians.

A similar conception of peace appeared in a parable of Jesus. A king began war on another king but found too late that his enemy's army was twice as large as his own, so he was forced "to sue for peace" (Luke 14:31–35). Why was this story told? Not as a lesson for kings, but to warn potential disciples not to commit themselves to Jesus unless they had given up all their possessions. The meaning of the term *peace* is clear, but its importance is marginal.

According to Random House, peace may mean freedom from civil disorders. This notion appears in the account of one of Paul's trials. The prosecuting attorney began his case against the apostle by flattering the judge. "It is through you, most excellent Felix, that we enjoy so much peace" (Acts 24:2). But such preservation of social order was of no concern to Paul.

I mention these texts for two reasons: first, as a reminder that many discussions of peace end in confusion because, though participants use the same word, they have quite different things in mind; and second, as a warning not to look to the New Testament for help in solving social conflicts, whether between races or classes or nations. The peace of which the Scripture speaks is indigenous to a very different thought world. To understand it, we must first enter "that strange new world in the Bible." I hope to help you migrate, at least for a time, into that world.

That journey requires more imagination and more effort than many migrants are willing to supply. One must be willing to leave the familiar world, whether academic or ecclesiastical, secular or sacred, and to adjust to a new community whose words have been translated into English but whose language relies on very different signals. In what follows, I want to use the term *peace* as a key to understanding those signals. If I succeed, it will be due to your readiness to migrate, at least for the time being, into a foreign world of thought.

God's Peace

The difference between the New Testament notion of peace and definitions from our modern dictionaries is the essential linkage of peace to the deity. Peace points to a specific human relationship to a very specific God. This is what one should expect among a people for whom the love of God is the greatest commandment. Where that is true, the relation to God can spell the greatest good, while a broken bond spells the greatest dereliction. Every change in thinking about this God is bound to affect the entire world of thought. It is God who determines and defines the true meaning of peace.

This primacy is reflected in the greetings typical of early Christian letters. "Grace and peace to you from God our Father . . ." (Rom. 1:7). Many inferences may be drawn from this greeting, which appears at least eighteen times. This peace is known by its source: the Father's gift to his children, forming a firm intimate bond with every member of a specific family of believers. These persons recall a time when they had known nothing of such peace, and a later time when they had first experienced it. The idea of peace was as different from other ideas as the idea of God was different from other ideas.[2] The word telescopes all that the good news of God's grace had brought to them, in contrast to previous isolation and ignorance. So the word became one of the boundary posts, separating the time before and the time after. The writer of each epistle was bound to each reader by this peace, both conscious of forming one family with the Father.

Before saying "peace," think of this God, this Father.

Letters that began with this greeting often closed with this farewell: "The God of peace be with you" (Rom. 15:33). In other words, this peace helps to distinguish this God from all others. He and his peace are inseparable; that is why recipients call him Father.[3] Whenever this family gathers, it can say, "The God of peace is with us." More than the source of peace, his presence *is* that peace. He himself is as present or as absent as his peace; his presence creates the cohesion, the solidarity of his family.

Before using the word *peace*, think of this presence.

We may now extend the orbit of thought by completing the greeting: "Grace and peace to you from God our Father and from the Lord Jesus Christ" (Rom. 1:7). That last phrase is essential. This Lord is the source of this peace; the gift is simultaneously his and his Father's. As Peter phrased it in his first sermon to Gentiles, "God sent this message to Israel, proclaiming good news of peace by Jesus Christ. He is Lord of all" (Acts 10:36). Or as Paul put it in his greeting to the Galatians, "Peace from the Lord Jesus Christ, who gave himself for our sins to set us free from the present evil age" (Gal. 1:4; also Rev. 1:5,6). Just as the Father/Son image dominates the relationship to God, so the Lord/slave image dominates the relationship to Christ. "He is our Lord; we are his slaves. Through his work he became our Lord and we became his slaves." It was through the life-death-life of this Son that the peace of God came to all of his siblings. As they responded to the story of what Jesus had done, that story revolutionized their God-relation, their God-thoughts, their God-talk — and thereby their peace-talk. The measure of this revolution is suggested by Paul when he wrote, May I never boast of anything except the cross of our Lord Jesus Christ, by which the world has been crucified to me, and I have been crucified to the world (Gal. 6:14–16). For Paul, peace came on the far side of that triple crucifixion. It was through that crucifixion that he received peace from Jesus.

When you say "peace," recall Jesus' entire story.

We may now estimate the range and depth of that peace by noting some of its specific results. For Paul, to believe in Christ is to be *in* Christ. To be in Christ means belonging to a new creation where everything old has passed away and all things have become new (2 Cor. 5:17). Paul believed himself to live under a new government in which every Christian is under new orders. "Let the peace of Christ rule in your hearts." Every congregation is called "in the one body" to live under that same government (Col. 3:15). Relevant to every congregation is the prayer, "May the Lord of peace himself give you peace at all times in all ways" (2 Thess. 3:16). So we ask, what are some of those ways?

For one thing, the inner world of the heart is transformed. "We have peace with God through our Lord Jesus Christ" (Rom. 5:1). The context of that assertion in Romans spells out some of the components of that peace. No longer does the memory of sins against God guarantee the wrath of God. Paul had been weak, ungodly, an enemy of God. No longer. Anxiety about the future had spawned despair. No longer. Once suffering had prompted resentment and fear. No longer. Now intensified suffering and danger produced hope. Now the love of God, poured into the heart, gave birth to forgiveness, trust, hope, and even the love of persecutors.

When saying "peace," think of those changes.

But there were broader social results as well. A radical change had taken place in the human habit of dividing all humanity into two segments, Jew and Gentile.[4] As a Jew Paul had belonged to the first type. With other Jews he had considered all Gentiles to be "far off." Now he believed that through Christ's death they had been brought near. Christ had made peace between them by creating in himself one new humanity, the new Adam. Centuries of alienation had ended. High and thick walls had crumbled. A new habitat for God had been created where he is now seen to dwell in the Spirit (Eph. 2:13–18). He had made obsolete economic, sexual, and cultural distinctions: slave and free, male and female, wise and foolish.

Before saying "peace," think of the demolition of those walls.

Our own resistance to such a revolution is as nothing compared to the resistance on the part of ancient Jews and Gentiles. Could they now eat together, the clean and the polluted? Could they agree to defy God's earlier commands for circumcision? Could they worship together, ignoring the laws of the Sabbath and accepting the hatred of the synagogue? Jewish antipathies to unclean Gentiles could not easily be jettisoned, or Gentile scorn of the fastidious conscience of Jews. What did "peace in the Holy Spirit" mean in polyglot congregations? The apostles answered: mutual acceptance and forbearance, refusal to condemn the immoral freedom of some, or the moral caution of others, absolute priority for the demands of love, readiness to let God be the judge. Many writings were occasioned by failures to realize the peace of Christ; those writings therefore insisted on doing "whatever it is that makes for peace" (Rom. 14:1–15:13). The peace of God was designed to produce peacemakers. The communal infrastructure became a fabric woven of mutual care and concern, self-discipline and self-sacrifice, the practice of returning good for evil, complete honesty in speech (1 Peter 3:8–10). Paul identified this communal peace with the advent of the kingdom of God (Rom. 14:17); James identified it with the harvest of peace produced by sowing peace (James 3:18).

Before saying "peace," think of these forms of peacemaking.

In the church at Corinth some of the greatest threats to peace erupted during moments when worship reached a peak of emotional intensity. Charismatic speech produced pandemonium. Many prophets wanted to reveal God's will at the same moment, and each revelation seemed too important to permit delay. The apostle felt obliged to call the meeting to order and to remind all the charismatics that their God was a God not of disorder but of peace (1 Cor. 14:33). The manifestations of ardor contradicted its origins in God.

We should not overlook the situations faced by wandering apostles as they carried the news from town to town. They had been charged to travel fast and light, with neither a picnic basket nor travelers' checks, wholly dependent on hospitality given to strangers. Often they were followed by truth squads who alerted synagogues to the arrival of troublemakers. The rules to be followed by Jesus' messengers were quite specific: "Carry no purse, no bag, no sandals. . . . Whatever house you enter, first say 'Peace to this house'. And if anyone is there who shares in peace ["a son of peace"] your peace will rest on that person; but if not, it will return to you" (Luke 10:5–12; Matt. 10:11–14). This was a dangerous calling. Each house needed to test the legitimacy of each visitor; each visitor, in turn, needed to judge the sincerity of a welcome, from one bed and breakfast stop to the next. Each potential guest brought responsibility and risk, for the host became accountable for the guest's deeds, whether good or bad (2 John 11; Acts 17: 5–9). Both hosts and guests were sons or daughters of peace who, after meeting each other, shared the same peace. Their common risk cemented the common bond.

We have now reviewed many of the forms taken by peace from God, from very simple if elemental gestures of courtesy to revolutionary crucifixions and resurrections. To summarize in more technical jargon: to comprehend this peace we must reckon with its ontological grounding, its eschatological origins, its cosmological ramifications, its sociological effects, its pneumatological manifestations, and its missiological orientation.

God's War

We have examined the roots and fruits of God's peace but have thus far overlooked evidence that contradicts the picture of Jesus as a dispenser of peace. Consider, for example, this warning that he addressed to his closest companions. "Do not suppose that I came to bring peace on earth. I did not come to bring peace. No, I came to bring a sword" (Matt. 10:34). What is this sword? And how is it related to peace? In any modern language the two are mutually exclusive—peace is possible only after hostilities cease—but in early Christian language, the two seem interdependent. This interdependence is reflected in the prophet's picture of

the sword coming from the mouth of the victorious Lamb, as well
as in the command issued from that Lamb to the four horsemen
to "take peace from the earth" (Rev. 6:4; 19:15,21).

What, then, is this sword? Jesus spoke most directly of the
divisions within families that would be caused by his call for followers. "In one house there will be five divided, three against
two . . . father against son . . . mother against daughter" (Luke
12:52; Matt. 10:34–39). This definition of the sword might be readily intelligible if it meant simply that loyalty to Jesus would create
family dissension as a regrettable by-product. But the sword cut
deeper than that. "I came *in order to* bring a sword." His work
and word were designed to arouse hostility as essential to the success of the mission — no less essential than Jesus' own cross. In re-
acting to this insistence, interpreters look desperately for euphemisms to hide the scandal, but Jesus resisted such euphemisms.
"A father will hand over his own son to death" (Matt. 10:21). Disciples would be murdered by their own parents. And his mission
was designed to produce such murders!

Moreover, the same sword cut through other circles than the
family. Followers would be ostracized from their religious home,
the synagogue. They would be publicly flogged by their neighbors. Hounded out of one town, they would be followed to the
next. Hailed before courts responsible for adjudicating conflict,
they would be condemned as enemies of Israel. Handed over to
Gentile governors, penalties would be inflicted by aliens who cared
nothing about Israel's God. "You will be hated by everyone for
my name's sake" (Matt 10:22). That is the sword Jesus came to bring.
He sent sheep out into a flock of snarling wolves. Or, to use a modern idiom, he enlisted soldiers for a kamikaze mission.

Before saying "peace," remember this sword.

One further aspect of this warfare should be noted. The dangerous mission of the lambs was motivated by concern for their
enemies, the wolves. It was a sign of God's love for those wolves.
Only by bringing his peace to those enemies could disciples become sons and daughters of this Father (Matt. 5:38–48). The example of Paul in changing from a persecutor to a victim of persecution was typical. This peace was very unusual, in that it seemed
to grow with the intensity of the warfare. How can one make intelligible, not to say credible, a mission to bring peace to enemies

by inciting them to murder the missioners (for example, Stephen, James, Peter, and Paul)?

A further dimension should be added. This warfare was not limited to strife within families, synagogues, and civil courts. It became visible there but its origin lay in an invisible conflict between God and Satan that spanned all times and places. That conflict had first been fought and won in heaven, from which Jesus had seen Satan fall (Luke 10:18; Rev. 12:7–9). His eviction had enabled Jesus to defeat Satan's most deceptive attacks on earth, including his mastery over demons. The same struggle pervaded the decisions of the early church (Eph. 6:10–17), which was sustained by the promise that "the God of peace will shortly crush Satan under your feet" (Rom. 16:20). Satan's power was the power of self-love; God's power was the power of enemy-love. The internal battles between these two loves were mirror reflections of the battle in heaven between God and Satan.

Before saying "peace," think about this heavenly warfare.

The implications of this peace may become clearer when we examine three benedictions in which participation in this cosmic warfare was seen as central to the Christian vocation. The first of these benedictions comes from Paul's letter to the Philippians. "The peace of God, which surpasses all understanding, will keep your hearts and your minds in Christ Jesus" (4:7). This text sounds altogether too banal until we recall the original setting. Paul was writing from jail, where the sentence of death was possible, and even probable (1:19–26). Such a sentence, then as now, carried with it disgrace, futility, the vindication of enemies, danger to friends, the possible destruction of the church. Paul was writing to a tiny new commune, poor, unpopular, subject to violence from both Jews and Gentiles. It had already survived one pogrom and, by sending help to Paul, had risked another. It was in turmoil over what strategy to adopt toward its adversaries. Some leaders were taking advantage of Paul's situation to argue for appeasing those adversaries. When Paul was writing, it appeared that those leaders might win. He called them "enemies of the cross of Christ" (3:18).

Now set that mild benediction against that background. Notice the verb: the peace of God will *keep*. The related noun *phroura* usually denoted a guard posted at the door of a prison. For a prisoner to use this verb in a benediction was far from accidental. He was being guarded. And by what? By peace. He viewed God's peace as an active force, capable of standing guard over prisoners. And what, in this case, was being protected? Hearts and minds. For a prisoner facing death, what was more vulnerable than heart and mind? The thrust of this benediction is clear: no matter how great the dangers you are facing, God's powerful peace will stand guard over your hearts and minds, so long as you are "in Christ Jesus."

The benediction has a relative clause: "the peace . . . that surpasses all understanding." That translation is too vague. Of course, the peace that enables a martyr to accept death does transcend normal understanding. But something more is suggested by the Greek verb *hyperechomai*, translated "surpasses." That verb belongs to a situation where two forces are in sharp conflict, and one of them establishes its mastery over its rival. In this case, presumably one force is God's peace and its rival is the human desire for self-preservation. God's peace is strong enough to overcome every contrary desire and temptation, including the devil's most deceptive seduction.

Now we should note that this benediction is really a promise: God's peace will keep. As a promise it is based on meeting certain conditions. *If* you do these things, that peace will stand guard. *If* you are fearless, stand firm, rejoice in your sufferings, give thanks, rely on Jesus' power "to subject all things to himself." Do these things, and God's peace will post a guard over your prison to protect your minds and hearts. Understood in this way, the benediction is a martyr's farewell to potential martyrs, promising them the same peace that guards him in his prison as he faces death.[5]

Second is John's account of Jesus' farewell to his disciples immediately before his arrest:

> The hour is coming, indeed it has already come, when you will be scattered, each one to his home, and you will leave me alone. Yet I am not alone, because the Father is with me. I have said this to you so that in me you may have peace. In the world you have persecution. But take courage! I have conquered the world. (John 16:32–33)

Among many possible inferences from this text, these bear on the idea of peace:

—The hour that has come is the hour of Jesus' martyrdom.

He faces that hour alone except for the presence of his Father. It is by accepting death from the world that he has conquered that world.

—The same hour has not yet come to his disciples. At his arrest they will scatter in panic, unaware of God's presence and unaware of Jesus' victory; therefore they will be strangers to his courageous peace.

—Their own hour, however, will come later, when they face persecution from the same enemy. Through their new courage they will then receive his gift of peace. In the world — persecution; "in me — peace."

—The warfare continues in which God's love for his enemies (the world) and Jesus' love for his enemies will be continued in the disciples' love for their enemies, producing both apparent defeat and this mysterious and miraculous peace.

The same basic message is conveyed by the other Johannine benediction:

> Peace I leave with you; I give my peace to you. I do not give to you as the world gives. Do not let your hearts be troubled. . . . The ruler of this world is coming. He has no power over me. (John 14:27–30)

The prospect of death represents Jesus' final battle with Satan, the ruler of this world. That battle has been won by Jesus' obedience to the Father. His defeat of Satan enables him to give his peace to the disciples; this peace is the opposite of anything the world can give. By implication, the world gives its peace to those who through fear of persecution conform to the world's demands. Fearful hearts signal the world's victory; fearless hearts, Jesus' victory. Here the inner psychic struggle is directly linked to the cosmic struggle. The battle line between Jesus and Satan coincides with the battle line within the hearts of the disciples between panic and peace.[6]

Before saying "peace," recall this battle line.

We find a third benediction in the Epistle to the Hebrews. Here an author addressed a church that had suffered greatly from earlier pogroms and was threatened by a violent recurrence. Some of its members were in prison; to visit them placed other members at great risk.

> Now may the God of peace who brought back from the dead
> our Lord Jesus, the great shepherd of the sheep, by the blood
> of the eternal covenant, make you complete in everything good
> so that you may do his will, working among us what is pleas-
> ing in his sight, through Jesus Christ, to whom be the glory
> forever and ever. (Heb. 13:20–21)

The pattern of thought is complex. The final appeal is to the God
of peace. His peace comes through the sealing of an eternal covenant with his people through the death and resurrection of the
Good Shepherd. All things are subjected to the transcendent glory
of this Lord. God's purpose in all this is this: "that you may do
his will." But such obedience is itself evidence that God is "working among us what is pleasing in his sight." When the human wills
coincide with God's working, then takes place the gift of God's
peace.

The author of Hebrews specifies the kind of actions that proceed from this convergence of human and divine wills. The faithful go outside the holy city, beyond its gates and protective walls,
to the profane place where Jesus suffered. There they share his
abuse. In doing this they look to him as the pioneer and perfecter
of their faith. They welcome this discipline that the Father inflicts
on all his children (13:6). Receiving his peace, they "strive for peace
with all others" (13:14). So in Christian parlance the word *peace*
comes to include all those individual and communal actions by
which God produces "what is pleasing in his sight through Jesus
Christ."

When we ponder the mystery of how all these separate wills
can become a single will within the orbit of ordinary human living, we begin to realize that previous ideas about God, about the
self, about such a community as the church, about the invisible
realm out of which desires emerge and actions are born — all these
ideas have to be radically revised. They begin to make sense in
a world of thought where old words are being used to point to
new relationships. Peace is one of those homespun words that
can be used as a key to this new language and to life in this new
world. In this new creation, peace refers primarily to the occa-
sions when the divine takes over the control center of the individ-

ual heart and when the Father, in being worshiped, takes over the control center of his worshiping family. This peace is not a condition to be described simply in psychological terms, nor is it something whose effects can be measured simply in sociological terms. It comes, as the benedictions imply, when crucifixion-like events are transformed through Jesus Christ into resurrection-like fulfillments.

Postscript

This world of thought is alien to most modern people. And it is true that early in its history the Christian church found other outlooks more conducive to its safety, popularity, and growth. When martyrdom is the price of sharing in God's peace, and when martyrs die for the sake of enemies who kill them in the name of their own God, not many will be found to accept a divinity who links discipleship to such demands. What, then, can be done with the universe of thought in which peace plays this role?

One answer is current among historians who by nature and professional training are inclined to have recourse to philosophical relativism. Like all other worldviews that once were entertained by past societies, this view is strictly relative to the conditions that spawned it. It may be interesting, and all the more interesting as it is esoteric and unique. But authoritative? No. At least not for a historian who wishes to remain credible as a historian.

Another answer is given by scholars whose thinking follows the rubrics of sociological analysis. For them, every such worldview must be judged in terms of the social structures of the ancient Roman world. It reflects the conflicts between rural and urban cultures, or between the rich and the poor, the powerful and the powerless. Prophets and apostles spoke for a tiny religious minority that was under deadly attack from a threatened religious establishment, a minority that projected its defensive mechanisms on a cosmic screen. As a weapon of defensive warfare, this perspective enabled the defeated to claim an illusory victory against its enemies. Like all other ideas, the idea of peace was a result of the complex interplay of economic and social forces.

Another method of dealing with the ancient worldview is

adopted by many church leaders, who have been convinced that the relevance of any religion must be demonstrated by its contribution to current desires for a more peaceful world. Professional credentials depend on offering the kinds of peace that the world seeks. The New Testament pictures of a peace that the world cannot give, a peace won by using Christ's sword — those pictures have little to offer to contemporary movements, whether left-wing or right. Unwittingly these leaders reflect their kinship to the adversaries of Jesus, Peter, and Paul. In the present scene they validate Kierkegaard's *Attack on Christendom.*

The very unanimity with which academics and clerics reject the early Christian perspectives should tell us something. At least it gives a negative testimony to the uniqueness and potential importance of those perspectives.

What can be done with the New Testament conceptions of peace? Instead of giving yet another answer, let me suggest a still more troublesome question. The question grows out of recognizing that the early Christian universe of thought centered in a revelation of God as a God of peace. The ultimate issue is this: does that God exist? Is this the true God? If the answer is no, then none of the correlative attitudes toward peace is worth salvaging. For many, that no is the only honest answer.

But what if the honest answer is yes? What if the God of peace is the only true God? If he is God, then he exerts an authority independent of succeeding changes in social crises, cultural developments, or philosophical systems. If he is God, his authority is quite independent of the alternate ways of measuring wisdom, power, or relevance. As the apostle shouted, "Let God be true, though everyone a liar" (Rom. 3:4).

I began with the recognition that there are many ideas of peace and with the desire to relate the early Christian ideas with the others. I conclude by recognizing with Paul that there exist many gods and many lords (1 Cor. 8:5) and by recognizing that the god of the New Testament is very different from all other gods, as the lord Jesus Christ is very different from all other lords. The ultimate issue is not the idea of peace, but how we are to think about this God of peace and, what is more important, how to enter the realm that is created by his "grace and peace."

NOTES

1. This essay is dedicated to the memory of my father, George L. Minear, who graduated from the Boston University School of Theology in 1901.

2. Paul S. Minear, *The God of the Gospels* (Atlanta: John Knox Press, 1988), pp. 60–66.

3. My task of describing New Testament thought requires that I use masculine nouns and pronouns: they are intrinsic to this metaphorical universe.

4. A witticism has much truth: there are only two types of people — those who divide all people into two groups, and those who do not.

5. See E. Lohmeyer, *Der Brief an der Philipper* (Gottingen: Vandenhoeck & Ruprecht, 1955), pp. 171–74.

6. See Paul S. Minear, *John: The Martyr's Gospel* (New York: Pilgrim Press, 1984), pp. 59–70.

PART III

Hindu and Buddhist
Views of Peace

8

The Rope of Violence and the Snake of Peace: Conflict and Harmony in Classical India

GERALD JAMES LARSON

ON REPUBLIC DAY in India there is a ceremony in New Delhi, the capital, called "Beating Retreat." It is an old British military ceremony, transformed now by the government of India to celebrate the inauguration of the Sovereign Democratic Republic of India on January 26, 1950. The ceremony occurs at sunset on the great avenue at the base of the hill leading to South Block, the main buildings of the government's ministries. As one looks up the hill toward South Block, one sees in the distance the looming presence of Rashtrapati Bhavan, the official residence of the President of India and formerly the home of the Viceroy. Looking the other way down the avenue, one sees the majestic India Gate. Just before sunset, government officials with their families, the diplomatic community, and various invited guests arrive at the ceremonial enclave. When everyone is seated, a motorcade brings the various members of the Cabinet and the Prime Minister of India. Shortly thereafter, the President of India arrives in a great horse-drawn carriage accompanied by a platoon of cavalry guards. The president is ushered to a great throne-chair placed in the center of the avenue and facing up the hill. At that moment the mounted soldiers of the Camel Corps in turbans and magnificent red and gold uniforms position themselves on the high walls of South Block. For a few moments there is an uneasy silence, while spectators absorb the deep reds and purples of twilight, the camels silhouetted against

135

the gathering darkness, the shadowed dome of Rashtrapati Bhavan in the distance. Then, from a distance one hears the first faint sounds of music as the Pipe and Drum Corps begins its slow march down the hill, followed after a few minutes by the Army, Navy, and Air Force bands of the government of India. The bands play separately, demonstrate their various disciplined maneuvers, and then finally, all together assemble directly in front of the President of India and the leadership of the government. At the moment of the setting of the sun over the horizon, the bands together then play one final selection before "beating retreat" back up the hill. It is the old Christian hymn:

> Abide with me: fast falls the eventide;
> The darkness deepens; Lord with me abide!
> When other helpers fail, and comforts flee,
> Help of the helpless, O abide with me.

I was there in 1987, profoundly moved by the occasion. Among the many impressions I had, three are relevant to the concern for peace. First, as a student of Sanskrit and Indology, I found myself reflecting upon this strange contrast between tradition and modernity. On one level was one of the world's oldest collection of cultures with its *kāvya* (formal poetry), *vyākaraṇa* (science of grammar), *purāṇa* (old tales), *itihāsa* (tradition), *darśana* (philosophical reflection), its Yogins and *sādhu-s* and pilgrims, and its plurality of tongues old and new, still "abiding" into the last decades of the twentieth century. On another level, that same culture celebrated its identity with the symbols of imperial power, pageantry, and ritual reenactment borrowed from the "eventide" of Western civilization's pretentious expansion to the ends of the earth, namely, the British Raj, symbol par excellence of the hoped-for *Pax Britannica*. The jewel is still extraordinary, but the crown is no more. Not simply tattered and worn, it is now little more than a museum relic and a somewhat bemusing cultural memory.

Second, as a student of the history of religions, I found myself reflecting upon the strange juxtaposition of the sacred and the profane. Here was the modern, secular nation-state of India with its largely Hindu and Muslim population and with its continuing agony over religion on almost all sides (Sri Lanka in the south,

Bengal and tribal unrest in the northeast, Kashmiri and Punjabi separatism by Muslims and Sikhs in the northwest), nevertheless celebrating and remembering its emergence into freedom after centuries of imperial domination with an old Christian hymn, "Abide with Me."

Third, and finally, as a student of comparative philosophy, I found myself reflecting upon and trying to recall the passage in Whitehead in which the old Christian hymn "Abide with Me" somehow played a role. I finally found it in *Process and Reality*. Says Whitehead:

> The best rendering of integral experience, expressing its general form divested of irrelevant details, is often to be found in the utterances of religious aspiration. One of the reasons for the thinness of so much modern metaphysics is its neglect of this wealth of expression of ultimate feeling. Accordingly we find in the first two lines of a famous hymn a full expression of the union of the two notions in one integral experience: "Abide with me: Fast falls the eventide."
>
> Here the first line expresses the permanences, "abide," "me," and the 'Being' addressed; and the second line sets these permanences amid the inescapable flux. Here at length we find formulated the complete problem of metaphysics. Those philosophers who start with the first line have given us the metaphysics of 'substance'; and those who start with the second line have developed the metaphysics of 'flux'. But, in truth, the two lines cannot be torn apart in this way; and we find that a wavering balance between the two is a characteristic of the greater number of philosophers.[1]

Later, in the concluding passages of *Process and Reality*, Whitehead returns to the theme:

> In a previous chapter (part 2, chap. 10) attention has already been drawn to the sense of permanence dominating the invocation "Abide with me," and the sense of flux dominating the sequel "Fast falls the eventide." Ideals fashion themselves round these two notions, permanence and flux. In the inescapable flux, there is something that abides; in the overwhelming permanence, there is an element that escapes into flux.

Permanence can be snatched only out of flux; and the passing moment can find its adequate intensity only by its submission to permanence. Those who would disjoin the two elements can find no interpretation of patent facts.[2]

In ordinary experience and usage the notion of peace is usually
associated with the yearning for permanence, with the quest for
wholeness, harmony, tranquility, happiness, and rest, whether in
personal life, the community, or one's place in the cosmos. The
notion of conflict, on the other hand, is often associated with flux,
change, dissolution, violence, hostility, deprivation, and frustration, states or conditions which most people seek to avoid. To be
at peace with oneself is to accept what or who one is and to have
stopped warring with oneself. To be at peace in community is to
make an agreement to end hostility, to live together in harmony,
accepting the presence of one another. To be at peace in the cosmos is to accept, largely on faith, that the universe is benign, a
more or less fitting habitat for the sorts of beings and forces that
dwell or operate within it.

The English word *peace* derives from the Latin *pacis* or *pax*,
via the French *paix*, and refers to the notion of making a "pact"
or agreement to end hostilities. *Paciscere* or *pacificare* is to "covenant" or "to make peace." The Hebrew שָׁלוֹם is the "state of wholeness possessed by persons or groups" or the fullness of covenant
with Yahweh and the absence of hostility. The Greek εἰρήνη refers to the absence of strife, from which we get our English word
irenic as opposed to *polemic* or quarrelsome. In Arabic the cognate of Hebrew שָׁלוֹם is *salām* which means "making peace" and
is related to the words *islām* and *muslim* in the sense of entering
into a state of peace or submission (*islām*) or one who has entered
into peace or submission (*muslim*). In Islam, *salām* or "making
peace" is one of the ninety-nine names of God. In Chinese the word
ho-p'ing (or the modern transliteration *heping*) is made up of
two characters, namely, "harmony" and "level" or "flat" and has
the sense of equalizing and balancing, as does the Japanese cognate *hewa*.

In classical Sanskrit the notion of peace is perhaps most commonly expressed by the word *śānti* from the verbal root *śam*, meaning to become quiet, be extinguished, go out, to fatigue oneself,

to come to an end, rest, be satisfied or contented. The noun form, namely, *śānti*, means tranquility, peace, calmness, extinction (of fire), happiness, bliss, good fortune, but also destruction, end, eternal rest, and, of course, death. Interestingly, many of the same meanings belong to the word *śiva* (as an adjective) or *Śiva* (as the proper name of the divine personification of one part of the *trimūrti* of the Ultimate), including auspiciousness, bliss, happiness, final emancipation, but also destruction, end, and death.

The etymology of the word *śiva* is not clear; possibly it is related to the verbal root *śī*, meaning "to lie" in the sense of "in whom all things lie," or possibly it is related to the verbal root *śvi*, meaning "to swell" in the sense of a dead body or corpse, *śava*, since Śiva is the Lord of Death; this latter verbal root is probably also related to *śūnyatā*, "voidness" or "emptiness." In the Upaniṣads, the ritual phrase *Om śāntiḥ, śāntiḥ, śāntiḥ* probably refers (at least according to Śaṅkara and other later commentators) to the three kinds of frustration (*duḥkha*) or suffering that people experience, namely, "personal," (*ādhyātmika*), "social" or "related to other beings" (*ādhibhautika*), and "cosmic" or "pertaining to one's destiny" or "the supernatural" (*ādhidaivika*). The various law books of classical India, the *Dharmaśāstras*, speak of *śānti* in the plural, that is to say, the need to perform *śānti*-s, referring to the ritual expiations that one may or must perform in order to ward off negative forces or to purify one's body or one's community.

Synonyms for *śānti* in classical Sanskrit include the notion of "connection," "combination," or "association" (*sandhi*) as opposed to "separation," "isolation," "hostility" (*vigraha*). Or again, the notion of peace is expressed negatively as the "absence of isolation" (*vigrahābhāva*) or the "absence of strife or war" (*yuddhābhāva*). The Minister of Defense in classical Sanskrit, or what we would call the Secretary of Defense, is simply *sandhivigrahakāyastha* or the bureaucrat in charge of matters pertaining to peace or war. Other synonyms for peace in classical Sanskrit include "indifferent to the alternatives or pairs of opposites" (*nirdvandva*), "weary" or "tired" (*viśrāma, viśrānti*, from the verbal root *śram*, meaning "to become weary"), "contentment" (*nirvṛti*, from the verbal root *vṛ* plus *nis*, meaning "to be satisfied"), "cessation" (*nivṛtti*, from the verbal root *vṛt* plus *ni*, meaning "to stop turning or cease"), "harmony" (*aikya*), "commonality" (*sarūpa*), "freedom

from commotion" (*nirupadravatā*, meaning "the state of not being assaulted," or negatively expressed, *upadravābhāva*, "the absence of being rushed at or assaulted"), and, of course, the variety
of cognate forms derived from the verbal root *śam* itself, including *śama*, *upaśama*, *praśānti*, and so forth, all of which notions
emphasize quiescence, tranquility, bliss, extinction, the absence
of conflict, or the attainment of peace.

While it is thus clear enough what the word *peace* means in
ordinary usage, problems arise as soon as one attempts to think
about its application. Consider, for example, the ceremony "Beating Retreat." Does it mark the harmony, permanence, and wholeness of the Indian nation-state at peace, its struggle for freedom
from imperial domination having been extinguished and won? Is
it a ceremony of quiet remembrance, rest, and tranquility at sunset after a long day of conflict and strife? Or is it only a brief re-
spite at the end of the day, fully mindful of the violence and conflict that will emerge with the coming dawn? Whitehead, in view
of his comments on the first two lines of the old hymn "Abide with
me: Fast falls the eventide," would suggest that it is not a matter
of either-or, but rather of both-and. Says Whitehead: "Permanence
can be snatched only out of flux; and the passing moment can
find its adequate intensity only by its submission to permanence."
The words *peace* and *conflict* can easily be substituted for *permanence* and *flux* in the passage, which then becomes: "Peace can
be snatched only out of conflict and the passing moment (of conflict) can find its adequate intensity only by its submission to peace."
Whitehead, of course, is in good company with the both-and argument, since it is a species of the genus "dialectical rationalism" which
has been a dominant informant of Western reflection almost from
the beginning.

The problem with the both-and argument, however, is that
it all too often blurs important distinctions and easily lends itself
to distortion and abuse that cloak what is really at issue, namely,
the struggle for power and the legitimation of power with the
discourse about peace. The Indian Army, currently occupying
the northern provinces of Sri Lanka, is referred to as the "Indian
Peacekeeping Force." United States Marines in Lebanon were referred to as "Peacekeepers." The obliteration of villages in South
Vietnam was described as a "Pacification" program. Jean-Paul

Sartre in his *Critique of Dialectical Reason* refers to what he calls an ongoing dialectic of "fraternity-terror." That is to say, "fraternity" and "terror" are not two separate entities. They are, rather, two related moments in an integral process, each presupposing and entailing the other in good Hegelian fashion. Or, putting the argument directly into its political form in the words of von Clausewitz in his treatise *On War:* "War is nothing but a continuation of political intercourse with the admixture of different means."

Philosophical reflection in India has been fascinated with the problem of error and illusion. The most common stock example of the problem of error is the conundrum of the rope-snake. While walking in the woods at dusk, one encounters what appears to be a snake. One reacts with fear, anxiety, or terror, possibly attempting to run away or to grab a stick in order to defend oneself. On closer examination, however, one discovers that the snake is just a rope. One realizes that one's initial reaction was an error, and when one realizes the error, the former snake experience together with its accompanying emotional state simply vanish. The philosophical issue is that of explaining the nature of the error involved. One could write a history of Indian epistemology based on the manner in which the various schools of Indian philosophy treat this problem. Śaṅkara in the opening comments to his *Brahmasūtrabhāṣya* refers to this problem as the key issue of "superimposition" (*adhyāsa*). He first offers his own definition of the problem as follows. "What, then, is this thing referred to as 'superimposition' (*adhyāsa*)? Simply stated, it is the following: it (superimposition) is the appearance, based on memory, of something that has been previously experienced, elsewhere (than where it should be)." (*ko 'yam adhyāso nāma iti. ucyate: smṛtirūpaḥ paratra pūrvadṛṣṭāvabhāsaḥ.*) Śaṅkara then concedes that other philosophers define it differently, and he briefly sets forth several other views regarding superimposition. He then, however, characterizes the general problem in a manner in which all would agree, apart from technical differences. Says Śaṅkara: "There would be no disagreement from anyone about the general issue, that is to say, that 'superimposition' has to do with the appearance of the qualities or attributes of one thing as linked with or related to another thing." (*sarvathā api tu anyasya anyadharmāvbhāsatāṃ na vyabhicarati.*)

Śaṅkara's analysis of the rope-snake problem is as follows. There is such a thing as a rope in ordinary experience, and there is such a thing as a snake. In at least one or more important respects, they resemble one another, for example, in their apparent form (long, curved, and so forth). When I encounter the rope-snake on the path, I have, on the one hand, a correct (albeit vague) perception of a rope and a correct memory of rope, *and* a correct memory of snake but no correct perception of a snake. My error or illusion occurs, then, because of projecting a memory into a situation in which there is no basis in fact for the projected memory. When my perception sharpens, the error simply vanishes, since it was never there to begin with as a genuine perception.

The point is not that there are no such things as ropes and snakes in ordinary life. There are, and they are quite different, even though they resemble one another in one or more respects. The point is that I have a tendency in ordinary life to project my memory states into situations where there is no basis in fact for those states, those common-sense, everyday contexts in which there is a rope *or* a snake present. In other words, when error or illusion occurs, there is the absence of a perception base.

On this level of analysis in Indian philosophy, there is nothing dialectical about ropes and snakes, as such. It is not the case that ropes entail snakes or snakes entail ropes, if only the analysis of perception is pushed far enough. There is nothing like a both-and argument being pressed. There is some sort of dialectic on the level of projective memory insofar as the rope memory and the snake memory clearly interact within the realm of memory awareness and their resemblances. But that is not the point of the rope-snake example. The point is that in ordinary life we experience things that are not really there, and that this occurs not because ropes and snakes are illusions, or in some sense entail one another, but, rather, that the illusions or errors have their locus in our own mental states which may or may not have a basis in fact.

On this level, then, classical Indian discussions of error and illusion would quickly cut through the bunk and hokum of much contemporary political discourse regarding "peace" and "war." When Marines are called "Peacekeepers," or the Indian Army is referred to as the "Indian Peacekeeping Force," or the obliteration of villages is called "Pacification," or world peace somehow entails massive weapons of destruction, or *fraternity* somehow comes to mean "terror," or *war* is described simply as "the continuation of political intercourse with the admixture of different means," and so forth, what we are really witnessing from the perspective of classical Indian thought is the juxtaposition of "the rope of violence and the snake of peace," and we need to recognize it for what it is, that is to say, illusion and error. The rope of violence and power is passing itself off as the snake of peace.

The rope-snake of classical Indian reflection, however, is not only concerned with identifying and explaining what might be called garden variety errors and illusions. It also is used, at least by Śaṅkara, for pointing to yet another level of experience, beyond both the illusory and the empirical, that raises questions about the adequacy of any rational or verbal account of what truly is, a level of ultimate (*pāramārthika*) peace that carries us beyond all distinctions whatever. This deeper, somewhat puzzling level evokes an experiential claim which is seldom heard in modern discourse, or outside the boundaries of South Asian reflection.

When I was asking whether the ceremony "Beating Retreat" should be construed as an experience of peace and permanence or an experience of conflict and flux, I suggested that in view of Whitehead's analysis of "Abide with me: Fast falls the eventide," the ceremony is best construed as a clear case of both-and, and I made a passing reference to the tradition of dialectical rationality in Western thought to which Whitehead clearly belongs.

Indian philosophy is also dialectical, but the framework for dialectical thinking is interestingly different in classical Indian thought. There is no separation of experience and reason in Indian philosophy; hence, there is little concern for formal logic in the Western sense, no distinction between a priori and a posteriori or between analytic and synthetic judgments. Truth is not propositional, although it should be quickly added that this does not mean that language is not important in Indian thought. Quite the contrary, Indian philosophers were superb grammarians and linguists. What it does mean, however, is that language, propositions, formal logic, and mind generally are not taken as in any sense a separate or enclosed realm. There is no mind-body dualism in Indian philosophy, no separation of thought and extension. In many ways, at least with respect to issues in the philosophy of mind, it can be argued that Indian thought comes close to what in modern Western thought is known as reductive materialism.

There is a deep suspicion in Indian thought regarding ordinary awareness or what we usually consider to be the intentional life of the mind. To be sure, awareness is always *about* something and to that extent is intentional, but the "phenomenology" of ordinary awareness or intentional awareness in Indian thought almost always turns out to be a phenomenology of error, at least with respect to *adhyātmavidyā* or that which pertains to consciousness, to what truly is. This does not mean that Indian philosophy makes no distinction between empirically verifiable common experience and illusory experience. That it clearly does so is evident from the rope-snake analysis already discussed. The illusory is what is called the *prātibhāsika*, the snake as a memory impression without a perception base. The empirically verifiable common experience is called the *vyāvahārika*, the rope. Indian thought, however, also raises questions about empirically verifiable experience. Our public experience is largely communal, consensual, and derivative and may not at all represent an adequate account of what truly is. What we think or believe we are may have a certain practical validity on the level of everyday life, but may be as misleading in its own way as the most obvious illusions or errors. We are inclined to act on the basis of convention simply because it is so widely believed. As a result, there is a recurrent quest in Indian philosophy (at least in Advaita Vedānta, Sāṃkhya, Yoga, Mādhyamika, and Yogācāra Buddhist thought) for a level of experience that transcends the vicissitudes of both subjectivity and objectivity, a longing for a direct experience of what truly is. This quest is not unlike what one finds in the later writings of Martin Heidegger. It seeks a direct experience of the Kantian "thing-in-itself."

But if what truly is cannot be confined to a distinct realm of reason; and if what truly is is not adequately represented in our ordinary, intentional awareness or our communal, consensual empirical apprehensions; then what is Indian philosophy talking *about* when it speaks of a direct experience of what truly is? Here Indian philosophy takes an interesting turn. Instead of speaking in terms of either-or, which it wisely confines to the level of the garden variety of the rope-snake (*prātibhāsika*), and instead of speaking of a dialectical both-and, à la Whitehead, et al., and the internal dialectic of language and thought (*vyāvahārika*), it proceeds, rather, in the direction of a dialectical "neither-nor" (*pāramārthika*). It follows a radically negative way, not in the sense that the ultimate experience is negative, but because what truly is finally escapes the determinations of all human constructions. It is as if what truly is is so overwhelming, so extraordinary, so utterly complete that one can only stand before it and say "na iti, na iti."

Śaṅkara describes what truly is in terms of pure consciousness (*ātman*), but it would be a mistake to reduce his understanding of pure consciousness to an empty abstraction. His pure consciousness is nothing less than everything that truly is. But what truly is must be allowed to show itself without any of the distinctions and determinations of human awareness, and just as the illusion of the snake simply disappears when a correct perception of the rope shows itself, so all determinations of ordinary language and thought will simply disappear when what truly is manifests itself. Similarly, Nāgārjuna describes what truly is in terms of *śūnyatā*, "voidness" or "emptiness." Again it would be a mistake to construe what is being evoked as an empty abstraction. Nāgārjuna's point is just the opposite. Emptiness refers to the limits of human conceptualization, to the internal dialectic and abstractions of language and thought, never to the vistas opened up when these abstract boundaries are finally transcended.

What, then, does classical India say about peace? It sends a double message. On one level, there is a no-nonsense appreciation for the hard realities of ordinary experience. Put negatively, as Indian philosophers are wont to do, there is a deep suspicion of the realm of phenomenal life. The human condition is frustrating and painful, and there is a continuing need to interrogate the details and conceptualizations of everyday life, separating the illusory from what is empirically valid, learning to be aware of language and verbalization (*vikalpa*), and remembering always that our verbal constructions are contextual, communal, and consensual. They may be useful enough for everyday communication, but they seldom tell you what experience really is. Peace, on this level, is a fluid and changing phenomenon, by no means illusory, but nevertheless shifting and always "to be snatched only out of flux," to use Whitehead's idiom. On another level, Indian thought invites us to undertake a journey into silence, beyond permanence and flux, beyond peace and conflict, beyond the rope and the snake, to an experience that answers the old question, "Why is there something rather than nothing?" with the simple response: "na iti, na iti."

In conclusion:

> asato mā sad gamaya,
> tamaso mā jyotir gamaya
> mṛtyor mā'mṛtaṁ gamaya!

> From the unreal lead me to the real,
> From darkness lead me to the light,
> From death lead me to immortality!
> (*Bṛhadāraṇakopaniṣad* 1.3.38)

And, of course, "Om, śāntiḥ, śāntiḥ, śāntiḥ!" (*Taittirīyopaniṣad*) 1.1

NOTES

1. Alfred North Whitehead, *Process and Reality* (1929; reprint ed., New York: Harper & Row, 1957), p. 318.

2. Ibid., p. 513.

9

Buddhism, Sri Lanka, and the Prospects for Peace

NINIAN SMART

MANY OF US WHO have admired the Buddhist tradition are somewhat perturbed that Sinhala nationalism in Sri Lanka has taken such a militant turn.[1] Buddhism is rightly thought to preach a message of peace. Tranquility and insight are what make up the blessed state of nirvana in this life. The Buddhist saint surveys the world with equanimity and compassion, and rejoices with those who rejoice and sympathizes with those who are unhappy. Kings are looked on with uneasiness, and the Buddhist knows that the use of force — the stick, or *daṇḍa* — has its problems even when intentions are good. It is therefore disappointing that often violent behavior is given a spiritual imprimatur.

For me, something of this disappointment occurred at a conference of the World Fellowship of Buddhists which I attended in Colombo, in the summer of 1984. Oddly, I had been asked by the Venerable Walpola Rahula to organize a seminar of international scholars, within the conference, on Buddhism's contribution to world culture. I found it a great honor, as I am not a Buddhist, but a Buddhified Episcopalian; I wondered how the World Council of Churches would react to having its chief academic offering run by a Christian-influenced Buddhist. Anyway, at the conference there were addresses by the President and the Prime Minister. There was no direct mention of the civil strife, and no attempt to hold out a Buddhist hand of friendship in a symbolic way toward Tamil Hindus and Christians, to show that the inten-

tions of the government were peaceful. I thought it was an opportunity missed.

It is, I think, useful to analyze the reasons for this rather militant Buddhist nationalism among many of the Sinhalese speakers
of the island. I do this analysis not in order to cast a stone in the
direction of Adam's Peak, but rather as a lesson to us all. I do not
even want to give the impression that Buddhist-style nationalism
is fiercer than the nationalism which has got mixed up with other
religions. It may be that it is in the last resort milder. But the analysis is intended rather to bring out ways in which we may reflect
on the relation between religion and internationalism, and more
broadly between faith and peace.

The first point to consider is how Buddhism relates to traditional Sinhala culture.[2] While in classical times through the Middle Ages there were at least a fair number of Tamil monks, in the
intervening period the Sangha has become virtually exclusively
Sinhalese. In modern times, the division between Sinhalese and
Tamils has been a religious one, save insofar as members of both
groups have converted to forms of Christianity. It may be noted
that there has been great intermingling between the groups, so
that there is a considerable genetic overlap. Many of each group
could pass as members of the other, if suitably dressed and speaking the relevant language. The division therefore is primarily a
cultural one. But it has been reinforced strongly by the fact of religious allegiance.

Now in one way one might expect that this division would
not be that severe. It is not really like the situation between Muslims and Hindus, where certain practices are mutually offensive.
In that case one group eats beef but not pork, and the other may
eat pork but not beef. One group loves graven images, and carries
them joyfully in processions, while the other abjures them as blasphemous. One is inclined to honor images, the other to smash them.
If you ascend to the doctrinal level, you could reconcile the two
easily enough: Rāmānuja and al-Ghazali could converse together
knowingly in heaven. But though the doctrinal dimension in the
two religious traditions need not be far apart, the mythic and ritual and ethical dimensions clash, and often bitterly and badly.

It is incidentally important to realize that the tendency to
look upon religions in terms of their ideas — a tendency very preva-

lent in theological modes of study and research, and normal in divinity schools — is misleading, because in the real world religions are multidimensional. It is above all in cases of clashes and divergences in the ritual dimension that there is likely to be trouble. These are typically connected to differences of institution in the social dimension and help to reinforce living divergences which in times of stress may generate actual and physical conflict.

But to summarize the situation in regard to Islam and Hinduism: here we have bitter differences about ritual and mythic representations of the One. In high theology, however, they are close, since theism is the dominant note in both traditions. But in the case of the relations between Buddhism and Hinduism in Sri Lanka the opposite occurs. The rituals can be harmonized, as is seen from the fact that Hindu-style gods — rather effete, I would admit — have their shrines within the Buddhist temple complexes, while the holy place of Kataragama is duly attended by masses of both populations in search of material benefits. Buddhists have no particular animus at all against Hindu images. It is true that they may think that traffic with such images is of merely this-worldly significance, and that it does not bring you spiritual merit which can get you onward and upward to heaven or holy life in this world. But there is immediately no great clash or tension between the rituals of the religions. There *is* a mythic problem at another level, which I shall later discuss, which constitutes a great reason for the animus between the two groups. In the context, though, of immediate religious practice, the symbolisms of the two groups are not terribly conflicting, though they are of course different. Śiva and the Buddha can live together.

They *can* live together: but do they? I remember getting a verbal reprimand from the Vice-Chancellor (President) of one of the universities in Sri Lanka, when I made a suggestion about the new Parliament building. This is a beautiful affair in the old Sinhalese style on a lake some miles out of Colombo. Its interior is modeled on the British system of government, with government and opposition benches facing each other (perhaps a mistake). Near the building, looking at it over the lake, is a huge Buddha statue. I remarked that it was a pity that they could not have added Śiva, Christ, and perhaps a minaret, all maybe a bit smaller than the Buddha statue. I thought it would be more in consonance with a plural society. The Vice-Chancellor, however, was very cold, and said that the Buddha was built on private land and people could do what they like with their property. But had the owner been a Hindu and put up a huge Śiva, there would not have been quite the same reaction.

Here is a hint of ritual clashes. In the meantime, we note that in regard to the ritual dimension there are not normally severe tensions. But it is in the doctrinal dimension that the great divergences occur. Buddhism is emphatically, in its Theravādin incarnation, not theistic. You may note similarities between *bhakti* religion in the Mahāyāna and similar motifs in Christianity and the Hindu world. But the Theravāda does not have its Amitabha and Pure Land. It did once in classical and medieval Sri Lanka, but not now in the Theravāda. No doubt the cult of statues of the Buddha owes something to earlier influences from *bhakti*-type Mahāyāna. But the atmosphere of the religion is really very different, and the doctrines remain clearly against the positing of a Creator. These points have recently been systematically presented in Gunapala Dharmasiri's *A Buddhist Critique of the Christian Concept of God.*[3] This is one of the reasons why the study of Theravāda Buddhism is so crucial to religious studies. Like Jainism, it is a vital nontheistic religion which does not even fit into such ideas of Ultimate Reality as may be found in more monistic systems such as those of Śankara and aspects of the Mahāyāna. This is why some of the dialogues between Japanese Buddhists and Christians are too easy. I have argued that Theravāda Buddhism and Christianity and other theisms cannot be merged in the Advaitin style of modern Hindu commentators, or in the style of Christian unifiers like W. C. Smith and John Hick. At best they are complementary. Perhaps, to take the matter from a Christian standpoint, the Holy Spirit stirred up such divergent religions in order to keep both sides honest. If God didn't want religious differences why did she allow them to unfold? But that is by the way. The point I wish to reinforce is that at the doctrinal level there are severe differences between any form of theism, including Hindu theism, and the spiritual atheism of the Theravāda tradition.

Another aside: the preoccupation among many Western scholars with the categories of theism, polytheism, and so on is natural

enough. God is after all the key concept in the major Western religions. It is however not appropriate to categorize the Theravāda
from Western assumptions. Theism does not happen to be an important concept for such Buddhists. The notions of Buddhahood
and nirvana are much more crucial. One could as well say that
Christianity is an important nonnirvanistic religion as that the
Theravāda is an important nontheistic religion.

But to return to our main theme: we have in Hinduism and
Buddhism religions which diverge very widely in theory — not just
in regard to ideas of God, but in relation to such other issues as
the applicability of the notion of substance. At the immediate religious level, however, their mythic and ritual behaviors are mutually tolerable and indeed overlap. Their ethical values are not very
different. Buddhism stresses the experience of meditation among
the elite, but an emphasis on Yoga is of course not absent from
the Saiva Siddhanta tradition which is important among Tamils.

Mythologically there are divergences too, obviously. These
concern the contrasting figures and stories about Śiva and the Buddha. But what really is most important here for understanding
the enmity between Sinhala and Tamils relates to nationalism,
which revamps an old tradition. It concerns the special relationship envisaged between Sri Lanka and the Buddhist *dhamma*. This
intimacy between national identity and faith has been underlined
and intensified in modern times because of nationalism. But the
notion that the Teaching was specially entrusted to the Sri Lankans
and more particularly to the Sinhalese is found in the great chron-
icle, the *Mahāvaṃsa*. Much of this text covers secular history, but
it also includes legends of the three visits of the Buddha himself
to the island and his associations with places of pilgrimage. Much
of it is taken up with the battles of the hero King Dutthagamini
against the Tamils. Later the same motif reappears in relation to
the reigns of the great medieval kings, Parakkrama Bahu I and
Parakkrama Bahu II. The history of the island was one of recurrent conflict between the Tamils of South India and the Sinhalese
speakers of Sri Lanka. But the struggles were much more confused
than would appear from a modern perspective. For one thing,
Theravāda Buddhism flourished in South India. For another, quite
a lot of Tamils were in medieval times Buddhists. But from a modern
perspective it is easy to see the Sinhala-Tamil struggle as essentially

a religious one—and this is how also it was represented in the chronicles. Thus Dutthagamini put a relic on the spear which he used as a standard and monks left the Order to fight.

Now such chronicles as the *Mahāvaṃsa*, which profess to be history, like modern history textbooks used in schools, are a vital ingredient in the myths of peoples.[4] We should not be deceived by the contrast we moderns sometimes make between myth and history. Essentially such stories help to give reality to a shared past and to underline the values prized in later times, namely, today or when such chronicles were written. They create identities through their reading and recitation. They can fit very easily into modern attitudes, where some may feel the fanciful character of heavenly myths, but are still beguiled by the reality of earthly stories. So the modern Sinhalese speaker is heir to these chronicles, and they reveal to the Sinhala two important "facts." One is that there is a special relationship between the *dhamma* and the island. The other is the long-standing friction with the Tamils, represented as sweeping south to take over the island.

In this connection it is worth pointing out that the Sinhalese suffer from what may be called the "majority as minority" syndrome. Though they are the majority population on the island itself, they also see themselves as the minority in the region—because they are heavily outnumbered by regional Tamils. The island Tamils or "Ceylon Tamils" are ancient migrants into the island. They form a culture distinct from that of the South Indian Tamils of Tamil Nadu, and therefore from those very recent migrants imported by the British from Tamil Nadu to work in the tea plantations in the hill country. But because of contemporary conflicts the island Tamils have been driven toward solidarity with the Tamils of Tamil Nadu. Thus they begin to conform to the image in the Sinhalese mind of a great horde of Tamils poised to take over the island. From this perspective the violent JVP reaction to the coming of the Indian Army after the agreement which President Jayawardene and Rajiv Gandhi made in 1987 is intelligible. The Sinhalese vision of a minority Sinhala population regionally threatened by a vast Tamil majority, backed by the great power of the Republic of India, has become a self-fulfilling prophecy.

In other words, Sinhalese Buddhism in modern conditions is not quite what we think it is. We think of it simply as a form

of Theravāda Buddhism. But it is more than the Theravāda. We
tend to think of the Theravāda in the life of the Sangha and the
laity, seen as loyal to the Buddha and treading an upward path
to ultimate liberation — a path delineated and expanded upon in
the Pali canon. It is these things; but it is more. It is the religion
of the Sinhala, who are sanctified by the special sacred relationship between the Buddha and the divine island. It is the religion
which opposes the dark designs of Tamils seeking to overthrow
Sinhala independence and so to destroy the *dhamma* in Sri Lanka.
You can get at the real religion on the ground by doing anthro-
pology, but you need also to be aware of its connection with a view
of the special place of the Sinhala people.[5] They have their own
sense of manifest destiny.

In short, Sinhala Buddhism is a syncretism between Buddhism
and national feeling, and in modern times this national feeling
has been fostered by a modern sense of nationalism. This has borrowed some important traits from mainstream European nationalism. We need then to look at this, and give it some analysis.

Modern nationalism has been the main political force since
before the French Revolution. It has fostered modernization, despite its nonrational and romantic roots. It has provided a scheme
for coalescing relatively large and continuous blocs of territory and
has often favored use of a common language to nourish a sense
of identity. New languages built on vernacular bases have been
fashioned by scholars and projected through universal education.
The same education that could create a literate working class and
a skilled middle class could also be used to recall history and foster a sense of belonging. Smaller segments of society were washed
away in the wider national identity. The two most potent signs
of this were the land or country ("My country right or wrong")
and the linguistic heritage, but to these was often added a religious heritage. Poles not only spoke Polish but were Catholics, in
contrast to the Lutherans of Prussia and the Orthodox of Russia.

Such a nationalism made its presence felt in Ceylon in the
period between the world wars. But the political evolution of the
country toward dominion status was steady, and the nationalist
feelings of Sinhalas were not exacerbated, oddly enough, until after independence. Their main expression was the Sri Lanka Freedom Party under the initial leadership of S. W. R. D. Bandara-

naike and then of his widow, Sirimavo Bandaranaike. This was
a fully evolved linguistic and religious nationalism, pinned to belief in the use of the Sinhalese language. The 1956 election slogan
"Sinhalese only" was potent, and it scared the Tamils. In 1958
communal riots confirmed Tamil fears. Because Sri Lanka is an
island it was easy to identify the sacred territory of the Sinhala
land with the whole island, and this led to a confused and sometimes repressive view of the Tamils. Other minorities such as the
so-called Moors or Muslims could be ignored, relatively speaking.
But the Hindu and Tamil problem would remain.

The fact is that Buddhism in Sri Lanka, as it was modernizing through the thought and work of figures such as Olcott, Anagarika Dharmapala,[6] Malalasekara,[7] and K. N. Jayatilleke,[8] failed
to provide a positive theory of other religions. It did not achieve
that remarkable synthesis produced by Vivekānanda,[9] Gandhi,
Radhakrishnan, and others, which saw a higher Hindu thought
and ethic summarizing the Truth toward which all religions ultimately point. That irenic theory lies behind the pluralism of the
Indian constitution, but no such ideology presented itself in Sinhalese Buddhism. So although Sri Lankan Buddhists had ample
contact historically with Hindus, and though Vishnu mythically
was supposed to have been deputed by Indra on the instructions
of the Buddha to guard Ceylon, there was no clear way for Sinhalese to think positively about Hinduism or, for that matter, Islam and Christianity. This showed itself in the politics of the period after independence.

The new elite in India expressed this ideology principally in
English, but Sinhalese nationalism in the hands of Mr. Bandaranaike led the retreat from English into an education system
dominated by Sinhalese. This new class of high school graduates
in Sinhalese formed the recruiting ground of the JVP, which staged
the great uprising of 1971, so nearly successful. Recently the JVP
movement, more explicitly nationalist in orientation, is at the forefront of violent agitation against the agreement with India. Its
ideology is quasi-Marxist and bears strong resemblances to the
thought of the Khmer Rouge. Thus the modern tragedy of the island is that it has the Tamil militants, notably the Tigers, and the
Sinhala militants, neither group being much inclined to eschew
violence. The peaceful values of Buddhism, much prized by great

defenders of the faith in modern times such as Dharmapala, have been overlaid by the new tendencies to warfare and guerrilla struggle.

The problem of Buddhism is that it has syncretized with modern nationalism without itself evolving a pluralist ideology. The Hindus *did* have such an ideology to offer, and insofar as ideas count in politics, those ideas made a lot of sense in trying to evolve a pluralist democracy in the Republic of India. But in Sri Lanka the Buddhist majority has made few political concessions to the Tamils, until perhaps too late. The Tigers in fact forced a measure of federalism on the government, and it is that which has been the basic thrust of Tamil policy throughout the period from World War II onwards.

It may be noted that the constitution which the British left in place was modeled on Westminster. Time and again this model has proved defective in the face of ethnic divisions — for instance in Northern Ireland and in those African countries which have opted for a one-party system because of dissatisfaction with the Westminster model. The reason ethnicity is a problem is that where parties form along ethnic lines, it is less easy to perceive the opposition as loyal. The Westminster system works with values coalitions, which are different from ethnic divisions.

What has happened is that Buddhist nationalism has gloried in a classical form of the Buddhist faith in Ceylon, namely, the great Anurādhapura and Polonnaruwa periods. It has therefore seen the role of government as living in a kind of symbiosis with the Sangha. The ancient kings became great patrons of and correcters of the Order. In a democratic state as at present there is no king or Parakkrama Bahu, but analogously to the ancient monarchs, the President and Prime Minister need popular support to rally the masses to their vision of a Buddhist society. This inevitably brings in the monks, whose support is crucial since they are potent vote-influencers in rural Sri Lanka. The politicization of the Order is a dangerous distraction from the true purposes of the Sangha. While there has been a great revival of those true purposes, through the development of meditation, the dissemination of Buddhist learning, and so on, there has also been an inflaming of the passions of monks in a patriotic mode.

Can a religion avoid these tendencies? Where stands Buddhist universalism in the face of nationalist politics? This is a general question which religions and ideologies have to face. Marxist universalism has been split by the conflict between nations, such as China and Vietnam, and inside Yugoslavia. Christian universalism has notoriously been the victim of conflicts in Europe and elsewhere in modern times.

It is not easy for an emerging Buddhist universalism to take the Hindu path. While some modern approaches, such as those of Guénon[10] and Hick,[11] seek a transcendental unity of all religions, this does not to my mind resolve the problem. This is so for various reasons. First, as we have seen, Theravāda Buddhism is itself a challenge to unifying credos. Second, there is also the vital question of secular worldviews. There is the question of what the religionist can say to the Marxist or the scientific humanist. Even if religions achieve some kind of notional unity, this leaves antireligious systems of thinking and acting out of account. Does one therefore have to despair of some theory of living together on the planet?

It may of course be commented that all we can do in forums like this one is to discuss ideas, and ideas are not potent. It is perhaps scratching at the surface of the problem to try to form a philosophy of living together. Beyond that the human race has to live together.

Of course; but ideas remain vital. It is our vision of the future which helps shape it. The Nazi phenomenon, the growth of Buddhism in Japan, the Meiji restoration, the October Revolution, 1776 – all these powerful moments in history, for better or worse, were shaped by ideas. Without these ideas, things would have turned out differently. Without the Nazi ideology the horror of the Holocaust would not have occurred, even if anti-Semitism, itself ideas-driven, had caused its own terrors. Without Marxism the October Revolution would have been merely a *coup d'etat*. Without the Enlightenment the events of 1776 would merely have been a colonial rebellion.

Now if such a peace-oriented faith as Buddhism can get itself drawn into bitter warfare and violence, do we have much hope of moderating human aggression? Yet we note also cases of peaceful coexistence where once it was absent – notably in Europe, and before that in other regions. Now, war in North America is virtually unthinkable, as in Scandinavia and through much of Latin America. Where there are troubles they have to do chiefly with unresolved ethnic tensions. The civil war in the Sudan is the struggle of a non-Muslim minority against, among other things, the universalization of Islamic *shari'a*. In Northern Ireland two groups conceiving of their mythic history differently have not reached a *modus vivendi*. In Israel there is the struggle between Palestinians and Jews. In Iraq and round about, the Kurds have been struggling for self-determination. In the southern Philippines the Muslim minority is fighting for independence. In Burma, the Karens fight; and in the Punjab, Sikh militants latch on to the dissatisfactions of the Sikhs in the wider fabric of Indian polity. In Zimbabwe recent violence has tainted relations between the Ndebele and the dominant Shona majority; and in Ethiopia Eritrea wishes for homogeneous imperial government. Unless we resolve such questions of ethnicity we are going to have much more trouble in the world. Now in the Soviet Union there are various open struggles — in the Baltic region and among the Armenians and Azerbaijanis.

Now a theory of the transcendental unity of religions might help in some cases. But as I have noted, the secular ideologies are also strong. Often Marx has been the inspiration of modernizing nationalist uprisings. Moreover, at one level the "all religions are equal" thesis does not work. It is resisted often by traditionalists, who may say, like Monsignor Ronald Knox, "comparative religion makes people comparatively religious." Is there an alternative irenic theory which has a greater measure of perceived truth?

We may note that there are often only two ways of resolving interethnic disputes peaceably. One is to give the oppressed group independence. Another is federalism. Even so, there will remain — and increasingly — the problem of ethnic minorities not distributed territorially. Some variation of the federal solution might be applied, by analogy perhaps with the Ottoman millet system. But it would be important to stress equality with otherness. In other words, one must respect varying cultural traditions. Such informal federalism begins to grow up in regions, such as Scandinavia, and wherever the mutual relations between nations are settled. Now in all this one of the binding, but at the same time dividing, forces is worldview, or ideology. As something which spans ethnicity, Christianity is a positive force for peace; in tension with

Islam, in Lebanon, it is a reinforcement of conflictual tendencies.

Now our aim may be stated as a system of ideas and ultimately of political arrangements which make the human race the community of ultimate concern — transcending and eventually dampening feelings of ethnic identity. Can we hold this aim while acknowledging the divisions between religious and other worldviews? Can we hold this in a nonrelativistic manner? For the notion of truth and the right way of living are built into worldviews, and we cannot reconcile them by wiping out their basis. Even if we reject all available worldviews it would still leave us with the notion that the worldview remaining (ours) which occupies the wasteland is somehow the truth or right. In short, can we provide a theory which would be acceptable to Theravādins as well as Muslims, and to Christians as well as Marxists?

It may be commented here, though, that some people are fanatics and prize their causes above humanity. They think that death with honor is a fine norm and are certain of the superiority of their beliefs to those of others. Sooner or later, of course, we must bump into the question as to who is entitled to use force. At present it is, by and large, the state and the nation. Am I implicitly arguing for a world government in saying that humanity is the community of ultimate concern? I am not sure. There can be uses of force, through the United Nations, which help to dampen conflicts, and which fall far short of world government. It would be dangerous to empower anyone as world ruler. It would seem to me better to tread the path of informal federalism, whereby sovereign states are drawn into working with one another in peace and can form ever larger and larger conglomerations. There are real advantages in preserving cross-cutting ways of dealing with world affairs — nation-states, multinational companies, transnational agencies, religious organizations — all cutting across boundaries. We might call this "transnationalism." We can now frame our question about worldviews. How can religious and other worldviews contribute to transnationalism? I suggest they can do as follows:

(1) They can encourage ecumenism each within each, because ecumenical modes of activity typically cross ethnic boundaries more fully than do nonecumenical attitudes.

(2) They can focus on the humanistic aspects of their own

traditions. Every religion has some notion or other of treating humans, and living beings in general, with respect. Similarly the humanistic aspects of Marxism and other secular worldviews can be underlined.

(3) They can emphasize ways in which each worldview has openings in its imagination for positive appraisals of other value systems.

(4) They can encourage friendly meetings with representatives of other worldviews.

(5) They can cooperate in ethical and social endeavors where concerns overlap, such as the spread of literacy.

(6) They can recognize that the underpinning of each tradition has its "soft" aspect. That is, a believer may be thoroughly dedicated and may have certain faith or certitude in her tradition's or worldview's teachings, and yet recognize that in a public, world community her faith is underpinned by nonconclusive, though maybe good, reasons.

On the basis of such moves a theory of universal toleration may be built. In other words, the spread of one's own viewpoint will be no longer a matter of force, but rather a matter of persuasion and debate. This debate need not be verbal. It may be a debate expressed in living examples, in qualities of life and the fruits of one's faith — a competition of saints.

This approach asks no worldview to abandon its own position or to cease from hope, if it so wishes, of becoming the universal belief of human beings. But it sets that hope in perspective and the means of achieving expansion under control. This suggestion is itself a kind of meta-worldview, depending on the notions that humanity is our community of ultimate concern and that worldviews can only be softly confirmed at best. Such a meta-worldview has the advantage that it gives as much as possible to the lower-order actual worldviews. It does not prevent a person from being a Buddhist or a Muslim, but only restricts the mode in which she holds to her worldview. To put it crudely, you can have 80 percent or more of your worldview, and so can everyone else. This contrasts with situations of forcible dominance where you can at best keep 20 percent. In brief, I here advocate soft non-relativism in a transnationalistic framework.

How would such an attitude affect Buddhism in Sri Lanka?

I think that it needs to work more on some of the items above, especially toward a theory under (3), seeing positive aspects of the Hindu heritage which are important for Buddhists to heed. The political message is that Sinhala Buddhist nationalism has to accept a federal arrangement. Only under such circumstances is it at all reasonable to hanker for a rebirth of the glory of classical Buddhist civilization.

There is much to build on, and this will be seen more clearly when the heat is gone and the dust has settled after the present conflict. There is the toleration of the great ideal emperor Asoka, who was the father of Therāvāda Buddhism in Sri Lanka. There is the rightful defense of Buddhist philosophy as being in line with modern science which was so well expressed by the late K. N. Jayatilleke, among others. This in turn implies an openness to other points of view. Such openness is necessary in the world if science is to go on flourishing and developing. There is the heavy traditional emphasis on not being too entangled in views, that is, not being too defensive in clinging to your own viewpoint. There is the peaceful and democratic ethos of the early Sangha — and much else besides.

The moral of the present crisis in Ceylon, as far as Buddhism goes, is that Buddhism has got too heavily enmeshed with Sinhala nationalism. Every religion is liable to such syncretism. As we saw, in an important way every worldview is syncretistic: Protestant evangelicalism with American patriotism; Marxism with a variety of national identities; Catholicism with the Polish struggle; Islam with Iranian nationalism — and so on. It is inevitable that such entanglement will happen to some degree. Ours is the age of nationalisms. But they can be tamed by being given some of their head. Football matches in due course substitute for wars. We do not suppress nationalism by trying to wipe it out, but by giving it some room in which to breathe. Loyalty to a national group need not be ignoble — but willingness to kill and oppress other humans because they do not belong to your group *is* ignoble.[12]

Above all, it seems to me, we must experiment in the world with new styles of and arrangements for pluralism. At the same time openness to other traditions and viewpoints is needful. Here religions and ideologies in particular need encouragement toward openness in their teaching. We can have a vision of a world community with great internal variety and many worldviews in harmonious competition. We can look toward a polydoxic world.

NOTES

1. See James Manor, ed., *Sri Lanka in Change and Crisis* (New York: St Martin's Press, 1984); and S. J. Tambiah, *Sri Lanka: Ethnic Fratricide and the Dismantling of Democracy* (Chicago: University of Chicago Press, 1986).

2. Richard Gombrich, *Theravāda Buddhism* (London and New York: Routledge & Kegan Paul, 1988); despite its title this book is overwhelmingly about Sri Lanka.

3. Gunapala Dharmasiri, *A Buddhist Critique of the Christian Concept of God*, 2d ed. (1988).

4. See my discussion in Peter Merkl and Ninian Smart, eds., *Religion and Politics in the Contemporary World* (New York: New York University Press, 1983).

5. Richard Gombrich felicitously combines historical and anthropological approaches in *Precept and Practice* (Oxford: Clarendon Press, 1971).

6. Anagarika Dharmapala, *A Message to the Young People of Ceylon* (1912).

7. See N. A. Jayawickrema, "Malalasekara," in *Encyclopedia of Religion*, ed. Mircea Eliade (New York: Macmillan, 1987).

8. K. N. Jayatilleke, *The Message of the Buddha*, ed. Ninian Smart (New York: Free Press, 1972).

9. See George M. Williams, *The Quest for Meaning of Swami Vivekānanda* (Chico, Calif.: New Horizons Press, 1974).

10. Pierre-Marie Sigaud, *René Guénon* (1984).

11. See especially John Hick's Gifford Lectures: *An Interpretation of Religion* (New Haven, Conn.: Yale University Press, 1989).

12. Ninian Smart, *Beyond Ideology* (San Francisco: Harper & Row, 1981).

10

Gandhi's Quest for a Nonviolent Political Philosophy

BHIKHU PAREKH

FOR MOST MEN AND WOMEN in the West and even in India, Mahatma Gandhi is a dated figure of local significance. In their view he was "essentially" a man of action, not of thought, and made little contribution to our understanding of humanity and society. He was too antipathetic to modern civilization to appreciate its great achievements and hankered after an irretrievably lost world of primitive simplicity. His principal contribution consisted in successfully leading his country's struggle for independence and providing a new method of political action whose practical value he greatly exaggerated.

I propose to argue that such an assessment does scant justice to the richness and depth of Gandhi's thought. Though not a theorist in the conventional sense, he was a creative and original thinker. He lived a political life of rare intensity and range, reflected deeply on his remarkable experiences, and distilled his insights in cryptic and unargued but pregnant and illuminating observations.

Political philosophers tend to fall into three categories. Some, whom we rightly call great, are both insightful and conceptually rigorous. Some others excel at theoretical rigor and rarely rise above conventional prejudices and wisdom in their understanding of political life. Yet others offer penetrating and profound insights into political life but lack the ability to organize them into a rigorous body of thought. Thanks to the mistaken theoreticist view of thought, we sometimes do not even call such writers philosophers.

Gandhi belonged to the third category. A thinker and not a theorist, he offered a loosely related "body" of important insights but not a tightly structured "system" of thought. If we are not to forfeit his insights, we must overcome the theoreticist prejudice against untheorized thoughts and think with and theorize for him.

I

Like many Indians Gandhi was deeply uneasy with the modern state, in his view the most abstract, rigid, and dehumanizing form of political organization invented by humankind so far.[1] For Gandhi the state largely speaks in only one language, that of authority; has only one means of action, namely, the law; uses only one way of securing compliance, namely, the threat of punishment; and has only one overriding concern, the maintenance of order. It is necessarily impersonal, that is, a system of rule by rules, and takes little account of the concrete circumstances and contexts in which human beings live and act. If a man is accused of committing a crime, say theft, it only asks whether he has or has not broken the law. His reasons, motives, circumstances, inadequately developed powers of will and self-discipline, the fact that he desperately needed the money to buy medicine for his dying mother, and so on, are of no relevance to its decisions. Like the courts of law, the bureaucrats apply rules more or less mechanically and without regard to their consequences in specific cases. The law is obsessed with regularity, predictability, and uniformity. It ignores human diversity and differences and defines justice as treating similar cases similarly. Since no two individuals are ever equal in their needs and circumstances, and no two cases ever similar, it often ends up becoming an instrument of injustice and inequality.

Since the state sees itself essentially as an instrument of order, Gandhi argued that it is anxious to secure unity of thought, will, and action in society. It uses educational, cultural, and other institutions and the power of public opinion to ensure that its citizens think and feel along acceptable lines and that their desires, affections, loyalties, and moral values remain within the permissible range of diversity. In Gandhi's view every modern state over-organizes and homogenizes its citizens as the very condition of its survival and smooth self-reproduction. The much-flaunted individuality of its citizens is either a mere sham or restricted to a narrow range of predetermined alternatives.

Following Tolstoy Gandhi thought that the modern state has a deep tendency to render its citizens amoral.[2] It encourages them to think that by its very nature it is either amoral or governed by its own separate moral principles, and that they should therefore not judge it by the principles of ordinary morality. It uses the sheer complexity and scale of political life to overwhelm and morally paralyze its citizens, and fosters a culture of moral apathy and inertia. Thanks to its abstract and autonomous nature, it encourages them to believe that its actions are not theirs and that they do not bear direct or indirect responsibility for them, and thus dulls their consciences. Not being forced to deal directly with their own political problems themselves, the people as citizens fail to develop and mobilize their moral energies and remain passive and dull.

For Gandhi then the modern abstract, overbearing, one-dimensional, rigid, hard, centralized, overorganized, and homogenizing state, obsessed with order and coercion, is a deeply dehumanizing institution and a constant threat to human dignity and individuality. Human dignity and moral development require that it should be humanized and integrated into the life of the community. How to do so is one of the neglected major problems of the modern age. Gandhi thought that even if his own answers were to be judged unsatisfactory, the problem remained and required the urgent attention of those who really cared for human dignity.

In Gandhi's view the modern state came into existence by breaking up long-established and preexisting communities and reorganizing the atomized individuals on a new collectivist basis. He thought this a grave historical mistake which the West should try to rectify. More importantly, he could not see why India and the other Third World countries, which were all beginning to enter the modern age, should repeat the European mistake. Almost all of them consist of ancient and more or less self-governing communities constituted on territorial, ethnic, functional, and other lines. These communities give their members a sense of belonging, a ready network of emotional and moral support, and a cultural and historical depth. They generally rely on the organized power of public opinion and manage to maintain social order without recourse to violence. They are also centers of power and offer vital safeguards against a centralized and overbearing state. India and the Third World countries should therefore explore an alternative *to* or at least an alternative form *of* the modern state, and evolve a polity deeply embedded in and deriving legitimacy and constant nourishment from these communities.[3] Far from weakening and fragmenting it, they give the polity depth and vitality wholly beyond the reach of the modern abstract state.

Such a polity is not an association of individuals but a community of communities. It exists not outside and above society but as an integral part of it, a living organism rather than an impersonal machine. Built from the bottom upward rather than from the top downward, it operates within the parameters set by and periodically renegotiated with its constituent communities.

Gandhi thought that many of the functions currently discharged by the state could be taken over by the constituent communities. One example suffices to indicate what he had in mind. As a lawyer, for example, he was convinced that the modern system of administering justice is a most unfortunate and easily dispensable institution. It is a concentrated expression of the modern state and shares all its objectionable features. It is expensive, dilatory, bureaucratic, and obsessed with uniformity. It treats human beings as passive objects in no way involved in the resolution of their conflicts, and reduces them to abstract cases to be settled by a trained legal establishment in an esoteric language. In spite of its claim to get to the truth of the matter, it privileges those capable of hiring the best experts.

Gandhi thought that as rational and moral beings, people are capable of discussing and resolving their differences in a spirit of good will and compromise and, if that fails, by accepting the arbitration of widely respected and mutually acceptable men and women in their community. That was how they had settled their differences in almost all premodern societies and do so even today in matters falling outside the jurisdiction of the state. In Gandhi's view the local communities should become the center of a radically redefined system of justice. They should be concerned not so much with the administration of justice as with the resolution of conflicts, and become moral and social rather than narrowly legal institutions. They should encourage their members to settle their disagreements themselves, and foster a climate in which allowing conflicts to occur, letting them get out of control, or failing to resolve them themselves would be widely regarded as a mark of personal inadequacy and a matter of shame. In cases where conflicts could not be so resolved, the local communities should provide people's courts made up of women and men enjoying popular trust and respect. The courts should act as communal forums rather than as agencies of the state, and exercise moral authority derived from the willing allegiance of the community rather than the narrowly legal authority derived from outside it. They should be concerned not so much to apportion blame and punish the guilty as to restore the ruptured fabric of society, to foster the spirit of fair play, and to increase the disputants' capacity to live together as members of a shared community.

In Gandhi's view such an arrangement has many advantages over the present professionalized and abstract system of justice. Justice here is swift, inexpensive, easily intelligible, and dispensed without an elaborate judicial and legal establishment. Since the modern state is unlikely to give up its monopoly of the administration of justice, Gandhi thought that citizens should themselves take the initiative and set up parallel popular courts on an experimental basis. As the courts became refined and widely known for the quality, speed, and cheapness of their justice, they would increasingly roll back the judicial frontiers of the state and reduce its judicial functions to the barest minimum. He thought that similar initiatives and processes could be launched in other areas of life, and the state transformed over time into a relatively minor though indispensable aspect of social life. It would then become an institution of the last rather than first resort as at present, and exist basically to facilitate social self-determination.

Gandhi also proposed what I might call a plural state. The modern state is based on two central assumptions. First, all its citizens are subject to the jurisdiction of a single legal system and governed by the same body of laws. To have different sets of laws for different bodies of citizens is considered inconsistent with the principle of equal citizenship lying at the heart of the modern state. Second, the modern state rests on a single source of legal authority from which all its institutions in one way or another derive their powers.

Gandhi could not see why either should be the case. In such societies as India and the Third World which had not yet become states in the modern sense, there exist ancient and long-established communities with their own distinct customs, traditions, and ways of life. Gandhi saw no sense in destroying them and creating an abstract state made up of abstract individuals. Thus, for example, the law may give the divorced wife a right of maintenance, leaving the different communities free to satisfy it in their own different ways. Some may ask her husband to pay; some may place an obligation on his family; yet others may make it the responsibility of the entire community or a charge on a collective fund. And these provisions may be enforced either in their own or in common courts. Gandhi thought that such a plurality of customs and practices would offer maximum cultural autonomy consistently with a shared civilized order.

Gandhi also challenged the second assumption of the modern state. The old and long-established territorial, occupational, and other communities within a state often preceded and grew up independently of it. They derive their authority not from the state but from the willing obedience and allegiance of their members. The modern state either dismantles them or turns them into its legal creatures.

It is true that the state speaks in the name of the entire society and enjoys a measure of preeminence over the narrowly based communities. However, the state is only a *legal* institution entitled to speak for society only in its *legal* aspect. It does not and can not presume to speak for it in moral, religious, cultural, and other matters. That right belongs to such groups as the church, the Brahmins, the cultural institutions, and the widely acknowledged moral leaders of society. Gandhi therefore rejected the doctrine of sovereignty, for neither in fact nor in principle can the state claim the right to regulate society in its totality.

He was particularly critical of the widespread view that the state is a moral institution.[4] The state is by its very nature a coercive institution whose every command is shadowed by a threat of violence. By contrast morality is a matter of uncoerced choice, and no action can be moral if done under fear of harm. For Gan-

dhi the state therefore can *never* be a moral institution. Furthermore the combination of legal and moral authority in the same
hands poses a grave danger to human dignity and freedom. It gives
the state a wholly illegitimate authority over its citizens' bodies
and consciences, and makes its laws binding not only in law but
also in conscience. It also dulls their legitimate suspicion of the
state and encourages them to direct their loyalty to it above all
others.

In Gandhi's view the state is basically a legal and adminis-
trative device, a "soulless machine." Far from being the organizing principle of society it is an institution of last resort, a necessary evil, and a standing indictment of our incapacity to organize
our affairs without coercion. In his later years Gandhi began to
appreciate that the state could become an instrument of social and
economic justice and engage in a redistributive program.[5] It is also
a custodian and critic of the public — and some aspects of private —
morality. Indeed one could even argue that when it levels up the
poor and the oppressed and bans such practices as untouchability,
the state puts into practice the supreme moral principle of active
love and becomes a moral and even a spiritual institution. Gandhi
resisted that conclusion, however. Though moral in their content,
these inherently coercive actions of the state are not moral in their
origin and motivation. People might have to be compelled, "treated
like beasts," under certain circumstances, but that neither makes
the state a moral institution nor represents a moral way of treating them.

Gandhi was deeply troubled by the violence of the modern
state. It is at work not only in such visible phenomena as wars
and internal repression but also in the silent and largely invisible
violence committed daily behind society's back and without a mur-
mur of protest in its prisons. Having been incarcerated for nearly
six years in India and seven months in South Africa, where he sometimes shared his cell with ordinary criminals, he was appalled by
the "utter futility" and "inhumanity" of prisons.[6] Since the modern state's indigenous resources consist primarily in its monopoly
on violence, it relies on physical punishment. The fear of punishment, however, has its obvious limits and can never solve the problem of order, as the experience of all states shows. More importantly, by making moral conduct a function of physical fear, it treats
men and women as animals and dehumanizes them.

For Gandhi order and disorder were abstractions and really referred to forms of human relationship. Order means nothing more than stable human relations; disorder signifies instability. Human relations are stable when they seem just to those involved. He believed that the good has the capacity to last; evil or untruth is inherently unstable. The so-called problem of order is thus basically about the quality of human relationships, and basically moral rather than legal in nature. The state has only limited competence in the matter, and it is wrong to pretend otherwise. At best it is equipped to put down disorder, but it can neither prevent nor reduce its occurrence, let alone create order. Rather than rely on its own resources, the state should lead the communal effort and mobilize and coordinate the moral energies of its citizens.

In such a polity, Gandhi went on, disorders are all seen as problems to be tackled by its citizens rather than left to the state. When a crime is committed, for example, citizens need to ask if it is a protest against a grievance. If so, they bear some responsibility for it and have a duty to remove the evil in question. If the crime is pointless or a product of ill-will, punishment is hardly the way to improve the criminal or to awaken his or her sense of moral responsibility. Rather than imprison criminals, the state should seek the support of family, friends, neighbors, and the respected members of the community, and give them all the help they need to reintegrate the criminal into his or her environment, using coercion most reluctantly and only as a last resort. In Gandhi's view the use of force represents a breakdown in the moral life of the community, and both indicts and challenges each of its citizens.

II

Social and political change is another area where Gandhi's thought contained important and original insights. He offered novel ways of understanding and opposing injustice and oppression.

For Gandhi all systems of domination rest on a profound misunderstanding of human nature, namely, that it is possible for one person or group to harm another without also harming themselves. Human beings are necessarily interdependent and form an organic whole.[7] Everyone owes his or her humanity to others and benefits from a world which she or he did not create. As Gandhi put it, everyone is "born a debtor," a beneficiary of others' gifts, and these inherited debts are too vast to be repaid. Even a whole lifetime is not enough to pay back what a person owes to parents, let alone all others. Furthermore the creditors are by their very nature unspecifiable. Since the debts can never be "repaid" or the favors "returned," all one can do is to "recognize the conditions of his existence" and continue the ongoing universal *yajna* by accepting a full share of collective responsibility.

Since humankind constitutes an organic whole and individuals are necessarily interdependent, every human action is both self- and other-regarding.[8] "I believe that if one man gains spiritually the whole world gains with him, and if one man falls the world falls to that extent."[9]

For Gandhi humanity is indivisible, and no one can degrade or brutalize another without also degrading or brutalizing oneself, or inflict psychic and moral damage on others without inflicting it on oneself as well. As Gandhi put it, no one "takes another down a pit without descending into it himself and sinning in the bargain."

Gandhi's concept of indivisible humanity formed the basis of his critique of systems of oppression and exploitation. Such dominant groups suffer as much as their victims and sometimes even more. White South Africans cannot deprive blacks of their livelihood and dignity without suppressing their inner doubts and tender feelings, damaging their capacities for critical self-reflection and impartial self-assessment, and falling victims to moral conceit, morbid fears, and irrational obsessions. In brutalizing the blacks they also brutalize themselves and are only prevented by their arrogance from noticing how sad, empty, and pitiable their lives has become. The colonial rulers met the same fate. They could not dismiss the natives as "effeminate" and "childlike" without thinking of themselves as tough, hypermasculine, and unemotional adults. In misrepresenting the natives, they misrepresented themselves and fell into their own traps. They also took home the attitudes, habits, and styles of government acquired abroad and corrupted their own society.

On the basis of his concept of human unity Gandhi arrived at a novel theory of social change.[10] He readily agreed that no dominant group ever gives up power without a struggle. However, he was convinced that the traditional theory of revolution was fundamentally flawed. In his view the fact that almost every revolution so far had led to terror, devoured its own children, and failed to create a better society was a proof of this.

These failures are not accidents but spring from the Manichaean view of the world lying at the basis of the traditional theory of revolution. The theory neatly separates good and evil and sees human existence as a mortal struggle between them. The belief that evil has no rights is the inspiring principle of revolutionary morality. Those identified as evil are deemed to have forfeited their humanity and the concomitant claims on their fellow human beings' understanding and charity.

Gandhi argued that far from being mutually exclusive, good and evil are conceptually and existentially inseparable. Nothing is good except in a specific context and within a specific pattern of human relationship; what is good in one context is not so in another; good turns into evil when pressed beyond a certain point; and what is good for one person might not be so for another. Every moral deed thus has a price, and good is necessarily shadowed by evil. Furthermore, in a world full of evil, good cannot exist — let alone be effective — without participating in evil, and no evil can last a day without some basis of goodness to give it strength and organization. Since good and evil are inseparable and at times indistinguishable, they can not be socially separated and attributed to specific classes or groups. Groups are composed of individuals, each a bearer of good and evil properties. Even the apparently innocent victims of an unjust social order actively or passively, wittingly or unwittingly, collaborate in their oppression and bear some responsibility for their predicament.

In Gandhi's view the traditional theory of revolution did not fully appreciate the subtle ways in which good suffers corruption in its struggle against evil. All means leading quickly and economically to the desired ends are considered morally acceptable. Since the so-called ends are in turn means to some other allegedly higher ends, everything ultimately gets reduced to a mere means, and human choices lack protection against moral cynicism. Violence, mendacity, cunning, duplicity, manipulation of the opponent, and so on are all considered legitimate. In resorting to them and borrowing its tools from its enemy, good subtly becomes transformed into evil and its victory is really its defeat. It is therefore hardly surprising that every revolution in history has involved massive terror and ended up replacing one set of masters with another. Every such disappointment weakens faith in the possibility of radical change, and the conservatives reap the political harvest.

Gandhi argued that we need a new theory of revolution grounded in the three principles of the unity of humankind, the indivisibility of means and ends, and a non-Manichaean view of the world. It must take its stand not just on the neglected interests of the oppressed but on the shared interests of all, including the oppressors. For Gandhi imperialism damages *both* the British and the Indians; and untouchability inflicts a grave moral and emotional damage not just on the untouchables but also on the caste Hindus. The revolutionary must appeal to these shared interests and common human bonds.

Like Marx Gandhi argued that revolutionary consciousness springs from intense sensitivity to human suffering which it is designed to alleviate, and thus has a special affinity with the oppressed, its natural constituency and concern. Unlike Marx, however, he insisted that the oppressed are neither wholly innocent nor free from their share of human failings, and that the oppressors are not totally evil and devoid of their share of human virtues. Even as no oppressive system can last without the cooperation of its morally implicated victims, it cannot be conclusively ended without the cooperation of its erstwhile masters. They must be persuaded and argued with and, since that often fails, subjected to the sustained moral pressure of *satyāgrahas*.

For Gandhi the means-end dichotomy lying at the heart of the traditional revolutionary theory was fundamentally false. In human life the so-called means consist not of implements and inanimate tools but of human actions, and by definition these cannot fall outside the jurisdiction of morality. Furthermore the method of fighting for an objective is an integral part of it. Every step toward a desired goal shapes its character, and utmost care has to be taken lest the steps taken distort or damage it.

Gandhi's theory of *satyāgraha*, the "surgery of the soul," as he called it, was his alternative to the traditional theory of revolution.[11] It is not so much a nonviolent *method* of achieving revolutionary ends as a novel way of *defining* the very idea of revolution. Like Trotsky's permanent revolution it is a form of constant social fermentation seeking to break down emotional, ideological, and moral barriers, to unfreeze the flow of social sympathy, and to cultivate a genuine sense of community.

For Gandhi the *satyāgrahi* rely on the power of suffering love. Confronted with untruth they seek dialogue with the opponent. When this is denied or reduced to an insincere exercise in public relations, they take a stand and accept whatever punishment is meted out to them. Since their sole concern is to evoke a moral response in the opponent, they do everything to put the opponent at ease and nothing to harass, embarrass, anger, or frighten him or her. In the meantime, they suffer the punishment without hatred or ill-will in the hope of triggering off in the opponent a slow, intensely personal, and highly complex process of self-examination. The moment the opponent shows willingness to talk in a spirit of genuine good will, the *satyāgrahi* suspend the struggle and give reason a chance to work in a more hospitable climate.

Like the rationalists, Gandhi stressed the importance of rational discussion; unlike them, however, he realized that what passes as rational discussion is often little more than alternative monologues or a public relations exercise, and that sticking to it under such circumstances is an act of irrationality. He knew that narrow rationalism and violence tend to feed off each other, and that the failure of rationality to deliver results renders violence morally respectable. Accordingly he sought to break through the narrow straitjacket of the reason-violence dichotomy lying at the basis of traditional rationalism. He imaginatively explored the uncharted terrain between reason and violence and arrived at new forms of political praxis. His *satyāgraha* was basically a new form of dialogue, a new conception of discussion, embedded in a richer and morally grounded theory of rationality.

III

Gandhi's conceptualization of political life and redefinitions of such central concepts as liberty (*swarāj*), equality (*samatā*), citizenship (*nāgarikatā*), rights (*adhikār*), obligation (*dharma*), and tolerance (*sahishnutā*) also contain important insights and deserve close study. The first three will serve by way of illustration.

Following the Hindu tradition Gandhi took little interest in the concept of human nature. Like most Hindus he took a radically individualistic view of humankind. Each individual is unique, follows his or her own path of moral and spiritual evolution, and has a distinct *swabhāva*, that is, a distinct and firm but relatively open and malleable constitution of nature.

For Gandhi the individual's *swabhāva* has two sources.[12] First, she is endowed at birth with a specific physical and mental constitution, temperament, tendencies, and dispositions, which are all a legacy of her previous life. Second, she is a member of a specific community which deeply shapes her habits, character, memories, ideals, and values and gives her personality a distinct tone and color.

The individual's *swabhāva* thus represents a unique blend of inherited and socially acquired characteristics. It holds him together, persists over time, and forms the basis of his personal identity. Since it makes him the person he is, it constitutes his ontological foundation or truth (*satya*). The Sanskrit word *satya* is derived from *sat*, meaning reality, the real, the ultimate, and that which endures over time. The opposite of *sat* is *māyā*, meaning illusory, ephemeral, transient, or only relatively real.

The *satya* or truth of an individual limits and guides but does not predetermine his or her choices and decisions. As a rational being endowed with such capacities as introspection, critical self-reflection, and choice, he or she is capable of becoming aware of some of these determinations, taking a critical and detached view of oneself, forming ideals and goals, and changing oneself. Many aspects of our constitution, however, are too deep to be excavated by even the most rigorous self-examination and remain beyond control. And some of those aspects are often too deeply entrenched and tenacious to be changed without superhuman courage. Human beings are therefore neither absolutely free nor totally determined. They are free within limits. The extent of the limits depends on such factors as their capacity for self-analysis, will power, and the kind of society in which they live. A cooperative and relaxed society in which people take affectionate interest in each other, are open in their relations, and thus help each know himself or herself is more conducive to human freedom than one in which they scrupulously keep their distance.

Not free will versus determinism, but how to change in harmony with one's truth was the problem for Gandhi, as for most Hindu thinkers. Unlike the liberal concept of individuality which stresses differences from others and is necessarily comparative, integration or wholeness in Gandhi's sense stresses the individual's relation to himself or herself and one's way of ontologically being in the world. An unreflective person, one not in the habit of reflecting on and reconstituting his or her being, is constantly in danger of becoming an eclectic collection of borrowed and discordant properties. Critical self-reflection is the source of self-knowledge, and hence a necessary condition of wholeness and sanity.

As a uniquely constituted and situated being, each individual necessarily sees and experiences the world differently and forms personal beliefs and opinions. For Gandhi, to force a person to act against sincerely held beliefs is to violate that person's truth. One might be mistaken, but one must discover that for oneself. Others have a duty to argue with him or her and show why they are mistaken, but if unpersuaded, the person should be left alone. Integrity or wholeness requires that one's views grow out of one's own way of looking at the world. Persuasion is thus qualitatively different from coercion. It respects and reinforces the persuadee's wholeness and ensures that the new way of looking at the world takes root in and grows out of that person's changed being. Gandhi thought that an individual can be legitimately compelled only when a matter is of grave social importance and the individual concerned can not be dissuaded from harmful conduct.

For Gandhi freedom consists in being true to oneself, in living by "one's own light" and growing at "one's own pace." It is a form of wholeness or integrity. Like many Hindu philosophers, Gandhi subsumes freedom under truth. To be free is to be truthful. To deny freedom is to deny "truth," to force one to be untrue and to live by someone else's truth.

Like freedom, Gandhi radically redefined the concept of equality. In much of the liberal and socialist literature on the subject equality is defined in comparative, contractual, competitive, and individualist terms. For Gandhi, however, people are necessarily interdependent, rise and fall together, only become human within a community, and are born subject to nonrepayable debts.

Since a human community is necessarily a fellowship of unique and interdependent beings, the concept of equality has to be defined in noncomparative, noncompetitive, and nonatomic terms. For Gandhi it basically consists in each individual enjoying full access to the community's economic, political, moral, and cultural resources in order to realize one's particular potential as a uniquely constituted being. As a progressive and reflective being the individual "grows from truth to truth" and strives to enrich, deepen, and reconstitute his or her being. Human equality consists in all alike being able to do so. It does not mean that I should get what others get, but rather that I should get what *I* need for my development as *I* define it. It is not only in my interest but in that of all others that they should treat me equally. Equality thus is not a mechanical concept or a synonym for uniformity. It is at bottom a relationship of mutuality and fellowship.

Gandhi also redefined the concept of citizenship.[13] As a political activist he knew that not consent, nor will, nor fear, but cooperation is the basis of the state.

Every government is tempted to misuse its power, and the democratic government is in that respect no different from the autocratic. What distinguishes the two is the fact that one does and the other does not succumb to the temptation. And that is so because a democratic government knows that if it did, its citizens would refuse to cooperate with it. Notwithstanding all its institutional checks and balances, a democratic government can easily turn evil if its citizens become apathetic, vulnerable to corruption and manipulation, or lose their sense of moral responsibility. For Gandhi the virtues and vices of a government are not inherent in it but derive from those of its people. It is the coward who creates the bully, the worm who encourages others to trample on it, the morally irresponsible citizen who creates a tyrant.

As a moral being a citizen has a duty to decide whom to support and under what conditions. Self-respect and dignity require that loyalty should not be unconditional or taken for granted. When a law is just, there is a "sacred duty" to give it "willing and spontaneous obedience." The duty has a dual basis: a general duty to do or support good and a specific moral duty to the community into which one was born and rooted, whose benefits one has enjoyed, and to whose members one is bound by ties of loyalty and mutual expectation. If a law is unjust or morally unacceptable, one has a duty to protest against and even disobey it. To obey it is to "participate in evil" and to incur moral responsibility for its immoral consequences.[14] In Gandhi's view it is a "mere superstition" and an attitude worthy of a "slave" to believe that a citizen should uncritically obey all laws. To be a citizen is to be coresponsible for the activities of the government.[15]

IV

Many of Gandhi's insights are original to him and make an important contribution to our understanding of moral and political life. Like all such insights they were products of deep reflection on his life experiences, and their persuasive power, or "validity," as he called it, lay in their ability to illuminate and guide human experiences. He did not claim incorrigibility for them. Indeed he himself kept revising and reformulating them. He said that they represented the truth as he had discovered it and were subject to correction in the light of new experiences.

For Gandhi experience is the only true test of ideas and insights. And experiences vary from individual to individual. An idea must stand alone, deriving its power only from its ability to illuminate others' experiences and win their uncoerced allegiance. As a man who deeply cherished nonviolence in life and in thought, he respected others' intellectual and moral autonomy and offered his insights tentatively, gently, in humility, only to stimulate their curiosity and to provide them with "some useful material" in their solitary intellectual journey. As he put it, he was not a preacher, a teacher, a guru, or even a guide, but an initiator of a conversation on moral and political matters who sought not followers but fellow seekers. In his view that was the only way free people should speak to one another, and the only morally acceptable manner in which moral and political philosophers should write about their subject.

NOTES

1. M. K. Gandhi, *Hind Swaraj* (Ahmedabad: Navajivan, 1938), pp. 31ff.; *Collected Works* (Ahmedabad: Navajivan, 1958), vol. 75, pp. 220ff. For a detailed discussion, see Bhikhu Parekh, *Gandhi's Political Philosophy* (London: Macmillan, 1989), chap. 5.

2. M. K. Gandhi, *Young India*, 12 August 1920 and 20 July 1926; *Collected Works*, vol. 17, p. 93.

3. M. K. Gandhi, *Harijan*, 26 July 1942, 14 January 1939, and 28 July 1946. See also Sriman Narayan Agarwal, *Gandhian Constitution for Free India* (Allahabad, 1946).

4. Gandhi, *Young India*, 4 December 1924. I am grateful to Dr. Geoffrey Ostegaard for his comments on this point.

5. Gandhi, *Harijan*, 5 May 1946 and 3 August 1947; *Collected Works*, vol. 24, p. 224.

6. Gandhi, *Collected Works*, vol. 32, pp. 150ff.

7. M. K. Gandhi, *From Yeravada Mandir* (Ahmedabad: Navajivan, 1932), chaps. 1–5.

8. Gandhi, *Collected Works*, vol. 50, p. 218; Raghavan Iyer, *The Moral and Political Writings of Mahatma Gandhi* (Oxford: Clarendon Press, 1986), vol. 11, pp. 552ff.

9. Gandhi, *Young India*, 4 December 1924.

10. Iyer, *Moral and Political Writings of Gandhi*, vol. 2, sec. 6.

11. Ibid., pp. 298ff.

12. Gandhi, *Harijan*, 2 June 1946 and 7 April 1946; see also the Preface to M. K. Gandhi, *The Story of My Experiments with Truth* (Ahmedabad: Navajivan, 1956), and *Collected Works*, vol. 50, p. 216. I have discussed this more fully in Parekh, *Gandhi's Political Philosophy*, pp. 92ff. As Śaṅkara put it, the real nature or disposition of a thing constituted its truth. (*Tasya bhāvah tattvam.*)

13. Iyer, *Moral and Political Writings of Gandhi*, vol. 11, p. 355.

14. Gandhi, *Young India*, 22 July 1920.

15. Ibid., 1 December 1920, 1 June 1921, and 5 January 1922; see also Gandhi, *Hind Swaraj*, pp. 80ff.

PART IV

Making Peace:
Prophecy, Protest, and Poetry

11

Christian Peacemakers in the Warmaking State

DANIEL BERRIGAN, S.J.

OUR RESOURCES, TO BEGIN at the beginning, are biblical, always from an ecumenical point of view. Our resources are also American, insistently. And upon each of these it seems profitable to reflect; and with these to walk. In the footsteps of ancestors of both kinds of history, Christian and secular. And so, never alone.

Our attention was drawn to General Electric and its weapons complex in King of Prussia, Pennsylvania, late in 1979. As I recall, the friend who opened the matter was a Mennonite lawyer, John Schuchardt. He pointed out that we and many others had stood and withstood at the Pentagon, the air- and sea- and land-based military centers, for many years. But no one had confronted the industrial complex. These gigantic martian musclemen, in utmost secrecy and unaccountability, continued unimpeded, stoking their forges, beating the world itself into the shape of a nuclear sword.

Vigilers and leafletters had stood outside the plant for a number of years. But now, Schuchardt felt, a more vigorous intervention was called for. The secrecy surrounding the weapons production was in effect an enormous protection for high crime. Under such conditions, in contravention to all public exercise of vote, debate, citizen alertness, literally anything could continue—any crime, any violation of international, national, divine, or human law, quite out of sight and mind.

The point was not that the forges of Mars at GE were off limits; everything nuclear was off limits. The point was that Mars had made himself both invisible and unaccountable. No one knew what went on in such factories and labs. Not even the workers were privy to the part they played. By and large, as we were to learn, the workers had only piecemeal responsibility. They created, as they insisted at our trial, only bits and parts of the bomb, and so laid claim to a more or less tainted ignorance.

Given the situation as "normal"—"nuclear normalcy" a grotesque oxymoron — a question arose. Where had democracy gone? What meaning could responsible citizenship hold? By hook and by crook a sleazy authority got hold of our dollars. They contemned and ignored our vote. Vote? In regard to nuclear weapons, we had, all said, no more voice in our future or that of our children than Russian one-party victims. Indeed nuclear arms were proving the great political equalizer. East and West, all people, children, adults, we were in the same boat; and the boat was leaking at every seam.

Once this was pointed out and reflected on, a great light arose in our souls. We had seen something. We had always seen it, but now we saw it as though for the first time. We were like the Texan bishop who told how he rode past the immense Pantex plant in Amarillo, hundreds of times. Every American nuclear weapon was assembled there, and the bishop rode past. And then one day he saw it, through those who had vigiled and prayed and been arrested there. He began to visit the prisoners, to inquire about their families, to carry the sacraments behind the walls, to ponder these events. And as he recounts, his life has never been the same.

We also had seen something. In consequence, we spent many months at prayer, reflection, discussion. We were seeking in Holy Scripture a metaphor, an image, that might lend strength to our nascent purpose.

Finally it came to us through Molly Rush, mother of eight, grandmother, founder of the Thomas Merton Center in Pittsburgh. She suggested the great image from Isaiah: "God will wield authority over the nations and render judgment over many peoples. They will hammer their swords into plowshares, and their spears into sickles."

All great moments are finally simple. Why not, we asked our souls, why not us, our hands, our hammers? And if not us, who?

So we took our small courage and our small household hammers in hand. And on September 9, 1980, we entered the GE Reentry Division Plant in King of Prussia, Pennsylvania. It was, I need not add, a watershed hour for our lives—and who knows, perhaps also for the lives of others.

We reflected long and long on those hammers. Each of us had sometime or other, clumsily or with skill, used a hammer. It seemed a tool of the common life, a symbol of the urge to humanize things. It was, by its modest heft, its adaptability, its gentle scope, a traditionally peaceful tool—for building homes and schools, hospitals and churches, for making toys, shaping metal, repairing and mending and enhancing the earth.

And more. Both Isaiah and Micah used the hammer as an implied symbol of spiritual rebirth, of conversion to compassion and justice, of a new face put not just on things, but on the soul. A new face turned toward God and one another.

And closer to our topic—the hammer after all is lifted, and falls, and falling, turns one thing into another—the hammer, falling on the weapon, transforms it. Thus the hammer becomes a symbol of the outlawing of war.

If war were outlawed, we asked ourselves, what would the world look like? What would that other, improbable, even unimaginable shape be?

Isaiah is a visionary, and a practical one. He sees what few saw in his lifetime, and only a few since; only a few kings and couriers and academics and students, churchgoers, consumers. He sees a new form of things, the shape of a world that has turned away from killing, turned its face toward the stranger and orphan and widow.

What he sees is what we all can see; but only in proportion as we have absorbed his vision. He sees a world in the form of—a plowshare.

But the plowshare was not yet forged. Isaiah's vision was not of a peace already accomplished. Nor did his vision stem from citizenship in a peaceable kingdom. Indeed in the Israel of this time, there was no peace, only war abroad and injustice at home. Peace was a lost art; unachieved and arduous, a work to be done, a work never quite accomplished.

Thus came his vision of peacemaking, in a strangely unpeaceable time. His century, the seventh before Christ, was turbulent

in the extreme: wars and rumors of wars. No matter. In the grand
tradition of the prophets of action, Isaiah intervened directly in
political, military, and diplomatic events. He predicted the invasion of Palestine; it happened twice. He lived to see the threat of
siege laid to his beloved Jerusalem.

But it was not merely his predictions that rubbed the powers
raw. Bad news they could absorb because it seldom or never fell
on their heads. Isaiah dared go further. Someone, he declared, was
responsible for making the news bad. He denounced the selfish-
ness and violence of those in power. Wars were not inevitable;
neither was domestic misery; these were the foul creation of those
who would put thrones above lives, riches above honor, excess above
human need.

No trust in armies and chariots, he cried; no trust in secret
deals with the powers, in the grandiosities of imperial ego. Whatever the pretensions of the nations, he insisted, God was in the
cockpit of history. More chariots, multiplied warriors? These were
vain divagations, the fits and starts of madmen. They would never
serve or save or succor; they could only multiply destruction and
disorder.

Let the great ones ignore or revile or punish, Isaiah persisted.
The crimes of the powerful, he declared, were paid for by the sufferings of the people. Before God, this was intolerable.

Politically passionate, mystically intense, Isaiah reminds us
of other, no less grand spirits of our own day: of Martin Luther
King and Gandhi and Dorothy Day. And indeed of Jesus, who
claimed him as spiritual ancestor.

They resemble Isaiah in this: in life and death, they are alter-
nately hated and feared, loved and celebrated. Thus a familiar
tradition, disclosing a common historical rejection, has Isaiah mar-
tyred at the end.

Swords into plowshares. It seems remarkable; a proclamation both simple and audacious, and all in the teeth of contrary
evidence. Isaiah spoke in a time of whetted swords and rusted plowshares, a time of immense violence and social conflict and neglect
of the poor. No plowshares, or very few. Little attention to the turning up of the soil, the nourishing of people, the lives of children.
Much attention to the arming of the nation; to swords, their forging, multiplying, whetting.

And in consequence of the social and military crimes, Isaiah saw something else: false worship. God could not be honored while the poor were dishonored. There could be no simultaneous sword making and true worship, any more than there could be a balancing off of swords and plows, of guns and butter. One could not be violent and nonviolent together, any more than one could be worshipful and blasphemous together.

Isaiah sensed it; the soul is not built upon such divisions. Neither is the community. In its debased balancing act of moral contradictions, the nation could only bring on itself and others ruin, betrayal, tradeoff, flight from sanity.

Isaiah is, among other good things, a wondrous psychologist. Again and again, he sees the nightmarish schizophrenia of soul and body politic that follows on the attempt to unite essential oppositions, to make of war a virtuous cover for arrogance, avarice, and conquest.

Against the filthy tide, he commended sanity and good sense. Only when the sword was transformed could healing occur. Once the plowshare was busy, the neglected earth would grow fruitful again. When structures of injustice and avarice were transformed, something of momentous public consequence would follow: there would be no more poor, because there were no more rich.

In so speaking, Isaiah flew in the face of something commonly understood as the facts, or realism, or big power diplomacy, or just war theory, or the curious game known as "interim ethic." He spoke as one who had better access than the conniving or compromising wisdom of the world. He spoke in consequence of a piercing intuition of history, of who were its true makers and breakers.

These were, to put matters bluntly, neither kings nor pharaohs nor commissars nor juntas nor shahs nor their armies nor chariots nor horses. Nor their bunkers nor laboratories, nor their nukes.

Those who made history pursued a far different task; they broke swords. Those who made history made plowshares.

Once the swords were rusty and the plowshares busy, we had an apt symbol for the conversion of society, its forms, attitudes, politics, priorities. No useless chatter about "reform," a luxurious berth on a Titanic. No, men and women must bend the instruments of death, structures of injustice, into a new form, a form in accord with the divine.

A new form? A plowshare was primordial, useful, appropriate to hand and earth. It was apt to the words of life, and the Giver of life. The image turned the blade aside, the old lethal stereotype of the settler sword: the sword that settles matters, once for all.

But the plow was something else. The plow was in harmony with the neglected and despised human, as with the neglected and despised earth. No one need be ashamed to put hand to the plow, that modest and appropriate instrument. But those who wielded the sword must be ashamed indeed; for they lost, first of all, their own humanity; in making of a brother or sister an enemy, and of the enemy, a corpse.

Word for word, we eight friends studied Isaiah in that summer of 1980. We knew we had come on our image.

We were intrigued by the verb of the text: "to beat, to refashion, to reshape, to forge." It was a word freighted with action, implying effort, cost, mental and physical drive. No miracles or magic are supposed. No act of God intervenes; nothing happens, as long as humans are unconcerned, cowardly, blunted in conscience, selfish, seduced by national myth, deaf to human suffering, politically naive or neutral, obsessed with law and order and money and security. No act of God intervenes, as long as believers regard themselves as citizens of a state first, and believers second, or third — or last of all (which option perhaps puts matters more honestly).

Hands, heart, courage, patience, peaceableness — all are presumed. Short of these, the sword remains the master and mastering image, the enslaving image of life in this world. Short of these, no sword in history has ever changed form or function. No nation in history has disarmed, by edict of the armed. No nuclear weapon, since Livermore Laboratory designed Fat Man to fall on Hiroshima — not one weapon has been dismantled by any nuclear nation.

Indeed the weaponry breeds outlandish illusion, perennially dusted off by political charlatans! The weapons make their true believers "drunk," "rolling in their own vomit." They weave a tale of a benign superstate, arming with reluctance, to minimal degree only, with due regard for the lives of noncombatants, against implacable outsiders, for a time of crisis only. Thereupon the crisis past or resolved, this entity resumes its tranquil way in the world.

Thus the illusion.

Isaiah is lucid. Swords beget not plowshares, but more swords. Nukes beget not disarmament (a word long abandoned even by the prestidigitators), nor even "arms control" (that weasel word signifying nothing). Nukes beget nukes. Nukes beget star wars. Terror, a more honest word than deterrence, but the same thing, is the iron destiny of the world, and of the peoples thereof.

In brief, then, the supremely practical vision of Isaiah, which the times make ever more urgent, is a call to rebirth of spirit and practice, to renewal of the skills of the human. Is the call issued in an inhuman time? No matter; issue it anyway.

The renewal includes in the nature of things such neglected virtues as compassion and justice toward the needy, the outcast and victimized. And above all, and first of all: "Don't kill. Have no part in killing, either enemy or criminal or the aged or the disabled or the unborn." Everything depends on this.

On September 9, 1980, disarmed by Isaiah, armed with small household hammers and vials of our own blood, eight good friends strode into GE's squat, cost-efficient matrix of the Mark 12A, a first strike "reentry vehicle" deployed currently on Minuteman 3, the Trident fleet, and the MX. The time was approximately 8:50 a.m. The shifts of workers were changing. We easily slipped by "security" notable for its laxity. We went unerringly toward a huge room whose entrance sign read: "Nondestructable Testing." We found before us the nose cones and components, and began their conversion — and perhaps our own as well.

Hammers and blood. The blood, we thought, was a reminder of our common parenthood in God, our common destiny, the bloodline that joins us to one another, for good or ill. The blood, as Exodus reminds us, is a sign of life, and therefore of the Lifegiver, and therefore sacred. It is a sign also of covenant, a common understanding — that the blood of Christ, once given, forbids all shedding of blood. "This is the new covenant in my blood" — a gift, a wellspring of justice and peace. No more genocide in our name, no suicide and murder by Mark 12A, Trident, MX, Cruise.

The rest is a kind of history. We had agreed that if stopped short of our purpose, we would simply drop the hammers, pour our blood around, form a circle of prayer, and wait for the consequence, which as we knew, is never slow to arrive.

But we went (better, were led) against all expectation, straight as unbroken arrows, to our quarry. I speak, I believe, for the others also. We were led there in spite of our second thoughts, our fears, fears of injury, fears of consequences. We were led almost in spite of ourselves.

We walked unhindered into a "high security" setting. There was no security worth the word. That was simply the fact; no security surrounding the weapons. And it continued to be the fact in the twenty-eight Plowshares actions that have followed our own, in our country, in West Germany, in Australia. No one to this day has been injured. And this in spite of warnings in many of these plague spots that "lethal force is decreed" against intruders such as ourselves. One cannot but reflect; the myth that the weapons are secure is matched, illusion for illusion, by the myth that the weapons supply security.

In both myths, I suggest that the controlling factor is fear. Fear that keeps the citizens in place, in lock step. We learned this on that fateful morning. Neither guards nor dogs nor hoses nor guns confronted us. But the fear that such dangers lurked in the building, this was almost as paralyzing as the dangers themselves. The dangers were nonexistent, as it turned out. Fear of the dangers could be mastered, we discovered, only by walking — with or without the fear. But walking.

Indeed the weapons are a monstrous monument to fear, as it moves both within the soul, and outward, to make of the nations lethal camps, socialized death rows. And of our people, hopeless and ill-fated victims.

Fear, nihilism, despair, anomie; and then the weapons that curse the human venture and lay their indelible stigma on our lives: a stigma of fear, nihilism, despair, anomie.

The weapons are a kind of demonic antisacrament, a sign of a mystery, of the sin that gives up. Despair of sisters and brothers, of human variety and beauty, of contesting forms of organizing societies. Most grievously of all, despair of the possibility of peacefully settling human differences.

The logic of hope, we thought, runs counter. What has been ill-made, immorally made, illegitimately made, secretly made — made without accountability of public debate or plain horse sense — this can be unmade.

This too we learned on that day, as we started a long trek down an iron corridor that seemed like a veritable last mile for humanity. We believed then, shakily, and our faith grew less shaky with every step we took.

And then, in sight of the horrid weapons, faith exploded into an epiphany. We had dared look Medusa in the face, and behold! We were not turned to stone. We raised our hammers, and the sound was like the knell of the Kingdom come; we were putting death to death.

We believe a mysterious providence accompanied us into that antiseptic charnel house, that nuclear Auschwitz. We believe the same providence led us to the deadly bric-a-brac, offered us ten or twelve minutes of noninterference, guided our hands and arms, protected us from injury.

Even while we hammered away, a knot of workers stood by, transfixed. The plant manager arrived, to blurt out the old canard, also repeated by the Secretary of War, Brown, at the Pentagon: "That's no way to get peace!"

And later, plant security, local police. The FBI, nonplussed at our timing and precision, asked fretfully: "How did they know where to go? They couldn't have done this without a leak!" Our agreement couldn't be more profound; we were led, in that place of moral incoherence and blindness, straight to the heart of darkness. And there, perhaps, were enabled to strike a small light.

The official aftermath was roughly predictable; one could outline the script beforehand. Hot wires to Washington and GE headquarters, illegal maneuvers, FBI prowling about, worried paper shuffling. We heard all day from our holding cells the frantic ringing of phones. We endured equably, as the down payment on our crime, eleven hours of enforced lock-up and fasting. And then toward evening, finally, an arraignment and a swollen vindictive indictment: thirteen charges, no bail. Deterrence indeed!

We finally came to trial in the winter of 1981. Many offers of reduced sentence, or no sentence at all, had been set floating about, if only we would plead guilty. Such goodies we saw as seldom sway in midair before felonious eyes: ample time in court to say our say to our very heart's content. No jail time, no fines, no parole. Plead guilty, walk free.

Indeed our brains reeled at the wondrous contradictions implied in the proffer. How plead guilty to nonviolent activity, on behalf of children, the future, the landscape, the plowshare that opens and releases life?

Thank you but no thank you. We were tried finally, in Norristown, Pennsylvania, a locale whose brand of justice would recall rural Mississippi in the late nineteenth century.

We defended ourselves, perhaps with more passion than prudence. At sentencing, our judge, quite beside himself after two weeks' exposure to our unchecked spirits, declared his regret "at not being able to send you all to a Siberian prison camp or a Puerto Rican leper colony."

I was unfamiliar with the first alternative so splenetically proposed. But I had worked with lepers briefly in Hawaii. Upon receiving news of this vindictive racism, a group of lepers wrote the judge, inviting him to "visit us, and perhaps yourself be healed."

Constrained by law to a less draconian course, this juridical wonder then sentenced us variously to two to ten years. The appeal, seven years later, is still underway in some judicial labyrinth.

The foregoing treats clumsily of our religious beliefs, how these might be thought to impinge on our public conduct, with respect to the law and its claim. I should like also to refer to our cultural or secular history as U.S. citizens. This history too is writ large on our souls.

We see ourselves as Christians first of all, but not to the exclusion of all. Our guideline in this matter of a double strain of ancestry is the apostle Paul, among others; he speaks of the Christian respect for "whatever is good, whatever noble, whatever just." Indeed. Americans to the bone. (I dare here speak for the other defendants, for those in prison, for the Douglasses, Sheats, Baranskis, Ellsbergs, Dellingers, and so many other noble unhousebroken spirits.)

We see ourselves as conservatives. We love our country and its people. Root and branch, for good and ill, weal and woe, we belong here. We take to ourselves a history of heroes and martyrs, civil libertarians, cross-grained writers and solitaries and pamphleteers, town criers, tea party tosspots, stamp act resisters, seditious printers of broadsheets, poets, myth makers, chroniclers.

Also, and of course, native Americans, slaves, indentured servants, poor artisans, radical farmers, multitudes of women, labor organizers, students, people of the cloth, political prisoners, philosophers. All those who from the start saw, dimly or ecstatically, something new. And declared it, pursued it, embodied it, dared be imprisoned for it or die for it. Taxation without representation is tyranny! Don't tread on me! Don't mourn, organize! Bread yes, but roses too!

We see ourselves in this bloodline. It is a line, it goes without saying, that prefers to give its blood rather than shed blood. We prefer, it goes without saying, such preference.

Thus perhaps we offer an illustration of our claim — to be conservatives. In such times as we endure, we see the good sense of such a claim. We claim, clumsily, to be conserving innocent blood. And to that degree, conservatives. Those who save lives.

Obviously, we are not in the camp of Tories or Reaganites. But something like this: we are modest custodians of a tradition that honors life and defends the wretched of the earth, poor people, the defenseless, the victims. And at present, since all stand at the edge of the nuclear precipice, and to that degree all are defenseless and victimized — to that degree we must help defend all the living.

12

Poetic Vision and the Hope for Peace

DENISE LEVERTOV

Is THERE A poetry of peace?

A few years ago I participated in a panel at Stanford University on "Women, War, and Peace." During the question period, someone in the audience, whom I could not see — we speakers were on a stage, and the house lights were down — but whom I afterwards learned was the distinguished psychologist Virginia Satir, said that poets should present to the world images of peace, not only of war: everyone needed to be able to *imagine* peace if we were going to achieve it. Since I was the only poet on the panel, this challenge was mine to respond to — but I had only a lame and confused response to make. Afterwards I thought about it, and I remember discussing the problem — the problem of the lack of peace poems — with some poet friends, Robert Hass and David Shaddock, a few days later. What was said I've forgotten, but out of that talk and my own ponderings a poem emerged which was in fact my delayed response.

Making Peace

A voice from the dark called out,
    'The poets must give us
imagination of peace, to oust the intense, familiar
imagination of disaster. Peace, not only
the absence of war.'

192

But peace, like a poem,
is not there ahead of itself,
can't be imagined before it is made,
can't be known except
in the words of its making,
grammar of justice,
syntax of mutual aid.
A feeling towards it,
dimly sensing a rhythm, is all we have
until we begin to utter its metaphors,
learning them as we speak.
A line of peace might appear
if we restructured the sentence our lives are making,
revoked its reaffirmation of profit and power,
questioned our needs, allowed
long pauses . . .
A cadence of peace might balance its
weight
on that different fulcrum; peace, a presence,
an energy field more intense than war,
might pulse then,
stanza by stanza into the world,
each act of living
one of its words, each word
a vibration of light — facets
of the forming crystal.[1]

This analogy still holds good for me. Peace as a positive condition of society, not merely as an interim between wars, is something so unknown that it casts no images on the mind's screen. Of course, one could seek out utopian projections, attempts to evoke the Golden Age; but these are not the psychologically dynamic images Ms. Satir was hoping for, and I can think of none from our own century, even of the nostalgic and fantastic variety, unless one were to cite works of prose in the science fiction category. And these, particularly if one compares them with the great novels of life as it is — with *War and Peace* and *The Brothers Karamazov*, with *Middlemarch* or *Madame Bovary* or *Remembrance*

of Things Past — are entertainments rather than illuminating visions. Credible, psychologically dynamic poetic images of peace
exist only on the most personal level. None of us knows what a
truly peaceful society might feel like; and since peace is indivisible, one society, or one culture, or one country alone could not
give its members a full experience of it, however much it evolved
in its own justice and positive peacemaking: the full experience
of peace could only come in a *world* at peace. It's like the old
song,

> *I* want/*to* be happy,
> *but* I/can't be happy
> *un*less/you are
> happy too!

Meanwhile, as Catherine de Vinck says in her *Book of Peace*,
"Right Now."

Right Now

> Right now, in this house we share
>   — earth the name of it
>   planet of no account
>   in the vast ranges of the sky —
> children are dying
>   lambs with cracked heads
>   their blood dripping on the stones.
>
> Right now, messengers reach us
>   handing out leaflets
>   printed with a single word:
>   death
> misspelled, no longer a dusky angel
> death in the shape of a vulture
>   landing on broken bodies
>   torn flesh.
>
> We look elsewhere:
> here the buds sliding out of their sheaths

unroll voluptuous green leaves;
we fill the garden-room with cushions
    hang wind-bells in the trees
toss the word "death" to the flames
    over which good meat is sizzling.

Messengers are sent away
but others arrive in endless procession:
    old women, weepy-eyed, speechless
    young ones with nerves exposed.
They have crossed the sierras
they have sailed in leaky boats
they have trudged through the desert
    to say:
"Our lives have no weight:
they are made of grass, of clouds
    of stories whispered at nightfall.
We are burning fields, we are fires
    fanned by the wind."

How can we mix this knowledge
    with the bread we eat
    with the cup we drink?
Is it enough to fill these words
    these hollow flutes of bones
        with aching songs?[2]

And terror is what we know most intimately — that terror and the ache of chronic anxiety Yarrow Cleaves articulates in "One Day."

One Day

When you were thirteen, thoughtful,
you said, "When
the bomb falls, I won't run, I won't
try to get out of the city like
everyone else, in the panic."

When I was a child,
younger than you, I had to
crouch on the floor
at school, under my desk.
How fast could I do it?
The thin bones of my arms
crossed my skull,
for practice. My forehead
went against my knees. I felt
the blinding light of the
windows behind me.
I knew what the bombs did.

"I'll find a tree," you said,
"and the tree will protect me."

Then I turned away, because
I was crying and because you are my child.

What if you stood on the wrong side?

What if the tree, like me, had
only its ashes to give?

What if you have to stand one day
in blasted silence,
screaming, and I can never,
never reach you?[3]

What about the testimony of peace on a personal level? Yes,
I do believe that poems which record individual epiphanies, moments of tranquility or bliss, tell us something about what peace
might be like. Yet because there *is* no peace they have, always, an
undertone of poignancy. We snatch our happiness from the teeth
of violence, from the shadow of oppression. And on the whole we
do not connect such poems with the idea of peace as a goal, but,

reading them, experience a momentary relief from the tensions of life lived in a chronic state of emergency.

Meanwhile what we do have is poems of protest, of denouncement, of struggle, and sometimes of comradeship. Little glimpses of what peace means or might mean come through in such poems as Margaret Randall's "The Gloves."

The Gloves

for Rhoda

Yes we did march around somewhere and yes it was
     cold,
we shared our gloves because we had a pair between us
and a New York city cop also shared his big gloves
with me — strange,
he was there to keep our order
and he could do that
and I could take that
back then.
We were marching for the Santa Maria, Rhoda,
a Portuguese ship whose crew had mutinied.
They demanded asylum in Goulart's Brazil
and we marched in support of that demand,
in winter, in New York City,
back and forth before the Portuguese Consulate,
Rockefeller Center, 1961.
I gauge the date by my first child
— Gregory was born late in 1960 — as I gauge
so many dates by the first, the second, the third, the
     fourth,
and I feel his body now, again, close to my breast,
held against cold to our strong steps of dignity.
That was my first public protest, Rhoda,
strange you should retrieve it now
in a letter out of this love of ours
alive these many years.
How many protests since that one, how many

marches and rallies
for greater causes, larger wars, deeper wounds
cleansed or untouched by our rage.
Today a cop would never unbuckle his gloves
and press them around my blue-red hands.
Today a baby held to breast
would be a child of my child, a generation removed.
The world is older and I in it
am older,
burning, slower, with the same passions.
The passions are older and so I am also younger
for knowing them more deeply and moving in them
pregnant with fear and fighting.
The gloves are still there, in the cold,
passing from hand to hand.[4]

In that poem — focused on a small intimate detail, gloves to
keep hands warm, and raying out from it to the sharing of that
minor comfort, and so to the passing from hand to hand, from
generation to generation, of a concern and a resolve — peace as such
is very far offstage, a distant unnamed hope which cannot even
be considered until issues of justice and freedom have been addressed and cleared. Yet a kind of peace is present in the poem,
too, the peace of mutual aid, of love and communion.

Our own Mel King, here in Boston, sent out a calligraphed
Christmas greeting a couple of years ago to people who had supported his various campaigns. "Peace," it reads,

On this planet
between nations,
On the streets
between people,
Of mind
within ourselves.[5]

A longing, a prayer — not a vision.

John Daniel, in his book *Common Ground*, writes of the
mystery of there being anything at all, and of love for the earth:

Of Earth

for Wallace Stegner

Swallows looping and diving
by the darkening oaks, the flash
of their white bellies,
the tall grasses gathering last light,
glowing pale gold, silence
overflowing in a shimmer of breeze —
these could have happened
a different way. The heavy-trunked oaks
might not have branched and branched
and finely re-branched
as if to weave themselves into air.
There is no necessity
that any creature should fly,
that last light should turn
the grasses gold, that grasses
should exist at all,
or light.

But a mind thinking so
is a mind wandering from home.
It is not thought that answers
each step of my feet, to be walking here
in the cool stir of dusk
is no mere possibility,
and I am so stained with the sweet
peculiar loveliness of things
that given God's power to dream worlds
from the dark, I know
I could only dream Earth —
birds, trees, this field of light
where I and each of us walk once.[6]

This is a clear example of the kind of poem, the kind of perception, which must for our time stand in for a poetry of peace. It
is an epiphany both personal and universal, common to all con-

scious humans, surely, in kind if not in degree. Whether they remember it or not, surely everyone at least once in a lifetime is filled
for a moment with a sense of wonder and exhilaration. But the
poem's poignancy is peculiar to the late twentieth century. In the
past, the dark side of such a poem would have been the sense of
the brevity of our own lives, of mortality within a monumentally
enduring Nature. Eschatology, whether theological or geological,
was too remote in its considerations to have much direct impact on
a poetic sensibility illumined by the intense presentness of a moment of being. But today the shadow is deeper and more chilling,
for it is the reasonable fear that the earth itself, to all intents and
purposes, is so threatened by our actions that its hold on life is
as tenuous as our own, its fate as precarious. Poets who direct our
attention to injustice, oppression, the suffering of the innocent,
and the heroism of those who struggle for change, serve the possibility of peace by stimulating others to support that struggle. Yes-
terday it was Vietnam, today it is El Salvador or Lebanon or Ireland. Closer to home, the Ku Klux Klan rides again, the Skinheads
multiply. Hunger and homelessness, crack and child abuse. There
are poems — good, bad, or indifferent — written every day somewhere about all of these, and they are a poetry of war. Yet one may
say they are a proto-peace poetry; for they testify to a rejection
which, though it cannot in itself create a state of peace, is one of
its indispensable preconditions. For war is no longer a matter of
armed conflict only. As we become more aware of the inseparability
of justice from peace, we perceive that hunger and homelessness
and our failure to stop them are forms of warfare, and that no one
is a civilian. And we perceive that our degradation of the biosphere
is the most devastating war of all. The threat of nuclear holocaust
simply proposes a more sudden variation in a continuum of violence
we are already engaged in. Our consciousness lags so far behind
our actions. W. S. Merwin has written in a poem called "Chord,"
included in his book *The Rain in the Trees*, about this time lag:

Chord

While Keats wrote they were cutting down the sandal-
    wood forests
while he listened to the nightingale they heard their
    own axes echoing through the forests

while he sat in the walled garden on the hill outside
the city they thought of their gardens dying far
away on the mountain
while the sound of the words clawed at him they
thought of their wives
while the tip of his pen travelled the iron they had
coveted was hateful to them
while he thought of the Grecian woods they bled
under red flowers
while he dreamed of wine the trees were falling from
the trees
while he felt his heart they were hungry and their
faith was sick
while the song broke over him they were in a secret
place and they were cutting it forever
while he coughed they carried the trunks to the hole
in the forest the size of a foreign ship
while he groaned on the voyage to Italy they fell on
the trails and were broken
when he lay with the odes behind him the wood was
sold for cannons
when he lay watching the window they came home
and lay down
and an age arrived when everything was explained in
another language.[7]

The tree has become a great symbol of what we need, what
we destroy, what we must revere and protect and learn from if
life on earth is to continue and that mysterious hope, *life at peace*,
is to be attained. The tree's deep and wide root system, its broad
embrace and lofty reach from earth into air, its relation to fire and
to human structures, as fuel and material, especially to water which
it not only needs but gives (drought ensuing when the forests are
destroyed) just as it gives us purer air — all these and other attributes of the tree make it a powerful archetype. The Swedish poet
Reidar Ekner has written in "Horologium" as follows:

Where the tree germinates, it takes root
there it stretches up its thin spire

there it sends down the fine threads
gyroscopically it takes its position
In the seed the genes whisper: stretch out for the light
      and seek the dark
And the tree seeks the light, it stretches out
      for the dark
And the more darkness it finds, the more light
      it discovers
the higher towards the light it reaches, the further down
      towards darkness
it is groping

Where the tree germinates, it widens
it drinks in from the dark, it sips from the light
intoxicated by the green blood, spirally it turns
the sun drives it, the sap rushes through the fine pipes
      towards the light
the pressure from the dark drives it out
      to the points, one
golden morning the big crown of the tree
      turns green, from all directions insects, and birds
It is a giddiness, one cone
      driving the other

Inch after inch the tree takes possession of its place
it transforms the dark into tree
it transforms the light into tree
it transforms the place into tree
It incorporates the revolutions of the planet, one after
      the other
the bright semicircle, the dark semicircle
Inside the bark, it converts time into tree

The tree has four dimensions, the fourth one
      memory
far back its memory goes, further back than that of Man,
      than the heart of any living beings
for a long time the corpse of the captured highway-
      man hung
      from its branches

The oldest ones, they remember the hunting people,
    the shell mounds,
    the neolithic dwellings
They will remember our time, too; our breathing out,
    they will breathe it in
Hiroshima's time, they breathe it in, cryptomeria
also this orbit of the planet, they add it to their growth
Time, they are measuring it; time pieces they are,
    seventy centuries
    the oldest ones carry in their wood[8]

Ekner causes us to perceive the tree as witness; and when we are stopped in our tracks by a witness to our foolishness, the effect is, at least for a moment, that which A. E. Housman described when he wrote,

> But man at whiles is sober,
> And thinks, by fits and starts;
> And when he thinks, he fastens
> His hand upon his heart.[9]

What of a religious approach to the state of war in which we live, and to the possibility of peace? The Welsh poet R. S. Thomas, an Anglican priest whose skepticism and pessimism, however, often seem more profound than those of secular poets, offers in "The Kingdom" a remote and somewhat abstract view of it and a basic prescription for getting there:

The Kingdom

> It's a long way off but inside it
> There are quite different things going on:
> Festivals at which the poor man
> Is king and the consumptive is
> Healed; mirrors in which the blind look
> At themselves and love looks at them
> Back; and industry is for mending
> The bent bones and the minds fractured

By life. It's a long way off, but to get
There takes no time and admission
Is free, if you will purge yourself
Of desire, and present yourself with
Your need only and the simple offering
Of your faith, green as a leaf.[10]

     Catherine de Vinck, from whom I quoted earlier, a Catholic writer all of whose work expresses her deep faith, adds to that prescription the ingredient of action: we must act our faith, she says, at the end of the last poem in her *Book of Peace*, by practical communion with others, offering up and sharing our bodily nourishment, the light of our belief, the living space we occupy. The time for peace, the title of this poem makes us recognize, is now.

A Time for Peace

We can still make it
     gather the threads, the pieces
     each of different size and shade
     to match and sew into a pattern:
       Rose of Sharon
       wedding ring
       circles and crowns.

We can still listen:
     children at play, their voices
     mingling in the present tense
     of a time that can be extended.

Peace, we say
     looking through our pockets
to find the golden word
     the coin to buy that ease
       that place sheltered
       from bullets and bombs.

But what we seek lies elsewhere
    beyond the course of lethargic blood
    beyond the narrow dream
        of resting safe and warm.

If we adjust our lenses
    we see far in the distance
figures of marching people
    homeless, hungry, going nowhere.
Why not call them
    to our mornings of milk and bread?
The coming night will be darker
    than the heart of stones
unless we strike the match
    light the guiding candle
    say yes, there is room after all
        at the inn.[11]

Muriel Rukeyser, in a poem begun on the trip to Hanoi she
and I made together, with one other woman, in 1972, shortly before Nixon's Christmas "carpet bombing" of the North, wrote of
the paradoxical presence of peace we felt there in the midst of
war:

It Is There

Yes, it is there, the city full of music,
Flute music, sounds of children, voices of poets,
The unknown bird in his long call. The bells of peace.

Essential peace, it sounds across the water
In the long parks where the lovers are walking,
Along the lake with its island and pagoda,
And a boy learning to fish. His father threads the line.
Essential peace, it sounds and it stills. Cockcrow.
It is there, the human place.

On what does it depend, this music, the children's
    games?
A long tradition of rest? Meditation? What peace is so
    profound
That it can reach all habitants, all children,
The eyes at worship, the shattered in hospitals?
All voyagers?
                    Meditation, yes; but within a tension
Of long resistance to all invasion, all seduction of hate.
Generations of holding to resistance; and within this
    resistance
Fluid change that can respond, that can show the
    children
A long future of finding, of responsibility; change
    within
Change and tension of sharing consciousness
Village to city, city to village, person to person entire
With unchanging cockcrow and unchanging
    endurance
Under the
          skies of war.[12]

On that journey I had felt the same thing—the still center, the
eye of the storm:

In Thai Binh (Peace) Province

for Muriel and Jane

I've used up all my film on bombed hospitals,
bombed village schools, the scattered
lemon-yellow cocoons at the bombed silk-factory,

and for the moment all my tears too
are used up, having seen today
yet another child with its feet blown off,
    a girl, this one, eleven years old,
patient and bewildered in her home, a fragile
small house of mud bricks among rice fields.

So I'll use my dry burning eyes
to photograph within me
dark sails of the river boats,
warm slant of afternoon light
apricot on the brown, swift, wide river,
village towers — church and pagoda — on the far shore,
and a boy and small bird both
perched, relaxed, on a quietly grazing
buffalo.   Peace within the
          long war.

It is that life, unhurried, sure, persistent,
I must bring home when I try to bring
the war home.
          Child, river, light.

Here the future, fabled bird
that has migrated away from America,
nests, and breeds, and sings,

common as any sparrow.[13]

Yes, though I have said we cannot write about peace because
we've never experienced it, we do have those glimpses of it, and
we have them most intensely when they are brought into relief
by the chaos and violence surrounding them. But the longing for
peace is a longing to get beyond not only the momentariness of
such glimpses but the ominous dualism that too often seems our
only way of obtaining those moments. Although the instant takes
us out of time, a peace in a larger sense experienced only through
the power of contrast would be as false as any artificial Paradise,
or as the hectic flush of prosperity periodically induced in ailing
economies by injections of war and arms-industry jobs and profits.

No; if there begins to be a poetry of peace, it is still, as it has
long been, a poetry of struggle. Much of it is not by the famous,
much of it is almost certainly still unpublished. And much of it
is likely to be by women, because so many women are actively engaged in nonviolent action, and through their work, especially at
the peace camps such as Greenham Common and elsewhere in

England or Germany, or here at the Nevada test site or the Con-
cord, California, railroad tracks, they have been gathering practical experience in ways of peaceful community. Ann Snitow, writing about Greenham in 1985, said:

> When I describe Greenham women — their lives in these
> circumstances — I often get the reaction that they sound like
> mad idealists detached from a reality principle about what
> can and cannot be done, and how. In a sense this is true. The
> women reject power and refuse to study it, at least on its own
> terms. But the other charge — that they are utopian dreamers
> who sit around and think about the end of the world while
> not really living in this one — is far from the mark.
>
> In a piece in the *Times Literary Supplement* last sum-
> mer, "Why the Peace Movement Is Wrong," the Russian emigre
> poet Joseph Brodsky charged the peace movement with be-
> ing a bunch of millenarians waiting for the apocalypse. Cer-
> tainly there are fascinating parallels between the thinking of
> the peace women and that of the radical millenarian Protes-
> tant sects of the seventeenth century. Both believe that the
> soul is the only court that matters, the self the only guide,
> and that paradise is a humble and realizable goal in England's
> green and pleasant land. The millenarians offered free food
> just like the caravans now on the Common: Food, says one
> sign. Eat till You're Full.
>
> But the women are not sitting in the mud waiting for
> the end, nor are they — as Brodsky and many others claim —
> trying to come to terms with their own deaths by imagining
> that soon the whole world will die. On the contrary, the
> women make up one of the really active antimillenarian forces
> around. President Reagan has told fundamentalist groups that
> the last trump ending human history might blow at any time
> now; the women believe that the dreadful sound can be
> avoided, if only we will stop believing in it.
>
> Greenham women see a kind of fatalism all around them.
> They, too, have imagined the end, and their own deaths, and
> have decided that they prefer to die without taking the world
> with them. Nothing makes them more furious than the apathy
> in the town of Newbury, where they are often told, "Look,
> you've got to die anyway. So what difference does it make

how you go?" These are the real millenarians, blithely accepting that the end is near.

In contrast, the women look very hardheaded, very pragmatic. They see a big war machine, the biggest the world
has known; and, rather than sitting in the cannon's mouth
hypnotized, catatonic with fear or denial, they are trying to
back away from the danger, step by step. They refuse to be
awed or silenced by the war machine. Instead they say calmly
that what was built by human beings can be dismantled by
them, too. Their logic, clarity, and independence are end-
lessly refreshing. Where is it written, they ask, that we must
destroy ourselves?[14]

There can be, then, a poetry which may help us, before it is too
late, to attain peace. Poems of protest, documentaries of the state
of war, can rouse us to work for peace and justice. Poems of praise
for life and the living earth can stimulate us to protect it. The work
of Gary Snyder, of Wendell Berry, comes to mind among others.
Poems of comradeship in struggle can help us — like the thought
of those shared gloves in the Margaret Randall poem — to know
the dimension of community, so often absent from modern life.
And there is beginning to be a new awareness, articulated most specifically in the writings of Father Thomas Berry, the talks and work-
shops of people like Miriam McGillis or Joanna Macy, that we humans are not just walking around *on* this planet but that we and
all things are truly, physically, biologically, part of one living organism; and that our human role on earth is as the consciousness
and self-awareness of that organism. A poem by John Daniel, who
almost certainly had not read Thomas Berry, shows how this real-
ization is beginning to appear as if spontaneously in many minds,
perhaps rather on the lines of the story of the hundredth monkey:

> a voice is finding its tongue
> in the slop and squall of birth.
>
>   It sounds,
>
> and we, in whom Earth happened to light
> a clear flame of consciousness,
> are only beginning to learn the language—

who are made of the ash of stars,
who carry the sea we were born in,
who spent millions of years learning to breathe,
who shivered in fur at the reptiles' feet,
who trained our hands on the limbs of trees
and came down, slowly straightening
to look over the grasses, to see
that the world not only is
                              but is beautiful —

we are Earth learning to see itself. . .[15]

If this consciousness (with its corollary awareness that when we exploit and mutilate the earth we are exploiting and mutilating the body of which we are the brain cells) increases and proliferates while there is still time, it could be the key to survival. A vision of peace cannot be a vision of a heaven in which natural disasters are miraculously eliminated, but must be of a society in which companionship and fellowship would so characterize the tone of daily life that unavoidable disasters would be differently met. Natural disasters such as earthquakes and floods do anyway elicit neighborliness, briefly at least. A peaceful society would have to be one capable of maintaining that love and care for the afflicted. Only lovingkindness could sustain a lasting peace.

How can poetry relate to that idea? Certainly not by preaching. But as more and more poets know and acknowledge that we are indeed "made of the ash of stars," as the poem said, their art, stirring the imagination of their readers, can have an oblique influence which cannot be measured. We cannot long survive at all unless we *do* move toward peace. If a poetry of peace is ever to be written, there must first be this stage we are just entering — the poetry of *preparation* for peace, a poetry of protest, of lament, of praise for the living earth; a poetry that demands justice, renounces violence, reverences mystery, like this Native American invocation of the Powers:

From the Hako (Pawnee, Osage, Omaha):
Invoking the Powers

Remember, remember the circle of the sky
    the stars and the brown eagle
    the supernatural winds
    breathing night and day
    from the four directions

Remember, remember the great life of the sun
    breathing on the earth
    it lies upon the earth
    to bring out life upon the earth
    life covering the earth

Remember, remember the sacredness of things
    running streams and dwellings
    the young within the nest
    a hearth for sacred fire
    the holy flame of fire[16]

NOTES

1. Denise Levertov, "Making Peace," in *Breathing the Water* (New York: New Directions, 1987). Copyright © 1987 by Denise Levertov. Reprinted with permission of New Directions Publishing Corp.

2. Catherine de Vinck, "Right Now," in *A Book of Peace* (Allendale, N.J.: Alleluia Press, 1985). Reprinted with permission of Alleluia Press.

3. Yarrow Cleaves, "One Day," printed by permission of the author.

4. Margaret Randall, "The Gloves," in *The Coming Home Poems* (East Haven, Conn.: Long River Books, 1986). Copyright © 1986 by Margaret Randall. Reprinted by permission.

5. Mel King, "Peace."

6. John Daniel, "Of Earth," in *Common Ground* (Lewiston, Idaho: Confluence Press, 1988). Reprinted with permission of Confluence Press.

7. W. S. Merwin, "Chord," in *The Rain in the Trees* (New York: Alfred A. Knopf, 1988). Copyright © 1988 by W. S. Merwin. Reprinted by permission of Alfred A. Knopf, Inc.

8. Reidar Ekner, "Horologium," *Northern Light* (date unknown). Reprinted by permission of the author.

9. "Could man be drunk forever" (no. 10) from *Last Poems*, reprinted in *Collected Poems of A. E. Housman* (New York: Holt, Rinehart & Winston, 1965).

10. R. S. Thomas, "The Kingdom," in *H'm* (London: Macmillan, 1972). Reprinted by permission of the author.

11. Catherine de Vinck, "A Time for Peace," in *Book of Peace*. Reprinted with permission of Alleluia Press.

12. Muriel Rukeyser, "It Is There," in *Women on War*, ed. Daniela Gioseffi (New York: Simon & Schuster, 1988). Reprinted by permission.

13. Denise Levertov, "In Thai Binh (Peace) Province," in *The Freeing of the Dust* (New York: New Directions, 1975). Copyright © 1975 by Denise Levertov. Reprinted with permission of New Directions Publishing Corp.

14. Ann Snitow, "Holding the Line at Greenham Common: Being Joyously Political in Dangerous Times (February 1985)," in *Women on War*, ed. Gioseffi. Reprinted with permission from *Mother Jones* magazine, © 1985, Foundation for National Progress.

15. John Daniel, "Common Ground," in *Common Ground*. Reprinted with permission of Confluence Press.

16. The Hako, "Invoking the Powers," in *The Magic World*, ed. W. Brandon (New York: William Morrow & Co., 1971).

Author Index

Adorno, T. W., 6, 106
Aquinas, St. Thomas, 44, 54, 67
Arendt, Hannah, 5
Aristotle, 78
Augustine, 2, 20, 54, 67

Bainton, Roland, 35
Bentham, Jeremy, 55
Berrigan, Daniel, 10–11, 181–91
Berry, Thomas, 209
Berry, Wendell, 209
Bismarck, Otto von, 108, 115
Bohr, Niels, 90
Bok, Sissela, 4, 52–72
Bonhoeffer, Dietrich, 107
Brodie, Bernard, 98
Brodsky, Joseph, 208

Childress, James, 42–43
Cleaves, Yarrow, 195–96
Crombie, Alistair, 76
Curran, Charles, 30–31

Daniel, John, 198–99, 209–10
Descartes, René, 76, 80
de Vinck, Catherine, 194–95,
  204–5
Dharmapala, Anagarika, 154
Dharmasiri, Gunapala, 150

Einstein, Albert, 102
Ekner, Reidar, 201–3
Eliot, T. S., 30
Erasmus, Desiderius, 4, 52–53,
  55–62, 67, 69, 75

Gandhi, Mohandas, 9–11, 154,
  162–78
Geyer, Alan, 34
Gilligan, John, 2–4, 15–32
Grotius, Hugo, 35, 73
Guénon, René, 156

Hegel, G. W. F., 55, 141
Heidegger, Martin, 144
Hick, John, 150, 156
Hobbes, Thomas, 62–63, 78–80
Hollenbach, David, 21–22
Hoskin, Michael, 76
Housman, A. E., 203

Jayatilleke, K. N., 154, 160

Kant, Immanuel, 4, 52–53, 55–
  56, 61–65, 67–69, 144
Kennan, George, 67
Kierkegaard, Sören, 130
King, Mel, 198
King-Hall, Stephen, 40

213

Subject Index